DS92
2007
Zisser, Eyal

Commanding Syria: Bashar Al-Sa

DS92
2007
Zisser, Eyal

Commanding Syria: Bashar Al-Sa

COMMANDING SYRIA

Commanding Syria

Bashar al-Asad and the First Years in Power

Eyal Zisser

I.B. TAURIS
LONDON · NEW YORK

Reprinted in 2007 by I.B.Tauris & Co Ltd
6 Salem Road, London W2 4BU
175 Fifth Avenue, New York Ny 10010
www.ibtauris.com

In the United States and Canada distributed by Palgrave Macmillan
a division of St Martin's Press
175 Fifth Avenue, New York NY 10010

First published in 2007 by
I.B.Tauris & Co Ltd
Copyright © Eyal Zisser 2007

Library of Modern Middle East Studies 60

ISBN: 978 1 84511 153 3

A full CIP record for this book is available from the British Library

A full CIP record for this book is available from the Library of
Congress

Library of Congress catalog card: available

Typeset in Bembo by Word Pro
Printed and bound in the Czech Republic
FINIDR, s.r.o.

Contents

Preface   vi

Introduction: The legacy of the late leader   1

Part I SYRIA UNDER BASHAR

1 The road to the top   19
2 Taking the reins of power   38
3 Bashar al-Asad – the man and his regime   47

Part II UNFULFILLED HOPES

4 A false spring in Damascus   77
5 Society and economy in the age of globalization   99

Part III SYRIAN FOREIGN POLICY
UNDER BASHAR

6 Bashar al-Asad in the international arena – the al-Aqsa
   Intifada, the September 11, 2001 events, and the war in Iraq   125
7 Syria and Israel in Bashar's era   148
8 Syria in Lebanon – the end of an era?   172

Conclusion: Why Bashar? Because there is no one else   198
Epilogue: Will Bashar al-Asad survive in power?   205

Notes   209
Index   224

Preface

For many years 'Abd al-Halim Khaddam was considered to be one of the mainstays, not to say a prominent symbol, of the Syrian Ba'th regime. He was Hafiz al-Asad's right-hand man, and even a close friend, and was known as one of the stalwarts of the Ba'th Party that has ruled Syria for nearly 40 years. After Hafiz al-Asad's death, Khaddam was appointed to be his temporary replacement, and in this capacity he issued the decrees that enabled Bashar al-Asad to become the ruler of Syria.

Thus, it came as a great surprise when Khaddam launched a sharp attack on Bashar's regime at the end of December 2005, and even expressed the view that it was most likely that Bashar would not survive the year 2006 as president.[1]

The blow that Khaddam inflicted on Bashar was only one of a series of blows the Syrian president suffered during 2005. Khaddam's attack was preceded in October 2005 by the publication of the Mehlis report, submitted by the German prosecutor Detlev Mehlis, who was appointed by the U.N. Security Council in April 2005 to investigate the February 2005 murder in Beirut of former Lebanese Prime Minister Rafiq al-Hariri. In this report Mehlis concluded that the Syrian regime was behind the murder of Hariri.[2]

It is difficult to determine whether Bashar al-Asad will remain in power in Syria, and for how much longer, but there is no question that the six years that have passed since he replaced his deceased father as president in Damascus have been difficult and stormy for both him and the country he heads.

The death of Hafiz al-Asad on Saturday, June 10, 2000 marked the end of an era in the history of modern Syria. Asad was often described, with considerable justification, as the founding father of the state or, at the very least, as the first effective president it had had since it attained independence on 17 April 1946. He left his imprint on many areas in the country, so much so that an argument can be made for the near total identification of the Syrian state with its leader.

Hafiz al-Asad's role as president of Syria was taken over by his son Bashar. This came as no surprise, for in the final years of his life

Asad Sr. did everything possible to assure his son's succession. Still, the transfer of power from father to son, smooth and free of turbulence as it was, evoked ripples of derision and criticism within and outside the country, especially regarding the suitability of the young son to lead the country at that time. The point was widely raised in this context that Bashar's journey to the top had begun only on January 21, 1994, following the death of his older brother, Basil, in a car accident. Basil had been his father's choice as heir, and was the focus of great expectations, while the selection of Bashar stemmed from the lack of an alternative and was essentially accidental. It was also accidental in terms of Bashar's personal career, which had been devoted until then to medicine rather than politics. Ultimately, the accident brought Bashar to the seat of the presidency.

Bashar's rise to power came at a time when Syria faced a crossroads, if not an impasse, in light of a series of challenges, some of them existential, in the realms of domestic political, social and economic policy. This reality inevitably raises questions about the ability of the Ba'th regime, which has ruled Syria since the Ba'th Party took over the government on March 8, 1963, to continue functioning in its present format. At the very least, it raises the question of whether the Asad dynasty, which has ruled the country over the past three decades, can retain its power in the aftermath of the demise of its founder.

By all accounts, one of Hafiz al-Asad's most definitive achievements was the establishment of a strong and stable regime – some would say a highly effective repressive regime. This gave Syria unprecedented political stability, enabling Asad to turn the country from a weak, ineffectual entity lacking legitimation to a regional power of stature and influence. By the mid-1980s, President Asad had reached the peak of his career and, conceivably, had attained repose and security, having managed to overcome rivals and enemies at home and abroad and acquire the status of a prominent and admired leader of the Middle East.

However, there was no guarantee of permanent immunity. By the late 1980s, cracks had begun to appear in the strong and secure image projected so successfully by Asad's regime during the 30 years of his rule. A series of factors were responsible for this setback, including the collapse of the Soviet Union, Syria's close ally and patron, and the ascendance of the United States to the status of the world's sole superpower; the spread of globalization, whose effects began to be palpable even in Syria; a spiraling birth rate and a stagnant economy which burdened the country increasingly during the 1990s; and Hafiz al-Asad's deteriorating health, which led to his decline and seclusion.

Nevertheless, so long as Asad retained his grip on power in Damascus, his presence served as a deterrent to any threat to the stability of his regime. With his death and the transfer of rule to his son, however, this deterrent vanished, resulting in uncertainty over the future of the Syrian regime and its new leader. Even assuming that Bashar and the dynasty founded by his father retain power over time, the question that remains is what direction Syria, or more precisely Bashar, will take. In light of the cracks that have appeared in the walls of confinement and fear built by Asad Sr. around Syria, will Bashar take action to reinforce and thereby preserve his father's legacy, as he indeed seemed to imply in some of his statements during his first years in power?[3] Or will he take steps instead to widen the cracks and bring about the dismantling of the walls, thereby putting Syria on a new path, distinct from that of his father?

This question became all the more imperative in the wake of the conquest of Iraq by American forces in the spring of 2003. The war in Iraq, which held the promise of major change in the Middle East, heightened pressure on Bashar and his regime both domestically (for policy change in the socioeconomic realm) and from abroad, especially from Washington (for a changed foreign policy). Initially, Bashar appeared uncertain as to how to navigate the Syrian ship of state to a safe harbor in the storm that had descended on the region, reflected in a series of blunders in his handling of the Syrian–American relationship. The immediate outcome was a collapse of Syrian–American relations, a further isolation of Syria in the region and in the world's affairs, and the expulsion of Syrian forces from Lebanon in April 2005 under heavy international but also Lebanese pressure. George Bush's remarks in late 2004 that Bashar was a weak leader not worthy of trust and, in early 2005, that Bashar was no better then the late Palestinian leader, Yasir 'Arafat, and thus should be isolated and ignored[4] were further evidence of the low state of American–Syrian relations and of Bashar's image in the eyes of Washington. Indeed, many observers anticipated another "war of liberation" in the region by the U.S., this time against Damascus. After all, it was Bashar himself who noted in an interview to *al-Sharq al-Awsat* in January 2005 that the current situation in the Middle East was more dangerous than at the time of the signing of the Sykes–Picot agreement a hundred years ago.[5] In March 2005 he admitted in an interview to the Italian *La Repubblica* that he was wary of the possibility that the U.S. might attack Syria.[6]

The answer to the question as to what direction Bashar will take in the future is not self-evident, for today, six years after assuming power, Bashar remains, in the view of many both inside and outside

Syria, an enigmatic figure or, as described by the former head of Israeli army intelligence, Uri Sagi, "unbaked dough."[7] Some believe that the apple hasn't fallen far from the tree and that Bashar is essentially a loyal follower in his father's footsteps, personality differences and changed circumstances notwithstanding. By contrast, others point out that he is, after all, a young man, amazingly young according to a Western leader who met him,[8] with an open mind and especially a deep acquaintance with the West. Apparently, moreover, he has an awareness of the deep gulf between Syrian and Western society, primarily in the realm of technological and scientific progress. This awareness once prompted him to state (before he assumed his governmental role) that "Bill Gates functions in a cultural and technological environment that helps explain his achievements and therefore, if Syrians wish to advance themselves in these areas, they must create a similar environment in Syria itself."[9]

In light of the crossroads that Syria faces in the aftermath of Hafiz al-Asad's death and against the background of Bashar's failure to deal with the consequences of the war against terrorism and the war in Iraq, an attempt to construct a profile of Hafiz al-Asad's heir is instructive. The image is that of a young man who, encouraged by his father, chose to study ophthalmology but found himself, not necessarily by choice, abandoning the corridors of the Western Eye Hospital in London for those of the Presidential Palace in Damascus. Ultimately, Bashar will determine Syria's path in the foreseeable future, at least by virtue of his formal role as president of the state, which grants him control over the country's governmental and bureaucratic systems, but also, and perhaps especially, by virtue of the fact that meanwhile no threat or danger to his status or his regime is perceptible. Still, he is a young leader at the start of his political career, which makes it difficult to assess, much less define, his personality, outlook or policy as applied in practice. This study, therefore, is not confined to compiling a political biography in the narrow sense, but surveys the wider arena of developments within the Ba'th regime, Syrian society and the state during the period of transition between Hafiz al-Asad's Syria and that of his son Bashar.

The book is divided into parts. "Introduction: The legacy of the late leader" sketches a portrait of Syria toward the end of Asad Sr.'s rule, focusing on the domestic as well as external impasse facing the country by the time of his death. Part I, "Syria under Bashar," deals with Bashar's journey to the seat of power and his father's efforts to entrench and secure his status as heir. This part also sketches a profile of Bashar's personal and political behavior during the first years of his administration, as well as a profile of the governmental system which he headed. Part II, "Unfulfilled hopes," surveys Bashar's domestic achievements and, more significantly, his failures during the first years of his rule, especially his unsuccessful effort to initiate reforms in domestic policy, social affairs and the economy. Lastly, Part III, "Syrian foreign policy under Bashar," focuses on Syria's regional relations. Emphasis is put on Syria's relationship with Israel in the wake of the outbreak of the al-Aqsa Intifada, and Syria's involvement in Lebanon, which came to an end in April 2005. Its role in international affairs in the wake of the events of September 11, 2001 and the war in Iraq is also surveyed.

Researching the subject of Syria's ruler and the regime he heads without the possibility of visiting that country undoubtedly constitutes a considerable drawback. Nevertheless, compensation is to be found in: a wealth of available primary materials – the press and electronic monitoring services during the period under review, including Syrian, other Arab and foreign sources; economic and political surveys and research published in Syria and abroad; and, of course, discussions and interviews with Syrians, other Arabs and Westerners who are permanent residents of Syria or who lived there in the past. Wide use was also made of secondary sources about Syria.

On a technical note, the English transliteration of Arabic names and terminology in the book follows the accepted academic style, with some simplification for the benefit of the lay reader.

Lastly, I would like to acknowledge all those who helped me write this volume. First and foremost, I want to express my gratitude to my guide and mentor, Professor Itamar Rabinovich, who has accompanied me from the start of my academic career and enriched me by his generous advice and abundant knowledge of Syria. I also thank colleagues in Israel and throughout the world for sharing information about Syria, with special thanks to colleagues and friends in Syria whose names, regrettably, still cannot be cited. Special thanks are due to friends in the Moshe Dayan Center for Middle Eastern and African Studies and in the Department of the History of the Middle East and Africa at Tel Aviv University for their support and encouragement over the years. Personal thanks are due to the Colton family, who generously granted me a scholarship that made it possible for me to devote my time to the study, and encouraged me while it was being written. Likewise, I should like to express my appreciation to Judy Krausz, who translated this volume into English. The publisher of the volume, I.B. Tauris, is to be commended for the devotion with which the manuscript has been prepared for publication. Last but not least, I thank my dear family – my wife, Shirley, and my children, Liron, Lilach and Toam – for their unfailing support.

The legacy of the late leader

Hafiz al-Asad, the "hidden" president

Hafiz al-Asad began his fifth seven-year term of office as president of Syria on March 11, 1999, arriving that morning at the People's Assembly to take his oath of allegiance. Viewers of Syrian television, which covered the event live, saw the president being received at the entrance of the Assembly building by his colleagues in the highest echelons of the regime, and thereafter taking the oath as president, an oath that consisted of one sentence: "I swear in the name of Almighty Allah to safeguard the People's Democratic Republican regime and to act to fulfill the aspirations of the Arab nation for unity, freedom and socialism." Later, Asad was shown briefly shaking hands with several members of the Assembly who approached him to congratulate him and express their support for him.[1]

That evening, the Syrian media gave wide coverage to a speech delivered by the president to the members of the Assembly and through them to the Syrian public as part of the inaugural event. The speech evoked great interest, for a public appearance by the Syrian president, together with a message to the people, was a rare event in Asad's Syria, especially during the last decade of his life. In fact, ever since his speech of September 11, 1994, on the occasion of the opening session of the People's Assembly following elections to the Assembly a month previously, President Asad had not spoken in public at all. Four years later, in December 1998, he was absent, for the first time during his rule, from the opening session of the Assembly voted in October of that year. His absence then was attributed by the Assembly's speaker to a severe cold.[2]

President Asad, in his unusual address of March 11, 1999, expressed pride in his achievements during the 30 years of his rule, describing them as "major and important [in that they] granted Syria a strong infrastructure which allowed it to stand fast [against its enemies] and continue to progress toward a brighter future." With this, Asad acknowledged that Syria still faced weighty challenges in developing the country. He called on the Assembly to prepare for these challenges and, particularly, to correct the many defects in the functioning of the governmental administration. He noted that "side by side with those who work faithfully and responsibly there are also some who have lost their sense of responsibility and have been slack or have neglected their task," warning: "We have no intention of tolerating these kinds of manifestations."[3]

While these contents were not new, and echoed remarks Asad had delivered on similar occasions in the past, there was one significant difference this time: he did not actually deliver his speech in person. Although the text begins with a direct address to the members of the Assembly – "I address you from this podium…" – indicating that the president intended to deliver it in person at the inaugural occasion, for some reason, apparently because of his health, he refrained from doing so. His speech, printed in advance, was distributed to the members of the Assembly, and that evening was read out by the radio and television news presenters. Yet the newscasters, like the press, which carried the speech in full the next day, refrained from noting that President Asad had not delivered his address himself.[4]

The "speech that wasn't delivered" was typical of Asad's management of Syria during most of his rule and especially during the last decade of his life, which was overshadowed by his deteriorating health. The speech, or, more accurately, the fact that he was unable to deliver it himself, was an apt illustration of Asad's rule as a "hidden" leader, or a leader with an "absentee presence," concealed in his palace, minimizing his public and political activity.

Asad refrained from touring the country during most of his rule, abstaining from visits to army bases, industrial plants, agricultural projects or educational and cultural institutions, much less walks through the cities, towns and villages to meet ordinary citizens. His daily schedule, publicized in detail by the Syrian media, revealed minimal meetings with foreign guests or with Syrian public figures, ministers, generals or any other senior members of the governmental, party or military apparatuses. In effect, he chose to rule Syria by means of a small nucleus of trusted leaders (*jama'a*) whom he had gathered around him during his rule and essentially from early on in his military and political career. Over time, he co-opted members of his family and tribe as well. This veteran group constituted a buffer between the president, elevated and removed from the people, and the day-to-day affairs of state, and especially the daily tribulations of the ordinary citizen, all of which Asad left in the care of his close circle and his aides. This arrangement was aptly described by the British journalist Patrick Seale, known to be a confidant of Asad, who wrote that "By the 1980s he had become for most people a dis-- embodied voice on the telephone." According to Seale, most of these officials never had the opportunity to meet their leader face to face, except at the inaugural ceremony at the start of their terms of office following governmental change (itself a rare occurrence in Syrian political life in the era of Hafiz al-Asad).[5] Asad thus stood at the top of the Syrian governmental pyramid, keeping a firm hold on the reins of the regime. Yet, whether he actually ruled, or, rather, whether in practice he managed the affairs of the state he headed, is doubtful.

Asad's seclusion basically illuminated his character: closed, cautious, wary and suspicious, reluctant to initiate any move, least of all any significant change in direction or policy. His success is attributable to the fact that underlying his image as a statesman was an experienced politician and a master of the art of survival. As one of Israel's most astute political personalities, Yosef Burg, once remarked about politicians like Asad, "When everyone takes care to walk between the raindrops, he prefers to stay at home and not get wet at all." He was a politician whose outstanding qualities were precisely passivity, the absence of initiative, and suspicion of taking action.[6]

Conceivably, too, he opted for seclusion within his office for fear of his life. Many of his acquaintances reported that the assassination attempt against him on June 26, 1980, was a traumatic experience which led to a change in his behavior as well as his lifestyle. The assassins, members of the Muslim Brotherhood, had penetrated the tight security perimeter surrounding Asad and were within grenade-throwing range, but missed their target. A loyal bodyguard threw himself on Asad and thereby saved his life.[7] Yet another contributing factor to Asad's disappearance from public life was his poor health. Following a serious heart attack on November 13, 1983, he cut back his work day drastically and ceased working nights entirely. Significantly, Asad in the 1970s had been known as a vigorous leader who maintained an intensive schedule and tended to work through the night, keeping high government officials in their offices until dawn waiting for his orders.[8]

The pattern of Assad's decline, seclusion and detachment from reality as a result of personality, security and health factors intensified during the 1990s. Asad in the last years of his rule became a shadow of the vital leader that Syria had known in the past – a forceful, strong-minded and disciplined figure, according to Western diplomats who had met him during the 1970s, 1980s and even early 1990s. In a well-publicized encounter in the summer of 1991, U.S. Secretary of State James Baker was prompted to wave his white handkerchief "in submission" after nine hours of exhausting discussions

with Asad, during which the Washington guest had to forbear going
to the washroom.[9]

The decline in Hafiz al-Asad's health, which accelerated in the
latter 1990s, became apparent in his appearance and in his physical
functioning, according to Western diplomats who met with him.
He also had difficulty concentrating during meetings he conducted
in the palace.[10] Several months before his death, the foreign press
reported that he suffered from dementia and was under constant
medical care.[11] American participants in the Asad–Clinton presidential summit in Geneva in March 2000, one of Asad's last meetings
with a foreign leader, reported that toward the end of the meeting,
when his medication had worn off, the Syrian president had difficulty speaking and relied on his translator, Buthayna Sha'ban, to
"assist" him in completing his remarks each time he faltered.[12] With
this, Syria- and Asad-watchers refrained from burying the Syrian
president prematurely, for he had outlasted many of his eulogizers
and had disproved the informed predictions by researchers as well
as physicians that his days were numbered following his heart attack
in 1983.

Still, the reports about his health during the last year of his life left
little room for surprise at his death on June 10, 2000. Although the
Syrian press reported the news under the headline "The Sudden
Death of the Eternal Leader,"[13] a close associate of Asad for over a
generation, Syrian Minister of Defense Mustafa Talas, who had first
met him in 1952 when they entered the Army Officers College,
remarked:

> When I met up with Asad at the Memorial Day ceremony for
> fallen soldiers on May 6, 2000, I sensed that his health was de-
> clining, although I hoped that this decline would be arrested and
> that he would manage to overcome his health problems, for these
> problems accompanied him for the last 15 years [ever since his
> heart attack in 1983] and he always managed to overcome them
> and regain his strength.[14]

Talas added: "President Asad himself felt that his end was near, and
about a month before his death he inquired when the Ba'th Party
Congress was scheduled. When we replied that it was scheduled for
June 17, 2000, he expressed surprise that it was to be so far off."[15]

Whether anticipated or not, the death of Hafiz al-Asad appeared
to be premature for many Syrians, especially in regard to the succession of his son Bashar. Although during the last years of his life
Asad had labored ceaselessly to guarantee his son's status as heir, these
efforts ran into a number of difficulties. In the perception of most

Syrians, Bashar remained an inexperienced young man lacking the necessary background to fill his father's shoes. Moreover, Bashar did not fill the mandatory requirement stipulated in the Syrian constitution that candidates for the presidency be at least 40 years old. Bashar, born on September 11, 1965, would be 40 only in 2005, the year his father would complete his fifth term as president.

During the final months of his life Asad appeared to become more aware of, or more concerned with, the deterioration of his health, prompting him to accelerate the process of his son's succession. He saw to the retirement of a series of figures in the highest echelons of the Syrian political and military/security establishment who might have challenged his son's status as successor. Additionally, he decided to convene the Ba'th Party national congress in June 2000, a step he had avoided for over 15 years. The congress was meant to confirm Bashar's appointment as a member of the party's leadership bodies, and possibly as the country's vice-president, thereby formally enhancing his status.[16] However, Asad passed away on June 10, 2000, seven days before the opening of the congress.

Possibly, his death was indeed somewhat premature for Bashar. Yet the reality in Syria in the late 1990s, at the end of the era of Hafiz al-Asad, suggests that, for the Syrian state, the president's death came very late, perhaps too late. His departure after 30 years of rule left Syria one of the most economically depressed states in the Middle East, sunk in political isolation, shunned by the international community, and embroiled in disputes with all its neighbors and with most of the Arab world. Syria also appeared more distant than ever from attaining its national goals, especially the return of the Golan Heights. Even its grip on Lebanon, practically the sole foreign-policy achievement by Asad during his long rule, was beginning to show signs of weakening. To a great extent, this bleak reality constituted the price of Asad Sr.'s survival or, put another way, was the indisputable result of the do-nothing policy he adopted, which preserved his rule for so many years.

Nevertheless, even accepting the view (shared by many Syrians) that the state would have benefited by Asad's retirement from the leadership a number of years earlier, any evaluation of his rule and his achievements and failures is a complex undertaking. Alongside the major failure to develop the Syrian state and society, and especially its governmental system, is the undeniable fact that Syria under Asad's leadership projected considerable power, which serves to counterbalance its weaknesses to a considerable degree. President Asad gained international recognition as one of the dominant leaders of the Middle East, praised repeatedly for his success in retaining a strong grip over his country for an unprecedented period by Syrian standards, and for imbuing the country with status and influence. His achievement in preserving political stability, perceived by many as his primary or even sole success, should not be underestimated, for he succeeded in an area in which all his predecessors had failed.

The struggle for Syria – an end that marked a beginning

Asad's ascent to power in Syria on November 16, 1970 is perceived as a turning point in the country's history for bringing an end to the "struggle for Syria," as Patrick Seale termed the power struggles that had plunged the country into turmoil ever since its independence on April 17, 1946. Intrinsic to the contest for control was a struggle over Syria's ideology, policy, identity and very existence.[17]

The termination of Hafiz al-Asad's prolonged rule prompted uncertainty over the country's future reminiscent of the insecurity during the period of the formation of the state by the French in the 1920s. Then, the sense of insecurity stemmed partly from the absence of roots or historical legitimation, for the Syrian state was established to serve the interests of France and not necessarily as a response to the will of its population. They, for their part, demanded the establishment of an Arab state covering the geographic area of Syria (*bilad al-sha'm*), and Iraq and the Arabian Peninsula as well. Uncertainty over Syria's future increased once the last of the French forces left the country in 1946, leaving behind a poorly functioning governmental system. This weakness was to characterize Syrian political life throughout its early years of independence till Asad seized power in that country.

Newly independent Syria also faced demographic, socioeconomic and regional challenges. Foremost of these was the factionalization of society along ethnic and communal lines, especially in terms of concentrated or compact minority groups which constituted majorities in their regions of residence. Syria's population contains Sunni Arabs, who constitute some 60 percent of the total, half residing in cities and half in rural and peripheral areas; Christians, constituting some 13 percent; Alawites, constituting 12 percent and living in the northern Alawite region; Druze, constituting approximately 5 percent and living mostly on Mount Druze; Kurds and Turkomans, constituting 10 percent and living mostly in the Jazira region; and the tiny Isma'ili population, constituting less than 1 percent. Moreover, a deeply rooted social gap existed between urban and rural populations throughout the country, along with an equally entrenched rivalry between Syria's two major cities, Damascus, the capital, and Aleppo to the north.

This traditional stratification blocked the acceptance of the Syrian state in the public mind and accounted for the failure to develop a widespread sense of loyalty to and identification with it. Rather, many Syrians tended to seek focuses of identity beyond Syria's territorial limits, e.g. pan-Arabism or, in certain circles, pan-Syrianism – the vision of a greater Syria. With this, regional, communal, ethnic, tribal and sometimes clan loyalty was also regarded as the basic and primary identity of the individual.

The lack of political stability in Syria evoked growing intervention by Arab as well as Western forces anxious to establish their influence in the country, to the point that the very existence of the Syrian state was undermined. The "struggle for Syria" reached a peak in 1958 when the Syrians opted to relinquish their statehood and form a united entity with Egypt, the United Arab Republic. However, three years later, in September 1961, the Syrians, disappointed with the implementation of the unification, disbanded it and from then on functioned independently.[18]

The Ba'th Revolution of March 8, 1963 was an important step in reinforcing the existence and viability of the Syrian state. It brought about a reversal of the governmental pyramid and in effect of the entire socioeconomic structure in Syria until then. The Sunni urban elite, which had controlled political, social and economic life for several hundred years, was replaced by a coalition of new political and social forces that emerged from previously suppressed sectors of Syrian society, namely minorities, rural populations and populations at the country's periphery.

The Ba'th regime, established in the wake of the 1963 revolution, entered into confrontation with key sectors of Syrian society, especially the Islamic elements, who were weakened and dislocated politically and economically by the regime change. The regime also became embroiled in an intense internal power struggle between a group of young Alawite military officers called the Military Committee (*al-Lajna al-'Askariyya*), headed by Salah Jadid, and the founders and veteran leaders of the Ba'th Party, led by Michel 'Aflaq and Salah al-Din al-Bitar. Although it was the Military Committee that had mounted the revolution in 1963, the rebels still needed the patronage and support of the old leadership of the party. Soon, a deep rift developed between the two camps over the direction and policy of the regime and, even more importantly, over who would control the state.[19]

The struggle ended in February 1966 with the victory of Salah Jadid over his rivals. The regime that he formed, known as the Neo-Ba'th, adopted a radical policy both externally (anti-Western and anti-Israeli) and domestically (namely, adopting the East European model of socialism), which proved disastrous. It led Syria into a deep economic crisis, heightened factionalization in Syrian society, and engendered rancor toward the regime by broad sectors of the population. Additionally, Syria was plunged into isolation in the Arab world and eventually dragged the entire region into the Six Day War of 1967.[20]

The crisis in Syria that resulted from Jadid's policy was one of the causes of the confrontation that occurred at that time between him and Hafiz al-Asad, his partner in the Syrian leadership, appointed Minister of Defense in 1966. Asad, an Alawite, as was Jadid, although from a different tribe, advocated moderation and conciliation in light of the complex reality in Syria, rather than the inflammatory policy pursued by the leader of the regime. The conflict between the two also had personal and communal motives. It reached a peak in 1969–70 when Asad, supported by the army and security forces, overcame his rival and took control of the regime in November 1970. For the first time, Syria was ruled by a single source of authority rather than a collaborative leadership arrangement. Moreover, Asad had no competitors or rivals in the domestic arena, for reasons that will be illuminated below.

Syria under Hafiz al-Asad

The secret of Asad's success lay in his ability to provide prudent responses to the challenges facing him and his regime, and possibly even to the fundamental problems of the Syrian state ever since its establishment. His responses accorded with the current reality not only in Syria but in its immediate region, in the Arab world generally and in the international arena. Four factors help explain his sustained success:

1. *President Asad, the "Eternal Leader."* A widely accepted and persuasive premise in the extant research about Syria under Asad is that the regional status acquired by Syria and the power projected by the regime were essentially the product of Asad's personal attributes. Syria itself was and remained a neglected and weak country, lacking both natural and human resources. It was Hafiz al-Asad who, by dint of his leadership and political acumen, carved out Syria's status as a regional power of influence.[21] Despite the depressed state of the country by the time of his death, Asad retained considerable support and admiration within Syria and outside it.

2. *Asad's regime.* Asad established a strong, stable, centralized regime that ended the prolonged period of political instability which had

characterized Syria ever since its independence. Decidedly ethno-centric, the regime relied on the support of the Alawite community from which Asad hailed, and which dominated the army and the security forces. The regime was also indisputably repressive, capable of going to great lengths to maintain its control, as exemplified by the crushing of the Islamic rebellion in Syria during 1976–82.

Asad's inner circle played a key role in this context. This group of trusted colleagues, family members and tribesmen, whose relationship with Asad went back as far as 40 or 50 years, conducted Syria's day-to-day affairs for him with unswerving loyalty to their leader and unshakable group solidarity. One startling exception, however, was Hafiz al-Asad's brother, Rif'at, who served for many years as the president's right arm and as number two in the leadership elite, but who turned on Asad when he fell ill in November 1983. Several senior Alawite army officers, including the commander of the commando forces, 'Ali Haydar, also criticized Asad outspokenly in a closed conference of officers in the summer of 1994. These, however, were exceptions. Notably, the political component of Asad's inner circle, including Vice-President 'Abd al-Halim Khaddam and Minister of Defense Mustafa Talas, were generally from the Sunni community, and displayed total loyalty to the president.[22]

3. *The composition of the ruling coalition: newly ascendant sectors of Syrian society.* Despite its weaknesses, the Syrian regime formed by Asad was more firmly rooted in the reality of the country than its predecessors had been. It was attuned to the political and socioeconomic order established in Syria in the wake of the Ba'th Revolution of 1963, which remained intact practically unchanged until the early 1990s. Structurally and in its human composition, the regime successfully reflected a coalition of social and political forces that represented most of the Syrian population. This coalition, moreover, consisted of long-repressed sectors of society, namely the minority groups, the rural sector and populations scattered at the periphery, and the lower classes, all of whom gained a dominant political voice with the advent of the Ba'th Revolution and even more so with the governmental takeover by Asad in 1970. The coalition was led by the Alawites, who constituted its hard core.

Upon taking power, Asad set out to pacify and draw in additional sectors who found themselves outside the governmental coalition and who resented or were hostile to the regime. The main target population was the urban Sunnis, whom Asad wooed with a policy of economic openness designed to restore some of their previous role in the country's economy. He also attempted to reach out to the Islamic elements, even prior to the Islamic revolt of February 1976 in Syria, by softening the secular image of his regime. Inter alia, he sought religious legitimation for his community, the Alawites. One result was that Imam Musa Sadr, leader of the Lebanese Shi'ites, handed down a religious judgment (fatwa) in 1972 recognizing the Alawites as Shi'ites and thereby as Muslims. Asad intensified these efforts following the suppression of the Islamic revolt, aiming at those Islamic elements who were prepared to accept the fact of his regime and even support it.[23]

Asad invested special efforts in establishing governmental institutions, namely the People's Assembly, the institution of the presidency, and an umbrella organization embracing all political parties permitted to operate in Syria – the National Progressive Front. Additionally, a series of popular organizations were established or institutionalized, including a farmers' union and a workers' union. This process of institutionalization was aimed at legitimizing Asad and his regime, guaranteeing him support by various sectors that had acquired governmental representation for the first time, and creating an atmosphere of stability in a state where instability and the absence of governmental and legislative bodies had been the rule for generations.

4. *A militant foreign policy but within acceptable limits.* Asad's foreign policy over time regarding the conflict with Israel, as with other regional and international issues, was another important element contributing to the esteem for him within Syria and outside it. This policy, skillfully articulated in the rhetoric of his regime (but, significantly, contrasting with Syria's moves in practice), reflected the perceptions of the ordinary Arab citizen – not only in Syria – regarding Israel and the West. Yet Asad took care to avoid crossing the line between inflammatory rhetoric and acts. In practice, his decisions were based on a realistic analysis of the world that Syria faced, and were typified by pragmatism and relative moderation. For example, following the October 1973 War, he maintained quiet along the border with Israel and even showed a readiness, when needed, to improve Syria's relationship with the West, including the U.S. Later, in the mid-1990s, at the height of the Middle East peace process, he displayed a preparedness to explore a peace settlement with Israel.[24]

What went wrong

While these attributes supported Asad in attaining stability in Syria and turning it into a viable state with status and influence, by the mid-1980s, and more apparently in the 1990s, the regime appeared to lose viability and no longer was able to meet the challenges facing the country, for the following reasons:

1. *Hafiz al-Asad, the "hidden president."* Asad was the linchpin of the regime, having molded it in his image. Until his last day of rule, he was viewed with respect by the Syrians, as by colleagues and rivals in the Arab arena, in Israel and throughout the world. Yet the fact that essentially he was non-functioning during the last decade of his life had a distinct effect on the regime he headed. The deterioration of his health, his seclusion and especially his avoidance of confronting the emerging issues facing Syria and making necessary decisions became an untenable burden for the country.

2. *The ruling elite – from asset to burden.* A pronounced manifestation of Asad's inactivity was his avoidance of making any significant changes or introducing new blood in the highest echelon of his regime. As a result, the Syrian leadership remained largely unchanged from the mid-1980s onward, and in some cases ever since Asad had taken over the government in 1970. A glance at the leadership lineup in the late 1990s reveals the average age to be in the seventies, some with health problems that hindered their functioning. Moreover, most had a pronounced Eastern European orientation and some had been educated in academic institutions in the former Soviet Union. Their world view had been molded in the 1950s and 1960s and they were unable to comprehend the changes that had occurred in the world, especially the globalization process, which had not passed Syria by despite its isolation.

3. *Disappointment in the articles of faith.* The regime itself, like the leadership, became anachronistic in its reflection and projection of world views that had lost their relevance. From the end of the 1960s onward, the pull of Arab nationalism waned, as did that of communism and socialism. For broad sectors of the population in the Middle East, Syria included, these ideologies were being replaced by a resurgence of Islam. One of the victims of this process was the Ba'th Party, known in the past as a vital ideological body with wide and authentic public support. However, the party gradually lost its vitality in the wake of the collapse of its precepts and became merely a bureaucratic body drained of content. Although data published by the regime in advance of the Ba'th Party regional congress in June 2000 showed a dramatic increase in membership since Asad's takeover of the government – from some 40,000 to approximately 1.25 million members[25] – these figures basically pointed to

the opportunism of the party's new members, who joined massively in order to ensure their personal future. Such data did not necessarily demonstrate the relevance of the party or its perceptions, or even the extent of its actual support within the Syrian public (see Chapter 3: "Bashar al-Asad – the man and his regime").

4. *Cracks in the ruling coalition.* The gravest development was the failure of the regime to reflect Syrian society any longer, while society ceased defining itself in terms of the structure, institutions and ideology of the regime. Notably, Syrian society had undergone vast changes during the decades since Asad had taken power. Foremost of these was dramatic demographic growth, the outcome of one of the highest rates of natural increase in the world, especially during the 1970s and 1980s (3.5–3.8 percent). Syria's population at the start of Asad's rule in 1970 was approximately 6 million, while in 2006 it approached 20 million.[26]

This significant population increase led to accelerated urbanization, turning Damascus, Aleppo and other cities in Syria into conglomerations of urban slums with millions of residents, most of them migrants from rural and peripheral regions who sought their fortune in the city but found themselves displaced and marginalized. Employment and housing were scarce, and education, health and welfare services inadequate. Consequently, these populations felt increasingly alienated from the state and its institutions.

This situation contrasted with that at the rise of the Ba'th regime, which succeeded in its goal of attracting and assimilating broad sectors of the disenfranchised, especially minorities and rural and peripheral populations. Under the leadership of the Alawites, these sectors formed a "coalition of the underprivileged" which brought the Ba'th Party to power in 1963 and later enabled Hafiz al-Asad to take over the government and retain control of the country for close to 30 years. By the 1990s, however, the regime appeared unable to sustain this achievement, namely to provide the necessary services for the spiraling populations in distress in the poverty-stricken quarters that had sprung up around the large cities, which led to a growing disconnection from the people.

One result of the widespread poverty, distress and alienation from the state was heightened Islamic sentiment, especially in the depressed urban quarters. Elsewhere, in such places as Egypt and Algeria, and in Syria itself in the mid-1970s, this mix of economic distress and deepening Islamic fervor led to outbursts of violent social protest with an Islamic coloration, threatening social and political stability.

5. *An irrelevant foreign policy that isolated Syria in a changing world.* The collapse of the Soviet Union in the late 1980s evoked concern in Damascus about the sustainability of the Syrian regime under Asad's leadership and the viability of the state he headed. The dramatic changes in Eastern Europe led to a breakdown of the Syrian defense perception, which had been based on two components: efforts to attain independent military capability vis-à-vis Israel, and reliance on the Soviet umbrella in the event of a threat to Syria by Israel or possibly by the United States. The collapse of the Soviet Union, moreover, engendered a new world order, and to some extent a new regional order as well, with the U.S. setting the tone. The potential ramifications of this development, for example the conceptualization of a "new Middle East," directly affected Syria's and the regime's regional and international standing. The regime was in danger of becoming anachronistic or irrelevant, its credo no longer attuned to reality.[27]

Clearly, a change of policy was needed. Indeed, from the late 1980s onward, Syria ostensibly changed direction, attempting to improve relations with the West, especially the U.S. As part of this effort, it joined the American-led anti-Iraq coalition during the Gulf crisis of August 1990 to March 1991. Furthermore, in October 1991 it logged on to the Middle East peace process, expressing a readiness in principle for the first time in its history, albeit equivocally, to sign a peace agreement with Israel. However, these foreign policy moves were hesitant and halfhearted, revealing no real desire to bring about a significant change in Syria's basic perceptions and world view. Moreover, Syria continued developing ties with Iran, and from 1997 made efforts to upgrade relations with Iraq. Not surprisingly, its relationships with the West, and especially with the U.S., remained frozen, showing no promise of a breakthrough (see Chapter 6: "Bashar al-Asad in the international arena").

The domestic challenge

Early in the 1990s, graffiti appeared on Damascus walls with the message "*Asadşescu*" and "*kul Ceauşescu biji yuma*" ("Ceauşescu's day will come"), hinting at the fate of Romania's ruler, Nicolae Ceauşescu, who was deposed and then executed in December 1989.[28] These street sentiments were further evidence, if any was needed, of the challenge posed to the Syrian regime by the collapse of the socialist regimes in Eastern Europe and later of the Soviet Union. Its very *raison d'être*, and the principles upon which it was established, were cast in doubt by the breakdown of the Soviet model, which had been a beacon for the Syrian regime over the years.

The significance of the collapse of the Soviet Union and its allies in Eastern Europe was not lost on the public or on the regime itself, including its highest echelon, which embarked on a series of social and economic reforms at the start of the 1990s. Furthermore, globalization, which began to be felt in Syria, as in most countries at that time, threatened to bring down the walls of isolation which the Syrian regime had built around the country and which it viewed as a guarantee of stability and endurance. These threats prompted the regime to introduce limited domestic change by adopting a policy of economic, and to a lesser degree political, openness, side by side with a readiness to shift national priorities and attempt to raise the standard of living of its citizens. Steps taken to create a sense of political openness included a cosmetic effort to impart a democratic character to referenda approving the candidacy of President Asad (the sole candidate) for additional terms of office in December 1991 and February 1999, and to the elections for the People's Assembly in May 1990, August 1994 and August 1998. The regime also broadened the authority and scope of the Assembly and, moreover, allowed a significant number of independent candidates who were not members of the Ba'th Party or its satellite parties to run for election. Another step was the release of thousands of political prisoners over the first half of the decade. Furthermore, the regime displayed a receptiveness to intensifying the dialogue with leaders of the Syrian Islamic movement, who in the past were among its bitterest enemies.

Economically, the government adopted a policy of greater openness and a limited measure of liberalization aimed at stimulating the Syrian economy and creating new sources of income and employment. This policy was also directed at easing Syria's integration into the world economy, widely perceived as a vital condition for guaranteeing the country's economic stability and prosperity in the future.[29] At the same time, the regime diverted significant resources to raising the standard of living of the population. From the early 1990s onward, large sums were invested in improving the country's infrastructure, namely the supply of electricity and water, communications, transportation, and education and health services. Nevertheless, despite impressive progress in these areas, the efforts made by the regime appeared to be insufficient to overcome the cumulative regression resulting from years of neglect, a lack of technological know-how and an absence of trained human resources. Moreover, the progress that was achieved could not keep pace with the spiraling demand for these services engendered by rapid population growth. Infrastructure crises in the supply of water, electricity, transportation and communications continued to preoccupy the regime and were a focus of sharp criticism of it by the public.

In summary, the limited process of change initiated by the regime did not appear to reflect a reformist vision or a new Syrian order. On the contrary, it seemed to be an essentially tactical step intended to preserve the existing order. If the Syrian regime from the late 1980s onward found itself facing a "window of opportunity," in the words of U.S. Secretary of State James Baker, then all it did was try to close that window or at the very least prevent winds of change from penetrating into the state.

Clearly, the main lesson learned by President Asad from the collapse of the Soviet Union was that every demand for change within the Syrian political system must be blocked, for such change could be the harbinger of disaster for the stability of the regime he headed and for his very existence. Not surprisingly, therefore, Asad repeatedly chose to highlight his country's "steadfastness in facing the challenges to it by its regional and international enemies" as the most significant accomplishment of his last 30 years. Syria, he emphasized, "preserved its independence, did not submit to pressure and scare campaigns, and refused to accept dictates that conflicted with its national interests."[30]

Apparently, the vast difference between Asad's perception of reality in the Syrian state and the perception of it by the West and Israel – along with many Syrians themselves – stemmed from his typically defensive, suspicious and essentially restrictive outlook. In this viewpoint, Syria's record under his rule was an unqualified success story. For, as even the sharpest critics of his regime admitted, all the threats to his country were successfully deflected by the regime, and even more so by Hafiz al-Asad personally, in maintaining relative stability in the state and in surviving, even though, as became clear, this was not enough. A glance at Syria at the end of the Asad era reveals a state at an impasse, having lost its direction and facing growing social strains that threatened to bring about the collapse of the socio-economic order and possibly the political one as well. Against this background, the claim that, alongside his ability to preserve stability during his rule, Asad's only other definitive accomplishment was assuring the succession of his son Bashar is understandable.[31]

This was the reality that faced Bashar al-Asad with the "surprising" death of his father in June 2000. Hafiz al-Asad's passing reawakened doubts raised in the past, but suppressed so long as he was alive, about the survivability of the Syrian regime for long. Undoubtedly, the regime had been sustained during the last decade of his rule, and in effect long before as well, by the dividends of past successes, namely his success in establishing a strong, stable government and preserving it for so long. Moreover, if the secret of Syria's success and viability during the preceding 30 years lay in the figure of Asad personally, as was widely thought, his departure presumably freed the restraints holding back a renewal of the struggle over Syria which in the past had nearly brought about the collapse of the state.

PART I

SYRIA UNDER BASHAR

CHAPTER 1

The road to the top

Beginnings

Friday, January 21, 1994 was to have been another routine day for Dr. Bashar al-Asad, a young ophthalmologist from Damascus serving as a resident in the Western Eye Hospital in London. Yet suddenly his world turned upside down. Word came from Syria that his older brother, Basil, had been killed in a car accident, and he was called upon to leave London immediately and return to Damascus.

Dr. Edmond Schulenburg, a senior ophthalmological surgeon at the hospital where Bashar was specializing, well remembers that bitter, stressful day:

> Bashar came to my office and said he had received bad news and must return to Syria at once. He didn't say a thing about his brother being killed in a traffic accident, or a word about his plans for the future. But we knew about it from the news broadcasts. I should add that his face was impassive and that he behaved with great restraint, giving no hint of his emotions.[1]

Bashar had arrived in London about a year previously, at the end of 1992. He had studied ophthalmology at the University of Damascus, graduating with high grades.[2] His choice of medicine as a profession may have been attributable to his father's affinity for it. In his youth, Hafiz al-Asad had wanted to become a doctor, but his family could not afford to finance his studies and he settled for an army career.[3] Nevertheless, he continued to show interest in the medical profession until the end of his life. He was known to be a hypochondriac, prompted in large measure by his major heart attack in 1983 and his concern about his health and his illnesses thereafter. Significantly, his eldest daughter, Bushra, also chose a medical field, studying pharmacology.

Bashar's choice of ophthalmology as a specialty was subsequently ascribed in the Arab newspaper *al-Hayat* to his "highly developed critical sense as well as his inclination toward an analytical, rational and methodical approach to everything he undertook."[4] This inclination was to be reflected distinctly, and even to an extreme, in his personal and his political conduct, eliciting the widespread view that he led Syria like an eye doctor and not necessarily like the leader of a state. Dr. Schulenburg, his supervising physician during his stay in London, observed:

> From my acquaintance with [Bashar], I think that what drew him to ophthalmology was his obsessive trait of doing things accurately. He had a high sensitivity for perfection. This is an important quality for an eye doctor, for we are not dealing with a profession that allows for mistakes. He also had great esteem for modern technologies. He was aware that Syria lagged behind the Western world in the field of ophthalmology and he wanted to study so that he could pass on the knowledge he acquired to his people.[5]

Bashar, born on September 11, 1965, was the third child of Hafiz and Anisa al-Asad. His older sister, Bushra, was born in 1960, followed by his brother Basil, born in 1962. His two younger brothers were Mahir, born in 1969, and Majid, born in 1972. Another daughter died in infancy in late 1959, when Hafiz al-Asad, then a promising young army officer on the rise, was in political exile in Cairo.[6]

The home in which Bashar grew up was infused with politics. Family life was conducted in the shadow of his father, who took over the Syrian government in November 1970 when Bashar was 5 and struggled in the early years to retain power. Bashar's older brother, Basil, once reminisced that he and Bashar saw little of their father, and that even when Asad was home he was immersed in reading official documents and dealing with affairs of state. Sometimes days would pass without his exchanging a word with them.[7] Fateful events in Syria during those years also left an impression on the family. During the October 1973 War the family was sent to the Alawite Mountains, in the event that Israeli forces threatened Damascus. Some years later, during the Islamic revolt against the regime (1976–82), the family again felt threatened, as members of the Muslim Brotherhood targeted leaders of the regime (including Asad) and their families for attacks. Basil, who was about 19 at the height of the revolt, recalled about that period: "Because of the random killing [perpetrated by members of the Brotherhood], people advised me not to go out, but I felt I could defend myself. All of us children were convinced that if anything should happen to one of us, it would have no political impact on our father."[8]

The long-range effect of the Arab and Syrian nationalist education that Bashar absorbed from home was analyzed by one of his
close acquaintances thus:

> In Israel and in the West it had been assumed that because Bashar
> was educated in the West [i.e. he spent his medical residency in
> London], he would be prepared to abandon his principles and
> thereby guarantee his rule [by means of Western support]. How-
> ever, in practice Bashar continued following his father's line, for
> Damascus, where he grew up, was and remained the incubator of
> resistance and struggle in the Arab world.[9]

Bashar himself, after assuming Syrian rule, attested that "whoever
thought that I would be more moderate than my father erred. The
Americans think that our political behavior is pragmatic, but in
practice my generation, including myself, show an even greater
adherence to national and pan-Arab principles than did my father's
generation."[10]

An analysis of Bashar's views reveals a person who grew up in a
Syria free of doubts and imbued with self-confidence in its right
as well as ability to maintain its existence as an independent state.
Indeed, remarks by him in praise of "the 10,000-year-old Syrian civilization"[11] confirm his definitive Syrian political identity, even if
cloaked in a broader pan-Arab identity. Possibly, Bashar inherited this
strong sense of Syrian identity from his mother, whose family, the
Makhlufs, were supporters of Antun Sa'ada, founder and leader of
the Syrian Socialist National Party (the P.P.S.).[12] More likely, he was
essentially the product of the "new Syria," which, under Hafiz al-
Asad's leadership, radiated strength and power and was no longer
the weak and unstable entity it had been in the early years of its
independence.

Bashar, like his brothers, attended the al-Huriyya School (*ma'had
al-huriyya*), a prestigious institution in Damascus that included elementary, preparatory and high school. Significantly, it was a public
school, for Asad Sr. followed, and imparted to his children, a modest
and even abstemious lifestyle. In 1979, at age 14, during his preparatory school studies, Bashar joined the Ba'th Party youth movement
and later became a party member. In contrast to his brothers Basil
and Mahir and his sister Bushra, Bashar was a quiet, shy child.[13] His
older brother, Basil, was considered a born leader with a strong, charismatic personality. His younger brother Mahir was said to have
resembled Basil in his vigor and the viability he radiated, but also in
his impulsiveness and, possibly, brutality.[14] Not surprisingly, Asad Sr.
groomed his eldest son, Basil, for greatness, steering him to a military
career at age 18.

Bashar's older sister, too, was known to be assertive and opinionated. The story of her marriage to the partner of her choice, Asaf Shawkat, or, more accurately, how she obtained her father's consent to the marriage, was one of the most talked-about items in Damascus in the early 1990s. Shawkat, an Alawite, born in 1950 in Tartus on the Syrian coast, was older than Bushra by ten years and, moreover, was thrice divorced. The fact that he held a doctorate in history from the University of Damascus (the topic of his thesis was the Syrian revolt against the French Mandate during 1925–27) did not placate Hafiz al-Asad or Basil, who opposed the match. Stories circulating in Damascus related that Basil had beaten up Shawkat and had him jailed in order to deter him from marrying his sister. In the end, however, Asad Sr. relented under the pressure of his daughter's entreaties, or possibly threats, and gave his blessing to the couple. The marriage, and especially the twins born thereafter (Hafiz and Naya, who were Asad's first grandchildren), clearly improved the atmosphere in the family and enhanced Shawkat's status. He was soon named to a senior position in the Department of Military Security, one of the key internal security bodies in Syria, and later was said to have become Bashar's closest confidant.[15] Nevertheless, rumor had it that there was tension between the "royal couple," as Asaf and Bushra were referred to surreptitiously, and Bashar, and especially between Asaf and Mahir. Reportedly, the two quarreled openly in the wake of a discussion within the family circle regarding Rif'at al-Asad. Shawkat, it was said, criticized Bashar's uncle sharply and was told by Mahir that he had best leave the matter to the family. When Shawkat retorted that he was part of the family, Mahir shot him and wounded him.[16]

Bashar's arrival in London at the end of 1992 to further his medical career marked his first exposure to the Western world. In the event, it was also to provide people in the West with a rare opportunity to get to know the future Syrian president. The impression he made on his colleagues at work was of an intelligent young man, a quick learner, well-mannered and polite, yet introverted, keeping his life private. Successful, although not highly impressive, at work, he was assigned to perform surgery within weeks of his arrival, at first minor procedures such as eyelid surgery, and later more complex operations.

Dr. Schulenburg, his supervisor, recalled:

When I first interviewed him for acceptance as a resident, I had reservations about this tall young man. People who come from a background such as Bashar's tend to be arrogant, but I was pleased to see that he was not arrogant. He was modest.... When he began working here as a resident, it was very important to him to show his recognition of the authority of his superiors. I called him by his first name and he called me Dr. Schulenburg.... He was a good and a pleasant resident. His behavior was reserved and gentle. He was well liked by my staff, [although] I don't think he had good friends among the other residents.... He gave the patients the feeling that their well-being was the only thing that concerned him. The patients liked the way he cared for them.[17]

The hospital secretary remembered that "as a resident Bashar was respected by his departmental colleagues. He was a very friendly fellow, quiet and polite." One of his colleagues in the department, Dr. Clive Migdal, observed, in a similar vein, that "Bashar was a polite person. I can't recall a single occasion when he behaved inappropriately towards anyone around him."[18]

Describing Bashar's lifestyle, Dr. Schulenburg stated:

He didn't put on airs.... He had no bodyguards. The patients knew him only as a young man named Bashar. I remember that for a time he didn't even have a car. One day he received a gift of a BMW, Model 318. He was very excited the day he received it. He talked about the car with great emotion. A BMW of the model he had is an expensive and fine car, but it isn't a flashy model that someone who has everything would get excited about. When I observed Bashar's emotion the day he got the car I thought to myself: Here is someone who isn't used to receiving the good things as a matter of course. This is not a person who was spoiled in his childhood.... I never saw him smoke, although he would take a sip of wine. He told me that he likes to listen to jazz and to Phil Collins [the Genesis soloist]. More than once he said that his life's ambition was to be an ophthalmologist. One of my colleagues once asked him about British politics and Bashar told him that the British politician that he liked was Margaret Thatcher.[19]

A relevant, if perhaps biased, evaluation by Bashar's relative and friend Rami Makhluf, who was in London at the same time, bears out the observations above:

Bashar showed himself to be a modest person, exactly like his father. He never used a driver to take him from place to place, and he was in the habit of clearing away his dishes from the table himself. When we would order in take-away food, he would scold us for ordering too much food. I remember that he particularly liked to cook and to read.[20]

Bashar returned to London in December 2002 for the first time since leaving it upon his brother's death. The occasion was his first official visit to the British capital as president of Syria. During the visit he frequently recalled his time there as a young resident. He was quoted as saying: "It is wonderful to be in London, a city I know well.... I lived here for two years. I worked as a physician and I got to know the English and the British in their daily lives, and I believe we formed bonds of friendship and mutual respect."[21] Or:

> When I lived here I preferred walking from my lodgings on Sloane Street to the hospital where I worked. My daily route took me past Buckingham Palace. I spent a lot of time viewing it and other sites. I familiarized myself with the British lifestyle and got to know how the ordinary person lived. However, I didn't have time to go out, as I spent most of my time in the eye hospital.[22]

During his extensively covered visit in London Bashar also stopped by the hospital where he had worked. Later he said of his return to the hospital:

> I was very pleased and excited about visiting the hospital from which I had parted nearly nine years previously. I asked the nurses and doctors how they were, and soon realized that nothing had changed except for the attitude of the director of the hospital. I remembered him as demanding and tough. He would shout at us and reprimand us when he discovered any kind of deficiency in our work. This time he addressed me in a tone of respect and said: "Welcome, Mr. President."[23]

Bashar's wife, the London-born Asma al-Akhras, accompanied him on this visit. She included in her itinerary a visit to the school she had attended. She, too, was excited by the visit, remarking: "To this day, I still think that the school I attended is one of the most beautiful places I have ever seen."[24] Bashar had met Asma, whom he would marry in December 2000 after he became president, during his period of residency in London. She was the daughter of Fawaz al-Akhras, a Syrian cardiologist of the Sunni community in Homs. Fawaz, born in 1946, emigrated to London in 1973, became a cardiologist and opened a clinic on fashionable Harley Street. He was a founder in 1984 of the Syrian Arab Society, which was dedicated to bringing together the approximately 10,000 Syrians living in Britain. Fawaz became an address for Syrians setting out for London. In 1991 he received a letter from Bashar al-Asad requesting assistance in locating a place to train in ophthalmology. Fawaz's acquaintance with Dr. Edmond Schulenburg paved the way for Bashar's acceptance as a resident under Schulenburg in the Western Eye Hospital, which was attached to St. Mary's Hospital in Paddington, London.[25]

Once he arrived in London, Bashar kept in touch with Fawaz and from time to time attended social and cultural events held by the Syrian Arab Society. It was at one such event that he met Fawaz's daughter, Asma, whom he probably knew before. Born in London, she was educated in English schools, including Queen's College, a girls' high school. Later, she attended King's College, graduating with honors in computer science. Her final project was an original soft-ware management program for the riding stable she frequented. Fellow students remembered her as an intelligent, sharp-witted, agreeable young woman. Western in every way, she dropped the 's' from her name during her early years at Queen's College – the name Asma commemorated her paternal grandmother[26] – adopting the popular English name Emma instead. At age 16, however, she re-sumed her given name as part of a return to her Arab and Syrian roots. "I can't say I was 'Emma'," she later observed. "I was 'Emma', as you call somebody sweetheart or sweetie or darling or so forth. I was born in London. I spent 25 years in London. But I also know that I am Syrian. I speak the language fluently. I read and write it. I am British and I am an Arab. I am not one or the other. I am part of both worlds."[27]

Upon completing her studies, Asma began working in mergers and acquisitions at J.P. Morgan Bankers and was later accepted to Harvard Business School. However, she abandoned these plans and resigned from her job in mid-2000 after Bashar proposed marriage. His proposal came as a surprise to many of their acquaintances, for the couple had kept their romantic attachment secret. Actually, rumors in Damascus had focused on various other young women as candidates for marriage to Bashar.[28] So effective was their secrecy that the announcement of the marriage prompted conjecture that the match had been arranged for political purposes, in as much as Asma was from the Sunni community. Later Asma revealed: "We were friends for a very long time. I came to Syria every year since I was born. [We met] through family friends who knew each other since childhood." Their friendship did not necessarily turn into something more when Bashar studied in England, as, she recalled, "we hardly saw each other at all. And, if we did, it was more on a friendly basis and nothing else." She did not know that she would be marrying him until he proposed.[29]

Bashar's residency in London was to have ended in 1994. Ac-cording to close acquaintances, he planned to return to Syria and establish a network of private hospitals in Damascus with the help

of a Saudi businessman friend, 'Akif al-Maghrabi. These plans, however, were to be relinquished entirely.[30]

Syria – the question of the succession

A review of Hafiz al-Asad's activity during the last decade of his life,
which ended with the transfer of the reins of power to his son Bashar,
gives the impression of a process carefully planned in advance. Yet
the question remains as to when Asad first conceived the idea of
choosing one of his sons as a successor. Was it on the very first day of
his rule? Was it after his heart attack in November 1983, which must
have prompted him to consider his mortality for the first time? Or
was it possibly in the early 1990s, when his eldest son, Basil, came of
age and was judged suited for the task and who may have even craved
the authority and the power of the office?

A study of the nature of the regime that Asad established in Syria
might provide a partial answer to this question, for not only was his
regime military-based but it was also ethnically based and to an even
greater degree tribal- and family-based. Above all it was a one-man
regime, identified with the moves and the persona of Hafiz al-Asad,
who entrenched it and sustained it throughout his prolonged rule.
Undoubtedly, he was also influenced by various Communist regimes
of a dictatorial family nature, with whom he kept close ties during
the 1970s and 1980s, especially Kim Il Sung's regime in North Korea
and Nicolai Ceauşescu's in Romania. At the same time, the Muslim
Arab heritage had a formative influence on the Syrian regime and its
leader. The dominance of the Alawite officer class over Syria under
the leadership of the Asad family was viewed by some as a revival of
the military sects that ruled the Islamic world from the tenth century
onward. These sects, which had a distinctly ethnic character, quickly
established hereditary dynasties in which rule was passed from father
to son. Nevertheless, describing one such dynasty – the Mamluke
sultanate in Egypt – Bernard Lewis noted in his *The Middle East:
2000 Years of History* that, with the death of the sultan, his son
inherited his crown for a period of time until the real effective successor would emerge.[31]

In the event, Asad refrained entirely from dealing with the issue of
succession during the early years of his rule and in effect left it an
open question. Notably, he had taken power in Syria at a relatively
young age (40), he was in good health and his political future appeared promising. Moreover, his two sons at the time were only 7
(Basil) and 5 (Bashar). It should also be pointed out that Asad emerged from a coterie of young officers with a shared outlook. While

they viewed Asad as first among equals, presumably they would have had reservations about, or would have opposed the notion of, Asad handing over the regime as an inheritance to one of his sons. They were, after all, a group of ardent revolutionaries raised on the Ba'th Party's socialist doctrine, with most belonging to its radical wing.

Still, Asad's early years at the helm of government witnessed the swift rise of his younger brother, Rif'at, to a position of power. He was put in command of the "Defense Squadrons" Division (*Saraya al-Difa'*), an elite military unit that was allocated generous resources, the best equipment and the highest-quality recruits, mostly from the Alawite community. This evoked a widespread assumption in the public mind that Rif'at was destined to succeed his brother, should Asad leave the political scene. Yet events proved otherwise. Apparently, Asad chose to rely on Rif'at for the reinforcement and entrenchment of his regime, but did not view him (or another brother, Jamil, who also played a central role in the Syrian leadership elite) as a worthy successor. Asad's equivocal attitude toward Rif'at is reflected in Patrick Seale's book *Asad of Syria*, which is based, inter alia, on interviews granted by the president himself. The depictions of Rif'at in the book are hardly flattering, especially in the section that deals with the struggle that broke out between the two brothers during 1983–84. Rif'at is described as unstable, brutal and corrupt. Moreover, the book hints that he was in effect a puppet in the hands of the Americans and the Saudis, who tried to use him to overthrow his brother.[32]

The question of the succession in Damascus surfaced acutely in the wake of Asad's heart attack in November 1983, which proved nearly fatal. Rif'at, to Asad's pronounced displeasure, promptly set about promoting himself as his brother's successor. The struggle between the two over the leadership of the regime threatened to disintegrate into a civil war, posing a challenge to domestic cohesion and to the survival of the regime over a period of six months. Ultimately, Asad emerged the victor, removing his brother from the positions of power he held and forcing him into a prolonged exile in Western Europe.[33] The episode had the effect of marginalizing the question of the succession in Syria. Nevertheless, it remained an unresolved issue, for, despite an improvement in his health, the Syrian president never regained his full strength, and his heart condition increasingly hindered his functioning.

Early in the 1990s, signals from Damascus began pointing to the likelihood of Asad grooming his eldest son, Basil, as his heir. Basil, who had reached adulthood by then, was successful in his military career and had gained a measure of popularity with the public. The signals, meant in part to test receptivity and possibly lay the groundwork for an official announcement of Basil as successor, took several forms. First, Basil's military career advanced meteorically. He was named, in the early 1990s, a brigade commander in the Republican Guard, an elite division in the Syrian army. He also participated in a series of military courses, including a staff command course and a tank battalion command course, which were prerequisites for advancement in the Syrian army. Second, Basil became more prominently exposed to the public and gained a measure of popularity. This exposure initially centered on his sports activity as leader of the Syrian Olympics equestrian team, and later on his work to promote computer awareness through the Syrian Computer Society (*al-jam'iyya al-ma'lumatiyya*), which he founded at that time and headed until his death. Third, in a new move, photographs of Basil were circulated next to those of his father during a referendum conducted in December 1991 for the ratification of Asad's candidacy for a fourth term as president. Moreover, Hafiz al-Asad began to be referred to as Abu Basil, although in the past he had often been referred to as Abu Sulayman, after his grandfather, Sulayman. Fourth, reports in the Arab press outside Syria began to appear about Hafiz al-Asad's intention to appoint Basil as his heir. Apparently, some of these reports were deliberately leaked from Damascus.[34]

Nevertheless, the plans made by Asad Sr., who was known to be pedantic, cautious and deliberate, went awry. On Friday morning, January 21, 1994, Basil met his death in a car accident en route to the Damascus airport. Driving at high speed, he had swerved to avoid hitting a roadblock put up for road repairs, and his car overturned. He was killed instantly, while a close friend who was traveling with him, Rami Makhluf, was badly injured. Rumors circulating in Damascus later suggested a plot to kill him. Basil's uncle Rif'at, who was undoubtedly distressed by his nephew's rise in status, was mentioned as a possible conspirator. Alternatively, drug dealers or smugglers, whom Basil had targeted in an anti-crime campaign, were cited. These rumors, however, were apparently unfounded.[35]

Basil's death at the age of 32 was a shock to Syria and beyond. The feeling in Damascus was that his untimely death constituted a loss of hope for the future not only for his bereaved father but for Syria as a whole. Basil had begun to be viewed in the public mind as the guarantor of continued political and economic stability achieved under Hafiz al-Asad.

Bashar – a jump start to the top

Shock was also the province of Bashar, Basil's younger brother, who all at once was called to the colors. If he had any doubts about the role he was now expected to play, he kept them to himself. Later, however, it was said that he tried to avoid accepting the burden his father was intent on placing on him, and that only under Asad Sr.'s firm pressure did he assent.[36] Syrian media coverage of the funeral procession and the mourning ceremonies for Basil showed Bashar by his father's side, supporting him and actually leading him by the arm. Notably, the Syrian media completely ignored another family member, Rif'at al-Asad, who was present among the mourners too. Later, the regime began circulating Bashar's photograph throughout Syria, at first as the third of a trio of photos of his father and deceased brother, and then alongside his father, or entirely alone.[37]

Apparently, as soon as he received the bitter news of Basil's death, Hafiz al-Asad made up his mind to hand over the reins of leadership to Bashar. However, he was aware that Bashar had a long way to go before he became an accepted and agreed-upon successor and, more importantly, a worthy and qualified successor. Bashar lacked knowledge and life experience of the kind that could help him fill the appointed task. Moreover, he lacked the image of a charismatic, capable leader fit to succeed his father. Perhaps the problem was not so much his image but the actual absence of these attributes in Bashar. Additionally, in order to ensure Bashar's candidacy as successor, Asad had to eliminate other potential contenders. These included Asad's own brother, Rif'at; army commanders and heads of key security services, for example Chief of Staff Hikmat Shihabi; and political leaders, especially Vice-President 'Abd al-Halim Khaddam.

Conscious of the need to prevent unnecessary shocks – especially prematurely – to the Syrian leadership elite, Asad chose to implement his plan gradually, cautiously and, most important, circumspectly. He avoided dealing with contenders for the succession – whether self-appointed or popularly perceived – by direct confrontation, whose final outcome would be self-evident. Typically, he used indirect tactics instead. He lulled them into a false sense of security, allowing them to pursue their dreams of the prize that would be theirs until they reached the legal retirement age in the various branches of public service. Then he forced them into retirement, backed by the provisions of the Military Service Law or the Civil Service Law.

Many Syrians and others tried initially to minimize the significance of Bashar's jump start (or, perhaps, push into the deep water of the Syrian political pool), especially as his chances of stepping into his father's shoes appeared slim, both because of his youth and inexperience and because Syria was, after all, a "people's democracy." For example, the head of Vice-President 'Abd al-Halim Khaddam's office conveyed a message to the author of this book that research I had published earlier about the accelerated promotion of Basil in the Syrian leadership had been far-fetched, and that I was repeating this mistake in the case of Bashar, for "Khaddam is the successor."[38] Chief of Staff Hikmat Shihabi, as well, continued to present himself to foreigners as "the number two man" in Syria.[39] Even the well-known researcher of Syrian and Lebanese history Elizabeth Picard believed that "the thought that Bashar might become president of Syria one day is foolish,"[40] which only shows the limitations of Western researchers and academicians who may have difficulty moving past their empathy for the object of their lifelong research, and in this case accepting the de facto transformation of the Syrian republic into a presidential monarchy.

Asad's plan was that his son should acquire education, knowledge and experience, mold his persona as a commander and leader, and generate status and personal support bases by means of a course of military training (however accelerated), rather than by assuming a position in the Ba'th Party or governmental service. This route showed that the army, or, more accurately, rising in the ranks of the army, and the establishment of loyal support bases in the officer elite remained an essential source of governmental legitimation and political backing for anyone seeking a career in high office. With this, the catapulting of Bashar, an eye doctor by profession, into the upper echelons of the army officer corps, which of necessity entailed marginalizing or dismissing senior officers with greater experience and higher rank, was an implied insult to the army leadership and evidence of Hafiz al-Asad's success in controlling the army and keeping it obedient to his wishes throughout his rule.

Soon after his return to Syria in January 1994, Bashar embarked on the military route of his father's design, the same route, albeit abbreviated, taken by his older brother, Basil. Included were a tank battalion commanders' course and a command and staff course, which together constituted an important portion of senior officer training in the Syrian army. Bashar also assumed the task of brigade commander in the Republican Guard Division, which Basil had led. Reports from Damascus traced Bashar's growing involvement in the running of the army and the other security services in Syria, namely in appointments and promotions in rank and in his regular presence in various training exercises.[41]

Bashar's progress up through the military ranks was also noted. When he returned to Syria in January 1994 he held the rank of first lieutenant (*mulazim awal*). In July of that year he was promoted to captain (*nakib*); by July 1995 he had risen to major (*ra'id*); and in July 1997 he became a lieutenant colonel (*muqaddam*). Syrian sources attributed this rapid advance to "Bashar's overall distinction in the command and staff course and the superior final project that he submitted for the course."[42] In January 1999 he was raised to the rank of colonel (*'aqid*), and upon the death of his father in 2000 he was named field marshal (*fariq*).[43]

In parallel, President Asad invested efforts in establishing support bases for Bashar within the Syrian military system. Apparently, this goal underlay a broad, unprecedented manpower shift in the highest command level, namely the divisional command. Young, mostly unknown Alawite officers were promoted to this level, evidently in the expectation that they would provide Bashar with the support he needed.

Bashar's public image

Side by side with advancing Bashar's status in the army and the security forces, Asad Sr., together with Bashar, focused on molding and marketing his image as heir apparent to the Syrian public, the Arab world and the West. The first goal was to put Bashar in the spotlight, as he was largely unknown in Syria or outside it until pressed into his new role upon his brother's death. Given wide attention by the Syrian media as soon as he returned home, he was projected as following in Basil's footsteps even during the mourning rites. Thereafter, he received extensive coverage when taking part in activities favored by Basil, including horse racing and conferences relating to computers. In contrast to Basil, Bashar did not actively race horses, but was shown awarding prizes to the winners. However, he did play an active role in promoting the Syrian Computer Society, becoming its chairman after his return to the country.[44]

The image created was of a vigorous, dynamic young man, with emphasis placed on his efforts to foster modernization and openness in Syria and heighten awareness of computer and Internet use. This aspect was also highlighted in interviews he began granting to the foreign press, during which he repeatedly stressed the need to advance Syria toward the twenty-first century. Describing himself as an experienced Internet surfer in an interview with the London-based *al-Hayat* in October 1997, he pointed out the importance of integrating the Arab world on the Internet so that the Arab point of view would be aired and the other side (Israel) be prevented from exerting a hegemonic hold over the medium.[45] In a similar vein, he told the editor of the Egyptian weekly *al-Usbu'*: "There is a need to ensure the existence of an open Arab medium that makes use of advanced technology to convey our positions. Only this type of medium, which respects the mentality of the Arab viewer, can influence public opinion and lead it to support our views."[46]

Additionally, Bashar was presented to the Syrian public and to the West as "Mr. Clean" – untainted, and responsive to the demand by the Syrian public for an uncompromising fight against corruption. Reports by foreign journalists in Damascus linked his name with the growing crackdown by the regime on corruption in governmental bodies.

He was also shown to have a common touch, open and accessible to the public, whom he encountered frequently during tours of the country, including major population centers his father had never visited during the entire span of his rule. An example was the city of Aleppo, which Bashar toured for several days in October 1999. During that visit he stopped to drink tea at a shop in the market, creating a sensation that was reported extensively in the Syrian and foreign press.

The Syrian press also began to relay signals, albeit tentative, that Hafiz al-Asad intended to pass on his rule to his son. The state-run daily *al-Thawra* published an article in January 1997 by a close associate of Bashar's, Dr. Bahjat Sulayman, who held a senior post with one of Syria's internal security bodies, hinting that such was Asad Sr.'s intention. "Bashar has proved in a short time that he is a branch of the blessed tree [the Asad dynasty], and has responded to the appeal of his countrymen to fulfill Basil's mission and preserve the heritage of the great leader on the road to the third millennium," Sulayman wrote.[47] Bashar's name was mentioned increasingly in literary columns in the press that published poems in praise of Hafiz al-Asad and his regime, while pictures of Bashar, mostly next to his father, began to appear on wall posters together with slogans designed to instill an awareness of him as heir apparent, e.g. "Basil was our symbol and Bashar is our hope."[48] The Mufti of Syria, instructed to mention Bashar's name in his sermons, stated in one sermon: "Bashar will take on and will succeed in carrying the burden borne by his father," a thought echoed by other preachers as well.[49]

In the late 1990s, Bashar began granting interviews to the media about his views in the context of his personal future, while carefully preserving the atmosphere of constructive opacity that he and his father had generated regarding the possibility of his inheriting the leadership of the regime. In an interview with the London-based weekly *al-Kifah al-'Arabi* in December 1999, he explained that he was not "seeking positions, yet should the leadership or the Party appoint me to a position, I am prepared to accept it."[50] In another interview with the London-based magazine *al-Wasat*, granted in February 2000, he stated:

> I believe in the need to encourage conceptual change and I ascribe greater importance to this issue than to assuming an official position of one kind or another. Syria has had a wonderful political leadership [under Hafiz al-Asad], and great effort must be made to create progress similar to that which we have attained in the political realm, as in the economic and social realms. The first steps have been taken, and I hope they will bear fruit soon. Our ability to enter the 21st century depends on our degree of readiness in these areas.[51]

Bashar in the inter-Arab and international arenas

Toward the end of the 1990s, when the awareness of Bashar's presence appeared to have become well accepted in the public eye, his father began granting him governmental authority and exposing him more extensively to the media, while still avoiding naming him as his successor. Father and son focused their efforts on foreign relations, reflecting a desire to impart vital experience to Bashar in an area viewed by Asad Sr. as critical, as well as imbue Bashar's candidacy with worldly legitimacy. Conceivably, Asad also preferred directing his son to the area of foreign relations before exposing him to the country's oppressive domestic issues, including the power struggles and grave social and economic problems which might have tarnished his image.

A pronounced sign of Bashar's new involvement in foreign affairs was a series of visits he made to various Arab countries during the year before his father's death, namely to Jordan, Bahrain, Kuwait, the United Arab Emirates and, lastly, Saudi Arabia, which he visited in July 1999, performing the 'Umra (a non-haj pilgrimage) there. Additionally, he made his first trip to the West in November 1999, visiting France, where he met with President Jacques Chirac. The French president was to become one of Bashar's most enthusiastic supporters and patrons in the West after he took over Syrian rule.[52] Bashar also sought out the Western media in an effort to gain support for himself and his aspirations. An unusual interview in the *Washington Post* in April 2000, shortly before his father's death, reflected this effective effort. The reporter, in a sympathetic piece, highlighted Bashar's commitment to promoting far-reaching reforms in Syria alongside his affinity for Western culture, writing:

> If change has been slow to come to Syria, that is in the nature of things here. Stability in the family, the culture and the society is

paramount, and no innovation – no matter how logical or urgent
it may seem by Western standards – is sanctioned without ex-
haustive discussion about the risks as well as the benefits.... But
that does not mean things will always be the same in Syria....
Bashar foresees a not too distant time when "the Internet is going
to enter every house," breaking [the present] barriers to information flow. "I would like everybody to be able to see everything.
The more you see, the more you improve.... Knowledge is lim-
itless.... [Yet] some... people [here] have their doubts [about
this].... The new generation wants new ideas. New hope."[53]

Plainly, Bashar had made a deep impression on the reporter, who
added:

Bashar Asad acknowledged: "I am ambitious." But, in contrast to
monarchical states where blood succession is the rule, he said he
would have to prove himself in a system that is politically complex
and heavy on tradition.... "You might find it strange, but we have
never discussed this issue [the inheritance of rule] in our family,"
he said. "Playing a public role is different from being prepared" to
take over.

Tellingly, the reporter described Bashar as "soft-spoken and con-
genial, a fan of Faith Hill and Phil Collins tunes downloaded to a
Walkman-like digital music player.... After cutting a ribbon to open
[an international information technology trade show in Damascus],
Bashar Assad spent nearly two hours wandering from vendor to
vendor, discussing the niceties of satellite phones and high-speed
servers."[54]

The Arabic media highlighted the network of relationships that
Bashar developed with the heirs apparent of his generation in the
Gulf states whom he met during his visits there and their visits to
Damascus. The warm relationship he developed with Jordan's King
'Abdallah was also emphasized in particular. 'Abdallah, returning
from a visit to Bashar and his father in April 1999, commented:
"Bashar is like me, a child of the Internet generation,"[55] reflecting the
common interests that the two found with each other and the fact
that Bashar was more open than his father to technological and scientific innovation.

In 1998 Bashar took charge of the "Lebanese file." Presumably,
President Asad entrusted it to him not only because of the importance he attached to it but also because Lebanon was no longer
viewed as a volatile issue, as the Syrians had imposed their control
over that state successfully. Another important advantage for Bashar
in handling the Lebanese issue was that it involved facing down

several powerful figures in Syria, such as Vice-President 'Abd al-Halim Khaddam and Chief of Staff Hikmat Shihabi, who had been responsible for Lebanon in the past and continued to be involved in developments there. Bashar's success, with his father's assistance, in supplanting them in the Lebanese arena contributed to his empowerment in Syria's domestic scene as well.

His involvement with the Lebanese file must have helped Bashar grasp the nature, essence and complexity of this neighbor of Syria's. However, whether his handling of the issue that was handed over to him made a strong impression in Lebanon or outside is doubtful. On the contrary, his approach to it may have raised doubts about his ability to deal with the complex reality that prevailed in Lebanon, or with even more complex issues that he would face as head of state. Many Lebanese perceived Bashar as trying to instruct them in handling their affairs, as a teacher instructing his students and expecting them to correct their ways, or as handing down directives in a bureaucratic fashion and expecting them to be followed exactingly. He appeared to minimize the importance of the personal touch as a means of leadership in managing Syria's affairs in Lebanon. The result was a break between the Syrian and the Lebanese political leadership, reflected in growing internal friction between the Lebanese politicians, who inevitably turned directly to Damascus to resolve their conflicts, often after they had reached the boiling point. All in all, Lebanon's political culture evoked a bureaucratic or "scientific" approach on Bashar's part.

The twilight of an era

A referendum held in Syria on February 10, 1999, ratifying President Asad's candidacy for his fifth seven-year term of office elicited 8,961,011 votes in favor, or 99.987 percent of the vote, with only 219 against and 917 disqualified votes.[56] Similar percentages were reported for previous referenda in Syria, although it was clear to everyone that any connection between these percentages, as reported by the authorities, and reality was purely coincidental. In practice, most of the population did not bother to take part in this regime-organized display of democracy.

President Asad took his oath of allegiance before the People's Assembly a month after the referendum, on March 11, 1999. However, unlike this occasion in the past, he did not address the Assembly in person, apparently because of his poor health. Instead, a printed version of his speech was distributed to the delegates.[57] Indeed, during the last years of his life, reports proliferated about his worsening

health. According to one such report, attributed to American diplomats who met with him, the Syrian president had difficulty
concentrating and expressing himself and seemed exhausted.[58] The
sharp decline in Asad's health in the last year of his life was accompanied by an evident effort on his part to accelerate the process of
transferring his rule to his son Bashar as his highest priority.

The struggle against Rif'at

One of the signs of the entrenchment of Bashar's status in the leadership elite was his preparedness to take on a fight to the end against
his uncle Rif'at, his father's brother. Rif'at, sent into a prolonged
exile in Western Europe early in 1985 following his attempted revolt
against his brother, returned to Syria in the summer of 1992 upon
the death of the Asad brothers' mother, Na'isa. Remaining in Syria,
Rif'at kept a low profile thereafter. Apparently, however, he did not
abandon his political ambitions and took covert steps, mostly outside
Syria, to preserve and reinforce his status as a potential successor to
President Asad. A main vehicle for this effort was various media
which he owned, especially the Arab News Network (ANN) under
his son Sumar's management, which began broadcasting from London in October 1997. Reportedly, Rif'at also sought to acquire
religious legitimation and support in the Alawite community by
adopting a religious lifestyle, growing a beard and praying regularly.[59]

These developments angered President Asad. On February 8, 1998,
a presidential order divested Rif'at of his title of Vice-President for
National Security Affairs – a title in name only – which he had held
since late 1984. The step was apparently designed to indicate President Asad's unequivocal rejection of Rif'at's candidacy as his successor.
Asad also constricted the latitude of another of his brothers, Jamil,
who in the late 1970s had been the political boss of the Alawite
region.[60] A break between Jamil and the president occurred during
the power struggle between Asad and Rif'at in 1983–84, apparently
as a consequence of Jamil's delay in aligning himself with Asad.

Rif'at, however, did not give up his quest, despite the blows delivered to him over the years by his brother. He continued building
up his public image by means of his media holdings, as well as by
cultivating political ties with personalities in the Arab world, to the
annoyance of the Syrian leadership. For example, Rif'at visited Saudi
Arabia often, meeting with his old friend Prince 'Abdallah, the heir
apparent. The wives of both men were sisters (although both men
had more than one wife). Rif'at attended the funeral of King Hasan
of Morocco in July 1999. The king had been another of Rif'at's
close associates. Notably, Hafiz al-Asad did not attend the funeral

because of the presence there of Israeli Prime Minister Ehud Barak. While at the funeral, Rif'at met with Chairman of the Palestinian Authority Yasir 'Arafat, which led to an invitation to Rif'at's son Sumar to visit the Palestinian Authority territories. This step angered the Syrian leadership, whose relationship with the Authority was in decline then.[61]

Asad and Bashar apparently viewed Rif'at's move as a challenge to Bashar. They decided to take action to demonstrate that his political pretensions would encounter firm resistance and, moreover, that Bashar was willing and able, despite his youth and lack of experience, to confront Rif'at without his father's help. At the end of October 1999, a series of arrests of Rif'at's supporters in the Alawite region was announced, while Syrian soldiers and security officers broke into a residential complex and an illegal harbor built by Rif'at on state land he had appropriated over time. Several security personnel and several of Rif'at's associates were killed during the incident.[62]

The eleventh hour

Reports from Damascus in April 2000 stated that the authorities planned to hold a Ba'th Party regional congress in June, the first such event since January 1985. The party congress at that time had taken place at the height of the power struggle between President Asad and his brother Rif'at. According to the party constitution, the congress was to be held every four years in order to elect the leaders of the party bodies as well as discuss and ratify its future course. Asad, however, chose to avoid convening this assembly after 1985, apparently in order to avoid unnecessary agitation within the Syrian governmental and Ba'th Party leadership in light of the vast changes that were taking place in Syria and outside it over this period.

Asad's decision to convene the party congress at last pointed to his intention to use it to solidify Bashar's status as his successor. Predictions in Damascus were that Bashar would be elected at the congress to one of the party's central bodies, and possibly might be appointed to an executive post, e.g. vice-president of Syria.[63]

However, a week before the scheduled opening of the congress, Asad passed away.

CHAPTER 2

Taking the reins of power

It is unfair that because of the fact that Bashar is the son of Hafiz al-Asad he should be denied the right to serve as president of the state. The Syrian constitution does not prohibit the son of the president from serving in the post filled by his father.

> (Minister of Information 'Adnan 'Umran to foreign correspondents
> following the approval of Bashar al-Asad's candidacy for the
> presidency by the People's Assembly,
> *al-Ahram*, 23 June 2000)

At 6.00 p.m. on Saturday, June 10, 2000, Syrian TV cut off all telecasts and the noted religious personality Marwan Shaykhu appeared on the screen looking grave. Shaykhu, who for some time had acted as patron of the "believing president," Hafiz al-Asad, and had been rewarded by a seat in the People's Assembly, delivered the following announcement in a voice choked by tears:

On the morning of June 10, 2000, an exceptional leader, a leader of rare wisdom, breathed his last and died. Today, a leader who stood firm in the defense of the rights of the nation and the homeland has passed away. The leader of exalted values, ideals, policies and way of life is dead. The leader who struggled for over half a century for the glory of the Arabs and their freedom, to preserve their honor and restore their rights, is dead. The leader who struggled against the raging storms and continued to stand fast against attacks without loss of courage or faltering vision has died. A leader whose perceptions remained firm and unwavering. He was the bravest in decision making, the strongest in delivering his nation from its enemies and rivals, and the most compassionate in love of man. Today, a star who lit Syria's and the Arabs' sky for over three decades, and gave of his wisdom, his body and his heart, has fallen. A leader who bore the burden with patience, holding the banner of the nation aloft. He fought the battle of jihad, struggled and bore the burden with forbearance and patience for the sake of the homeland so that it will be safe, prosperous and strong. He was like a lion in dealing with the tragedies, the hardships and the storms. He was a soldier and a fighter who believed that life has no value without the existence of the precious, free and unified homeland. He was a president conscious of his responsibility in building up the homeland, responding to its needs, and struggling to liberate its captured land. He was a father, a father who loves his subjects. He felt their sorrows and shared their joys. Brothers, today we have lost our brother, comrade, friend, guiding father and teacher.[1]

This announcement might easily be dismissed as rhetoric had it not evidently expressed the feelings of many Syrians and others that Asad's death marked the end of a significant era – the formative era of Syria's history as a modern state. Moreover, since Asad was widely viewed – with considerable justification – as the cornerstone of the regime he had established and had led for a generation, his passing elicited fears for the continued viability of this regime and, by extension, of the political stability he had maintained in Syria throughout his rule.

As if sensing these fears, Syrian TV did not screen Qur'anic verses, as was customary in the Arab states on such occasions, but instead switched to a live telecast of the hastily convened session of the People's Assembly. The purpose of the session was to approve an amendment to Article 83 of the constitution, the article which stipulated the minimum age of the president as 40, a condition widely perceived as one of the obstacles to Bashar's ascendancy to the presidency. A revised version for consideration by the plenum, which was eventually ratified, fixed the minimum age at 34, Bashar's age.[2]

The next day, June 11, 2000, the acting president, First Vice-President 'Abd al-Halim Khaddam, announced two decrees: Decree No. 9, which appointed Bashar as commander of the armed forces, and Decree No. 10, which promoted him to the rank of *fariq* (field marshal), the highest military rank, which his father had held. That evening, the Syrian high command, led by Minister of Defense Mustafa Talas and Chief of Staff 'Ali Aslan, pledged their allegiance to Bashar.[3]

The alacrity of the response to Asad's passing showed that his end was anticipated, that a consensus had been reached in Damascus regarding filling the vacuum he would leave and, by extension, that a plan had been in place should his death come suddenly. This indeed was the case, for he died early in the morning of June 10 during a telephone conversation with Lebanese president Emile Lahhud.[4] The first rumors of his death spread through the Syrian capital in the early afternoon,[5] while the official announcement was made, as discussed above, in the early evening. The announcement was evidently made after the inner leadership circle had prepared a well-organized and rapid transfer of power to Bashar.

The first step in this process was the altering of the constitution, followed by the appointment of Bashar as commander of the army. A week later, the authorities took advantage of the scheduled Ba'th Party Congress, convened in an atmosphere of mourning for the leader of the party and the nation, to appoint Bashar as secretary-general of the party and, as such, a member of its highest bodies – the National Command, the Regional Command and the Central Committee. Reading out the reasons for the election of Bashar as leader of the party, the assistant to the secretary-general of the Regional Command, Sulayman Qaddah, noted that "Bashar has personal qualities with which the late leader was also graced, including intelligence, courage, the ability to contend with difficulties, and an absolute commitment to the interest of the people."[6] In the same vein, the editor of the party organ *al-Ba'th*, Turki al-Saqr, declared: "Bashar has inherited the wisdom, courage and political acumen of the leader Hafiz al-Asad, and is the most suitable [candidate] to steer the ship of the homeland at a time when it faces dangers and challenges and sails in stormy seas."[7]

Later, the Regional Command of the party chose Bashar as its candidate for the presidency of the country. According to the Syrian constitution, it is the Ba'th Party Regional Command that chooses the candidate for president. The candidate must then be approved by the People's Assembly, and thereafter by the Syrian public by means of a referendum. The members of the party's Regional Command in explaining their choice, stated:

> In his personality and his acts Comrade Dr. Bashar embodies the link between generations – between the generation that brought about the great turning point and change in Syria's history [the Ba'th Revolution] and amassed experience during the years of struggle it led, and the young generation which grew up under the wing of the Reform Movement [an appellation for Hafiz al-Asad's ascent to power] and which today works with all its strength to develop and promote modernization in the state. The link between these two generations, embodied in the candidacy of Bashar for the presidency, is essential in order to ensure continuity and modernization, and especially the continuation of the progress of the state. Presenting Bashar's candidacy also constitutes a response to the will of the masses and is essential in meeting the challenges to our country, challenges whose motto is "Renewal based on continuity."[8]

The People's Assembly convened on June 26, 2000, and approved Bashar's candidacy for the presidency. Thereafter, his candidacy was submitted for approval by a referendum. The entire process of approval was accompanied by demonstrations of support for Bashar throughout Syria, which had begun in effect the day Asad had died and were organized at least partially by the authorities.[9] The referendum was held on July 10, 2000. According to official figures, 8,931,623 voters took part, of a total electorate of 9,442,054 (a 94.59 percent rate of participation). Bashar obtained the support of 8,718,689 of the voters, constituting a majority of 97.29 percent. Negative votes amounted to 22,439, or 0.25 percent of the voters, with 219,319 disqualified votes.[10] Syrian spokesmen hastened to point out that the fact that Bashar obtained 97.29 percent of the vote and not 99.99 percent, as his father used to attain during his rule, was evidence of the authenticity of the referendum. However, as in the past, foreign observers cast doubt on the credibility of the results.[11]

Bashar took his oath of loyalty before the People's Assembly on July 17, 2000. Addressing the delegates on that occasion, he outlined the main points of his policy, which he called "Change alongside Continuity and Stability," i.e. a sustained commitment to his father's legacy while introducing imperative changes in the Syrian way of life. In particular, he emphasized the need to "present new ideas in all areas, while also improving ideas that no longer suit the existing reality, or even relinquishing old ideas that are no longer useful." He added that "supervisory apparatuses, a sense of responsibility, and respect for the law must be reinforced, while wastefulness and corruption must be combated, and culture and values must become permanent features in the political life of the state." With this, Bashar warned against demands for fundamental changes in the Syrian reality:

> Democracy is obligatory, but we must not enact the democracy of others. The Western democracies stemmed from a long history which produced leaders and traditions that created the present culture of democratic societies. We, by contrast, must adapt a democracy distinctive to us, founded on our history, culture and civilization and stemming from the needs of the society and reality in which we live.[12]

Bashar's speech sent a promising signal to a broad stratum of intellectuals as well as pragmatists who viewed it as a prelude to a campaign of long-range reform in the state. Yet, whether this was Bashar's intention is doubtful. Very likely, he himself did not have a clear vision of the course he wished to chart for Syria's future. Essentially, his speech, like many of those to follow, was replete with slogans but lacked any mention of his operative intentions.

First shadows

The sole challenger to Bashar's election as president was his father's brother Rif'at, living in exile in Spain for the last decade. An announcement attributed to Rif'at on the ANN satellite TV network he owned questioned the legitimacy of the installation of his nephew as successor. The manner in which it had been accomplished, said the report, constituted "a knife in the back of the [Syrian] constitution and cause for the negation of the constitutional legitimacy of the institution of the presidency, so that by extension he is ignoring the will of the people."[13] Rif'at's son, Sumar, followed this up by calling the referendum that approved Bashar's candidacy illegitimate, and saying that, in contrast to Bashar, his (Sumar's) father, Rif'at, was the person who had support and legitimation from the Syrian public. The demonstrations of support for Bashar, Sumar said, were "a fake exhibition."[14]

Nevertheless, once it became clear that the transfer of power to Bashar had been accomplished smoothly, and that Rif'at's appeal to the Syrian public had not elicited any response, Rif'at ended this criticism. Moreover, he announced that he supported the parts of Bashar's inaugural speech which he found "positive," and that these statements were evidence of the start of a "new reform movement under his leadership."[15] Syrian sources reported, however, that an arrest order was issued against Rif'at should he attempt to enter Syria, pointing to Bashar's suspicion of him.[16]

Rif'at's challenge to Bashar, marginal as it was, inasmuch as he had evidently lost his stature in the Syrian public eye and within the power bases, nevertheless cast a shadow over Bashar's rule. The rivalry between Bashar and Rif'at (as well as between Bashar and another of his father's brothers, Jamil) demonstrated that the extended Asad family did not uniformly support Hafiz al-Asad's son and heir. Indeed, Rif'at continued to be a nuisance to the young ruler in Damascus. Reports during the months that followed the inauguration pointed to contacts made by Rif'at and Sumar with the leaders of the Syrian Muslim Brotherhood in exile in London aimed at testing the possibility of attaining a cease-fire between these traditionally bitter enemies and establishing an alliance under Rif'at's leadership that would topple Bashar. Later reports indicated an attempt by Rif'at to make contact with representatives of Israel in Europe with the goal of ensuring support for him from Jerusalem should he attempt to return to Syria.[17] At the same time, he continued using his influence with the Saudi elite to persuade Bashar to reconcile with him and allow him to return to Damascus.[18]

Criticism of the manner of Bashar's ascendance to the presidency as a warning signal for Syria's future was also expressed within the country. A particularly blunt critic, Riyad al-Turk, leader of one of the factions of the Syrian Communist Party (the Communist Party – Political Bureau), was quoted as stating that he would not vote for Bashar in the forthcoming referendum, for "Asad Sr.'s management style had turned Syria into the private property of his family, and the state was nothing but one large prison." Turk labeled the manner of changing the minimum age requirement for the presidency from 40 to 34 "ludicrous."[19] In the early months of 2001, Turk and many others were to attempt to take advantage of the regime change to challenge the political order established by the Ba'th in Syria, but were to pay dearly for it.

Notably, side by side with the display of grief upon the death of President Asad and the enthusiastic expression of support for Bashar, other, more equivocal reactions toward the Asad dynasty were also evident. For example, reports from the city of Hamah, which had endured brutal treatment by the regime during the suppression of the Islamic uprising that had flared up in February 1982, indicated the absence of any atmosphere of mourning over the death of Hafiz al-Asad. The mourners' tents set up by the authorities for representatives of the regime to receive the condolences of the public stood empty. Some residents dared tell foreign reporters: "Too bad Asad died a natural death and was never punished for the evil he perpetrated in this city."[20] This reaction was a warning sign that the Islamic protest suppressed by the iron fist of the regime in the early 1980s was still palpable, albeit beneath the surface, and could yet burst out anew and constitute a real challenge to the regime.

Why Bashar?

Despite the apparently sweeping support for Bashar by the Syrian public, and not least from the power bases in the country, President Asad's choice of Bashar as his successor, and even more so the ostensibly smooth transfer of power to him after his father's death, raised questions on the part of seasoned Syria-watchers. Besides his youth and the obvious absence of experience and self-confidence, along with other lacunae in the personality of the new ruler in Damascus which were quickly noted, these observers were in agreement that Bashar lacked charisma and leadership ability or, as one Syria expert put it, "Bashar lacked the killer instinct so essential to anyone interested in ruling that state."[21] Notably, the Israeli coordinator of his country's activity in Lebanon, Uri Lubrani, bluntly forecast a bad end for Bashar soon after his election: "They went and crowned a lad of 34 to rule over Syria. They made him a commander overnight. What are the generals in the Syrian army thinking now – that this Alawite boy will give us orders? Does he have experience, courage or ability? I barely give him a fifty–fifty chance of survival."[22]

This line of thinking was well expressed by Dr. Schulenburg, under whom Bashar had trained in London. In an interview approximately a year after Bashar's election as president, he acknowledged:

> To tell the truth, I thought that the Bashar al-Asad whom I knew was too delicate a man to be president of a state. I did not think he would be assertive or tough enough to rule Syria. Yet, I would not underestimate his determination. As a resident, Bashar was highly focused. He worked stubbornly in order to reach the goal he had set himself, to be an ophthalmologist, and perhaps this quality of determination can help him.[23]

In the Arab world, too, Bashar's ascendance to power was viewed with unconcealed derision toward the man and especially toward the Syrian state – the Democratic People's Republic which Hafiz al-Asad and his sons had turned into a family dynasty.[24] Even in Syria itself Bashar's ability to lead the country was in doubt, as shown by the widespread response in the Syrian street to the question: Why Bashar and, more specifically, what quality does Bashar have that makes him a worthy successor to his father? The most popular answer, as reflected in the opinions of taxi drivers in Damascus, was: "There is no one else [*ma fi ghayru*],"[25] indicating that many Syrians viewed Bashar's rise to power as a choice by default in the absence of any other worthy candidate for the presidency. This reality had been molded, in no small measure, by Hafiz al-Asad himself, who devoted his last years precisely to this goal: ensuring the succession of his son, inter alia, by removing every other potential candidate from the scene.

Apparently, Bashar was the unexpected beneficiary of this situation. The choice of Bashar, therefore, may be viewed not only as a choice by default but, conceivably, as a conscious decision by the power brokers in Syria not to determine the long-range succession at that time. Deferring this permanent decision to the future, they were satisfied with Bashar for the transitional period that would bridge the era of the Asad dynasty and the era to come. This strategy, moreover, reflected Hafiz al-Asad's success in taming and neutralizing the army, which in the past had constituted the greatest threat to the politicians.

Bashar's success in taking the reins of power was attributable, therefore, to a series of factors. First, the Syrian governing elite recognized the importance of quickly filling the vacuum left by the passing of Hafiz al-Asad, the founder and unchallenged leader of the regime, so as to prevent any threat to the stability of the regime or to its very existence. The fear of power struggles in the governing elite over the vacant office was particularly salient, for such contention was liable to shatter the regime from within. Second, Bashar was the only relevant candidate in the domestic arena, inasmuch as most of the other candidates, or at least those who viewed themselves or were mentioned as possible candidates to succeed Hafiz al-Asad, had been removed from the political arena before his death. Third, the fact that he was his father's son, and the chosen son, worked in Bashar's favor, giving a measure of legitimation to his rule and imbuing his succession with the status of continuity. Fourth, Bashar was not perceived as a threatening figure or as intrinsically having power or stature that could endanger the status of the governing elite or the other power bases in the state. Neither his personality nor his world view – which was considered to be generalized and undefined – was perceived as a threat either to the status quo in Syria or to the power brokers themselves. This was aptly expressed by Syrian Defense Minister Mustafa Talas, a friend and confidant of Hafiz al-Asad, who explained:

> There was an option that [Vice-President 'Abd al-Halim] Khaddam would be a candidate, or even that I would serve as a candidate, but this never entered my mind because I am nearly 70, as is my colleague, and if one of us were to be elected president, we would have had to elect a president every two years. The election of Bashar is a way of expressing thanks to Asad, who has given so much to Syria.... Bashar is a promising young man deserving of confidence, and we will assist him in every situation.[26]

Fifth and last, a point to be emphasized is that Bashar was perceived by wide sectors of the Syrian public, especially intellectuals, the business community and the younger generation, as someone who could bring about change and even a turnabout in the Syrian reality. This perception is reflected in remarks at that time by the dean of the Law Faculty at the University of Damascus, Professor 'Aziz Shukri, who had become one of the Syrian spokesmen in the West over time: "I am very optimistic about him. We are speaking about a person with an open mind who demonstrates a credible ability in real politik. He will win because the people are with him, and sooner or later, with the backing of the people, he will reorganize the [Syrian] house."[27] This support for Bashar did not escape the notice of the Syrian elite, who were anxious to fill the vacuum left by Hafiz al-Asad's departure with a minimum of agitation, and reinforce their own position through the support for Bashar in wide sectors of Syrian society.

One way or another, Bashar, carried aloft on a wave of anticipation of change, and backed by a measure of support from the power bases of the state under the leadership of the old guard who had surrounded his father, ascended to the presidency. Some said the move came too soon, others that it was too late. All that remained was to wait and see whether the six years of work by his father to prepare him for this moment were sufficient.

CHAPTER 3

Bashar al-Asad – the man and his regime

The Syrian Ba'th regime inherited by Bashar al-Asad from his father was a personality-based regime revolving around the figure of Hafiz al-Asad, its founder and long-time leader. The central pillar of the regime, Asad Sr. served as the force that unified its varied, and sometimes rival, components. His character, and especially his image both within Syria and outside it, constituted a source of power that fueled the regime and that he used skillfully to rally support from various sectors of Syrian society.

At the same time, the regime was also family-run, or even tribal, in view of the central role played in it by Hafiz al-Asad's family and tribe – the Kalbiyya tribe. Moreover, it was also a communal regime in its reliance on the support of the Alawite community. This group constituted an important element in the regime – in effect the element that held the other components of the regime together. In this respect, the regime reflected the ascendance of the Alawite community in the second half of the twentieth century from a minority of inferior status to an elite sector.[1]

Ultimately, the regime established by Hafiz al-Asad might be described as multi-faceted. Sometimes it displayed its personality-based character, and at other times its family-, tribal- or community-based character, depending on circumstances or, more accurately, the challenges faced by its leader. Moreover, the regime also had a party coloration as a Ba'th regime, as well as a military character in that it relied on the support of the army and the security forces.

Historically, the regime was the product of a social and political revolution that took place in Syria in the wake of the Ba'th Revolution of March 8, 1963, and as such reflected the socioeconomic and political system entrenched in the state thereafter. The format of the system was a ruling coalition composed of the following forces: 1) The Alawite community, which constituted the dominant element, guaranteeing the coherence and viability of the regime by means of its relative power and advantaged status. 2) The rural Sunni community located in the peripheral regions and constituting a senior partner in the coalition. The strength and prominence of this sector in the Syrian regime was evident in the composition of the Syrian political elite – at least the observable leadership – in which the Sunnis constituted a majority. 3) Other minorities in Syria – Christians, Druze and Isma'ilis – who were partners in the coalition. These minorities viewed, and continue to rely on, the Alawite dominance as a guarantee of their own status as well as of their personal and economic security. 4) The gradual integration of another group into the ruling coalition over time, albeit as a marginal partner – the Sunni economic elite, primarily in Damascus. This sector was able to capitalize on the policy of economic and political openness adopted by Asad's regime in 1970 and gradually enhanced from the early 1990s onward.[2]

Bashar al-Asad thus inherited a functioning, if aging, governmental system, which granted him a certain grace period which he would need at the start of his rule. Relying on the system, he nevertheless attempted to introduce certain changes aimed at integrating additional sectors of society into mainstream life, with an emphasis on reinforcing Syria's non-governmental institutions (the government, the People's Assembly, the officially recognized political parties, extra-parliamentary organizations and even non-establishment organizations). This effort apparently stemmed from Bashar's awareness that the key to Syria's future lay in the improved functioning of its governmental system, especially its social and economic institutions; in diffusing the atmosphere of political suffocation that had prevailed for nearly 40 years; and in co-opting population groups outside the establishment into the productive development of the state. Yet these attempts at reform, however limited, were unsuccessful, at least initially, and Bashar soon chose, or was forced to make do with, the old order.

Much has been written about the new direction that Bashar sought and seeks for Syria. Clearly, however, he did not have an overall reversal of direction in mind. He did not contemplate adopting the Western democratic model. In fact, he warned his audience in his inaugural speech against unrealistic expectations of dramatic change which, he said, Syria did not need and for which it was not prepared:

> Administering democracy is a must for us, but we must not implement the democracy of others. Western democracy is the product of a long history from which leaders and traditions emerged to create the present culture of democratic societies. We, in contrast, must adopt a democracy that is distinctive to us, founded on our history, our culture and our civilization, and stemming from the needs of the society and the reality in which we live.[3]

In the course of the struggle that he inevitably conducted against the reformist camp in Syria, Bashar explicitly defined the limits of the public debate which he sought to stimulate, and by implication pointed to the issues that were off limits: 1) his late father's life work; 2) the question of the status and role of the army and the security forces; 3) the leadership status of the Ba'th Party in Syria, anchored in the constitution; and 4) the socialist world view, which still constituted the regime's guiding light.[4]

Interviewed in the London-based *al-Sharq al-Awsat* on February 8, 2001, the young president explained how the public debate in Syria, which he wanted to encourage, should be conducted, and what the true meaning is of the political openness he sought to introduce in the state:

> We ought to remember that the homeland is a family, and it is surely unacceptable for members of a family to discuss their problems at home when they are outside the home. If they did, they would lose the respect of others. Even if one perceives the Arab states as kinfolk in an extended family, it is unacceptable for a member of the nuclear family to discuss personal problems with relatives, though they be part of one's extended family.[5]

This message also illuminated the claim by the reformist camp that Hafiz al-Asad had turned Syria into a family legacy and that essentially Bashar sought to preserve this legacy as it was, even if he wished to make it prosper and blossom through greater openness and freedom than in his father's day.[6]

Bashar – the leader and his image

Bashar did not seek to offer an alternative political model of rule to the existing one molded by his father, i.e. a model of presidential rule based, ultimately, on the image and personality of the leader. In fact, during his first years as president he acted vigorously to fill the vacuum left by his father and entrench his status as first among equals in the Syrian ruling elite and in the public eye.

At first, however, he made efforts, at least outwardly, to tone down the cult of personality of "the Comrade, the Leader, the President Hafiz al-Asad," which had characterized his father's rule. He ordered the removal of his pictures from walls, and a moderation of the flattery that the Syrian press had habitually used in referring to his father, such as the use of the title "the Eternal Leader."[7] The state-run newspaper *Tishrin* promptly praised Bashar for his modesty, informing its readers that apparently his father, too, "had silently opposed the cult

of personality that enveloped him, but the people insisted on bestow-
ing honor and respect upon him as an expression of loyalty to the
leader, and Asad had no choice but to overlook it."[8] Notably, however, the pictures of Bashar were not removed, and a survey of the
Syrian newspapers since his inauguration reveals no significant change
in the treatment of him as compared to that of his father. Indeed, the
Syrian media promptly mounted and sustained a laudatory campaign
surrounding Bashar once he took over the presidency, with necessary
alterations made in light of the differences in personality between
father and son.

Bashar was projected as a young, vigorous president of great vitality – honest, industrious, devoted, intelligent, quick-witted, open-
minded, accessible to the public, and yet a man of principle and a
guardian of the nation and the homeland. Descriptions of the young
president by pro-Syrian newspaper editors to whom Bashar granted
long interviews during the first years of his rule clearly reflect the
image he wanted to project. With this, these accounts also reveal an
authentic difference between Bashar and his father, and conceivably
between Bashar and other leaders in the Arab world.

The editor of the Jordanian *al-Majd* reported, after meeting Bashar
in May 2002:

> This young leader is not the usual type of president of a republic,
> but someone with the potential to be an outstanding Arab leader.
> He is destined to fill a distinctive role in the history of [the Arab
> nation] and to restore to the Arab leadership the honor and credi-
> bility it has lost. In my encounter with him I found him to be
> likable and modest, with a sense of self-confidence, willpower, in-
> depth experience and an open approach. His capacity for broad
> vision and clear rhetoric is evident. He is consistent, determined
> to challenge the existing reality, true to the principle of resistance
> and struggle, attuned to the mood in the street, and he believes in
> the ability of the [Arab] nation to overcome its difficulties.[9]

The editor of the Lebanese *al-Liwa'*, who met Bashar two years later,
in July 2002, wrote:

> When you enter the Presidential Palace in the Muhajirun Quarter
> [of Damascus], you sense that everything around you signals sim-
> plicity and clarity. And when you sit beside the young president,
> you quickly grasp that he is a new type of leader, whose demeanor
> conveys calm and quiet and whose behavior reveals wisdom and
> an iron logic. His lucid, friendly remarks show you that here is a
> leader who believes in democratic dialogue as a way of life. He
> keeps long hours, day and night, for he promised in his inaugural

address to work for his people. Nothing interests him except his work, and the truth is that the work that awaits him is vast.[10]

And finally, the editor of the Kuwaiti daily *al-Qabas*, who met with Bashar in July 2003, testified that he was surprised to find out how the palace where he met Bashar, al-Rawda, had no guards. He added that "Bashar speaks freely and smoothly and expresses his ideas in a clear-cut way, reflecting openness and warmness towards his interlocutors, something that is difficult to find among other Arab leaders."[11]

Western journalists, too, were similarly impressed by Bashar. A London *Observer* reporter who interviewed Bashar and his wife, Asma, in preparation for a feature article about Asma during a visit by the couple to Britain in December 2002 related that at the end of the interview the young president asked for the microphones to be turned off and the reporter's notebook to be put away. The reporter noted: "He wants to chat, but it is not an interview. And for a moment, with the constraints of protocol and diplomacy stripped away, as they sit together on a sofa, you have an insight into their life together: a lively, humorous dialogue in which they lob ideas between them like a tennis ball."[12]

A similar impression was gained by Western leaders. One prominent European figure noted that Bashar displayed a good mastery of detail and did not require the assistance of his advisors or prepared cards or notes in order to conduct a relevant and purposeful dialogue. Bashar, he reported, talked freely with his guest about the obstacles placed in his way by several of his colleagues in the Syrian leadership to block his efforts at reform. Another Western leader observed that he found Bashar to be an intelligent and friendly conversationalist who displayed great curiosity and a thirst for information. Even when the question of the Israeli–Arab conflict came up, the Syrian president's tone remained matter-of-fact and free of emotion, even if ultimately he showed hostility, and especially suspicion and lack of trust, regarding his neighbor to the south. Nevertheless, the many Western leaders found Bashar to be "amazingly young." Indeed, the question that these Western leaders who met Bashar asked themselves was whether the qualities with which he was endowed, such as intelligence, intellectual curiosity and analytic ability, were sufficient to enable him to rule Syria. The discussions he held with them sometimes revealed his weakness vis-à-vis his colleagues in the Syrian leadership elite, e.g. Foreign Minister Faruq al-Shar', who on several occasions in the first years of Bashar's term in office interrupted his leader or even corrected him, behavior that was unacceptable in Arab political culture.[13]

One way or another, however, Bashar and his regime conveyed a message to the Syrian public regarding their new leader's image and personality that emphasized the following aspects:

1. *Continuity and commitment to his father's legacy.* During the first years of his rule, and especially after he was burned in his attempt to initiate certain processes of change in the state, Bashar made pronounced efforts to project himself as following in his father's footsteps. As British journalist Patrick Seale, a confidant of his father, pointed out, loyalty and commitment to his father's heritage was ultimately the source of legitimation of his rule.[14] Moreover, in some of his statements Bashar suggested that his generation (and, by implication, he himself) was more committed and devoted to pan-Arab values than was his father's generation.[15] This stance, apparently, was part of Bashar's attempt to assume his father's role as leader of the rejectionist front, or at least as leader of the Arab camp that advocated an aggressive, inflexible approach to Israel and to the West.

   Bashar also remained devoted to his father's guiding principles in the socioeconomic (i.e. a socialist approach) and political (i.e. one-man rule supported by the military) realms, and in any case refrained from proposing any real alternatives. Forced to defend his father's legacy against attackers, he often described his own work, and even more so his vision, as a continuation of his father's: "All I aspire to is to augment the edifice my father established,"[16] or: "Syria experienced wonderful political leadership [under Hafiz al-Asad], and a significant effort must be made to bring about development similar to that which we achieved in the political as well as economic and social realms during the period of his rule."[17]

   This point merits emphasis in light of the identification of Bashar as belonging to the "Internet generation." Apparently, the first to use this term in reference to Bashar was the Jordanian monarch, King 'Abdallah, who thereby expressed the hope that Bashar would emerge as someone who thought along Western lines. However, in contrast to 'Abdallah, who had spent years, and especially the formative years of his life, in Britain and the United States, Bashar had spent most of his life in his father's home in Damascus. Indeed, when asked about his relationship with King 'Abdallah, Bashar explained:

   > There is a special link between us that was formed before I became president. It is only natural that the fact that we were the same age and had the same hobbies influenced the relationship that developed between us. But when a person reaches

a position of influence and responsibility, he becomes part of the society to which he belongs and in which many age groups and outlooks are to be found. Thus, my path often crosses that of King 'Abdallah, as of many other rulers, especially in our approach to domestic matters, but at the same time there are many differences [in our operative approach] stemming from the extant difference between our countries.[18]

Still, quoted statements by Bashar suggest that his commitment to his father's legacy may not have been as total or absolute as had appeared during the first years of his rule, and that he was aware of the need to detach himself from this legacy when the opportunity presented itself. In an interview with the *Washington Post* even before he assumed office, he acknowledged, as will be recalled, "that the difference between my father and my grandfather was amazingly slight, as life at that time changed very slowly. The difference between me and my father is very great… and the difference between me and those younger than me by only ten years is even greater."[19] This pointed to Bashar's awareness that time cannot be held back and that Syria could not remain fixed at the point at which his late father had left it.

2. *Ushering in progress and modernization.* Bashar made a point of projecting himself as the person who would lead Syria into the twenty-first century. This goal was emphasized repeatedly by him as well as by the Syrian media. Typically, the announcement of Bashar's candidacy for the presidency released by the Ba'th Party national leadership stated:

> Comrade Dr. Bashar embodies in his personality and his activity the link between generations – between the generation that brought about the great turning point in Syria's history and that gained experience during the years of struggle which it led, and the young generation that grew up under the wings of the corrective movement [an appellation for the ascendance of Hafiz al-Asad to power], and which works with all its might for the development and the promotion of modernization in the state.[20]

Tishrin informed its readers on July 10, 2000, just before the referendum on Bashar's candidacy, that "Bashar opened the door to technical knowledge as a way of thinking, thereby spreading vitality throughout the state and initiating modernization."[21] Two days later, the newspaper added: "The nations of the world are engaged in this century in a race for progress and scientific technology. Syria has no choice but to join this race and surmount all obstacles on the road to this goal."[22]

However, Bashar, along with many other Syrians who hoped for change under him, was to discover that the road to progress and modernization was long and difficult. A glance at the measures he sought to introduce since assuming office, most of which were foiled by his colleagues in the leadership elite or by the Syrian entrenched power structure, reveals Bashar's inexperience, although, with this, his true desire to bring about change and progress in his country. Examples are his abortive attempts to implement reform in the economic realm, or his effort to weaken the grip of the Ba'th Party on the government. However, whether Bashar had a clear set of goals or a vision of Syria in the future was doubtful, and whether he had the capacity to implement such a vision even more doubtful. In a telling remark in the summer of 2003, he stated that he envisioned not change but the development of the state, that is, gradual progress along the same track as in the past.[23]

3. *Energy, vitality, openness and accessibility to the public.* From the start of his rule, Bashar radiated a sense of youthful energy and joy of creation. A comparison between the scope of his public activity (meetings, visits, issuing laws and orders) and that of his father clearly favors the son. In an interview with *al-Sharq al-Awsat*, Bashar detailed a crowded daily schedule that began at 7.30 a.m. and ended at 11.30 p.m. He had no time for hobbies, and certainly not for entertainment, he said. He allowed himself reading, primarily history, and watching documentary films. Speaking to the Russian newspaper *Izvestia*, he added that he enjoyed jogging, riding bicycle, swimming and weight-lifting and that in his youth he used to play football.[24] However, Israeli sources claimed repeatedly that the image of an active, energetic president was a façade, and that Bashar relaxed frequently by playing computer games and watching television. Former head of the Israeli Mossad Ephraim Halevi even described him as a "young man who suffers from mental problems that do affect his political as well as personal behaviour."[25] Yet even if his daily schedule was indeed crowded, Bashar did not differ in this respect from many other Arab leaders, including his late father albeit secluded from the public eye, or the late King Husayn or his son, King 'Abdallah II.

Like several of his fellow rulers in the Arab world, and in complete contrast to his father, Bashar was anxious to convey openness and, even more importantly, accessibility to the public. While he did not wander the streets of Damascus in disguise, as did his colleague

King 'Abdallah of Jordan, he toured his country often, at least by Syrian standards, and certainly in comparison with his father. Following the collapse in June 2002 of the Zayzun Dam in northern Syria, resulting in extensive flooding and tens of thousands being made homeless, Bashar promptly visited the disaster zone. Dressed informally in slacks and a short-sleeved shirt – a new image for a ruler of Syria – he arrived at the tent camps put up for the flood victims and spoke with the people. A filmed report of his visit showed him exploring the question of the cause of the disaster and whether the authorities in charge were taking the necessary steps to ease the victims' plight.[26] On one evening in January 2005, he held a surprise visit to the main hospital of Damascus. He was surprised to find how bad the conditions of the hospital were and how poor was the treatment ordinary visitors got there. He then asked the Health Minister and other senior officials to join him at the hospital so that they too could learn about the situation there. He visited the hospital a few days later to see what had been changed since his previous visit.[27]

In this context, Bashar's high-profile visits in late 2002 to two "vipers' nests" – the 'Umar Ibn al-Khattab Mosque in Hama and the al-Tawhid Mosque in Aleppo, where he attended prayers on the last Friday of the Ramadan fast, and the *'id al-Fitr* prayer, respectively[28] – merit mention. The visit to Hama, stronghold of anti-Ba'th Islamist rebels in the early 1980s, was intended to convey Bashar's self-confidence and, conceivably, send a conciliatory message to the Syrian Islamist community. The important point is that Bashar did not avoid these visits, even though the residents' animosity toward the regime even two decades later was known. Both visits suggested a pragmatic approach to problems. Similarly, Bashar was not deterred by the prospect of undertaking several media-saturated visits to Western countries that were liable to – and in some cases did indeed – prove discomfiting to him. In June 2001, shortly after a visit to Syria by Pope John Paul II, during which Bashar made several statements with anti-Semitic connotations, he visited Paris and was criticized sharply for these remarks in meetings with members of the French National Assembly and the Municipal Council of Paris.[29] Notably, thereafter he made no further anti-Semitic comments and in effect ceased referring to Jews at all in his statements.

4. *An intellectual.* Bashar projected himself as a thinking man, stating in an interview in 2000 that he habitually allocated time in his daily schedule for contemplation.[30] This intellectual attribute, however,

was difficult to detect in Bashar's somewhat awkward, dry demeanor. His speeches reflected a didactic element and showed a pretentiousness in their lengthy, detailed analyses of the issues he addressed. They were widely viewed as boring, vague and above all lacking in vitality or a personal touch, delivered like lectures to students or presentations of medical cases to fellow physicians.

More than that, Bashar's listeners often found it difficult to understand his thoughts and intentions. Thus, for example, when Bashar was asked in an interview he granted to the *Daily Telegraph* in January 2004 whether Syria was developing non-conventional weapons as it was accused of doing by Israel and the U.S., Bashar chose to deliver a long lecture about the theoretical right of Syria to develop non-conventional weapons because it was in a state of war with Israel. The British journalist, who failed to understand the difference between the theoretical and the practical, was quick to publish that Bashar admitted that Syria was developing such weapons. The Syrians were embarrassed and official spokespersons were quick to deny that this was Bashar's intention and argued that he had been misread.[31] It also seems that many of the misunderstandings between Bashar and the American administration stemmed from similar answers given by Bashar to the Secretary of State, Colin Powell, in May 2003 when the American side demanded that Syria close the offices of the terrorist Palestinian organizations which were operating in Damascus and stop the Syrian aid to Hizballah.[32]

Multiple identities

Ostensibly, Bashar's commitment to Arabism required no substantiation. He frequently stressed his loyalty to the Arab nation in public statements and depicted Syria as a fortress of Arabism. As *Tishrin* wrote in 2002:

> Bashar al-Asad is the clearest and most explicit national voice today, articulating the goals of the Arab nation and its values and principles with vigor and courage but also with logic, wisdom and discretion. He represents not only Syria, which in itself constitutes an Arab and a regional force of importance, but the aspirations of the [Arab] nation wherever it is, from the [Atlantic] Ocean to the [Arabian] Gulf, its hopes and its fears.[33]

Bashar himself explained, in this context:

> Many have tried in the past to destroy the Arab national perception by attempting to position it in confrontation with feelings of

"local patriotism" which ostensibly are contaminated by separatism. Some tried to position Arabism in confrontation with Islam.... Others even tried to turn Arabism into the equivalent of backwardness and isolationism.... But none of this, of course, is correct.[34]

Still, despite his resolute statements regarding his commitment to Arabism, Bashar was sometimes perceived as having a Syrian nationalist identity no less salient, and perhaps even more pronounced, than his Arab identity. This was not far-fetched, for he had grown up in "Asad's Syria," a state unencumbered, as it had been in the past, by insecurity over its capacity or even its right to exist as an independent entity. His commitment to this state, therefore, was free of any doubt or impediment.

Statements by him over the years, starting before his rule, reflect a Syro-Arab ideology that sanctifies the territorial Syrian state and views it as a cornerstone of the regional policy formulated by Damascus, albeit with an Arabist coloration.

An explicit example of this Syrian-centered outlook is to be found on the Internet site of the Syrian Computer Society, chaired by Bashar. The site, inaugurated by him in April 1998, informs the surfer that events that transpired in Syria, or, more accurately, in the Syrian Lands, made a decisive contribution to civilization, namely "the invention of the first alphabet, the first musical composition, the first agricultural revolution, the planting of wheat, the first musical instruments known today... and... the first database management and library system ever." Moreover:

> Throughout the hundreds of thousands of years of Syria's history, since the first human beings lived there, Syria never started an aggression against another country, she was invaded by many but the great heart and deep roots of Syria managed to turn that into a true interaction and contributed to every civilization she dealt with. [For example,] Syria gave [the] Roman [Empire] five... emperors and one of the greatest architects ever: Appolodoros the Damascene.[35]

Bashar: between Alawite and Islamic identities

The question of Bashar's Alawite origin appeared to be barely relevant during his first years of rule, whether in his personal and political behavior or in his choices of governmental office holders. Evidently, he did not have to rely on his Alawite identity to recruit support from his community, in as much as the transfer of power to him had been smooth. Possibly, too, the fact that he had grown up in

Damascus and not, as his father had, in a village in the heart of the Alawite region allowed him to feel comfortable with his Syrian identity, which was more meaningful and actual for him than his Alawite identity. Ultimately, he did not have to pave his way to the Presidential Palace, as did his father, who, surrounded by a loyal coterie of Alawite army officers to reinforce him, overcame his political enemies in a series of relentless power struggles.

Not surprisingly, therefore, Bashar married a woman of Sunni and not Alawite origin. Furthermore, his attempt to accelerate the process of "Shi'ization" of the Alawite community, begun during his father's time with Iranian backing, was also understandable in light of his non-communal proclivities. Starting in the 1980s, Iranian clerics were sent to Syria, followed in the 1990s by Shi'ite clerics from Lebanon associated with Hizballah, to preach in the Alawite villages. At the same time, Alawite youngsters were sent to study in Iranian religious institutions. Apparently, this development was not aimed at actually Islamizing the Alawite community or turning them into orthodox Shi'ites, but simply at legitimizing the community, and by extension the regime, in the eyes of the Sunni majority.[36]

Essentially, Bashar appeared to have inherited his father's perception – the perception of the Ba'th Party – of the role and status of Islam in Syria. This view regarded Islam as an important and even central element in the history and cultural heritage of the Arab nation, although it did not recognize it as the law of the land. Significantly, the founder of the Ba'th Party, Michel 'Aflaq, envisioned Arab nationalism as a new "religion" that would substitute for or inherit the role played by Islam in the life of the individual, society and state. However, once he came to power, Hafiz al-Asad retreated somewhat from 'Aflaq's approach and instead adopted an "Islamic" policy that turned Syria into a "Muslim state" – a state (or, in the event, a dynasty) that rallies support and religious legitimation by co-opting Islam and its institutions into its governmental functioning. In this it resembled other Arab states in the Middle Each such as Egypt and Jordan, in which Islam played a central role in the life of the individual, society and the state.

Still, Bashar avoided opening his inaugural speech at the People's Assembly with the salutation "Bismillah" (In the name of Allah the compassionate and merciful), an element that is *de rigueur* in the speeches of every self-respecting politician in the Arab world today. In this he followed his father's practice of avoiding incorporating any Islamic religious motif in his speeches.[37] In fact, Bashar's speeches and interviews consistently reflect a secular perception without any Islamic religious undertones, a trait observed by Dr. Edmond

Shulenburg – Bashar's superior when he was an ophthalmological resident in London – who recalled that the young doctor was in the habit of having a glass of wine.[38]

With this, one of Bashar's first acts as president was to annul an order issued by his father in 1982 forbidding female pupils in schools throughout the country to wear headscarves. The order had been issued by Asad Sr. after he had succeeded in suppressing the Islamic revolt against his regime and bringing about its demise.[39] Three years later, in June 2003, it was reported from Damascus that the regime had promulgated a decree permitting soldiers in compulsory service to pray in the military camps despite the fact that the policy requiring the dismissal of any officer suspected of religious inclinations had remained unchanged.[40]

Bashar and his family

Bashar's statement, quoted in *al-Sharq al-Awsat*, that Syria is like a family, and that the family's dirty laundry is never washed in public, suggests that his world view is strongly molded by the heritage and especially the sociocultural reality of Syria.

Committed to the image of head of the Syrian family, Bashar married Asma al-Ahras after a brief engagement on January 1, 2001, choosing, for reasons of his own, a modest private ceremony away from the eye of the media. He attributed this decision to the suffering of the Palestinian people struggling under Israeli occupation. A great deal was written at the time about the political implications of Asma's Sunni origin,[41] although Bashar's marriage to her did not appear to have earned him any immediate political gains. This contrasted with his father's marriage to his mother, Anisa, who came from the important and powerful Makhluf family in the town of Qardaha, the birthplace of both partners. A year after Bashar and Asma's wedding, their first child, a son, was born, named Hafiz for his paternal grandfather. In October 2003, the couple's first daughter, Zayn, was born, and in December 2004 the couple's second son, Karim, was born.[42]

Asma emerged as a vigorous, vital presidential wife. In contrast to her mother-in-law, Anisa, who had avoided appearing in public, whether at her husband's side or alone, Asma joined her husband on official visits throughout the world, during which she stood out by her Western appearance and self-confidence. In accordance with accepted norms among wives of Arab leaders, she became involved in advancing welfare and social issues, initiating the establishment of the Firdus (Paradise) Foundation for development in Syria's villages, which focused on backing small and medium enterprises in peripheral regions. Toward this end she traveled widely in rural areas of the country, receiving full media coverage.[43]

In an interview with the British *Observer*, Asma revealed that she had spent the first months of her marriage traveling incognito in jeans and t-shirt around the rural areas of the country.

> I wanted to meet ordinary Syrians before the world met me. It was my crash course. I would just tag along with one of the many programs being run in the rural areas. Because people had no idea who I was, I was able to see people completely honestly, I was able to see what their problems were on the ground... what the issues are. What people's hopes and aspirations are.... It wasn't to spy on them. It was really just to see who they are, what they are doing.[44]

Undoubtedly, Asma was an asset to Bashar in promoting his image as a modern leader who devotes his energy to advancing his state. Hinting at their relationship and the balance maintained between them, she stated:

> I let my actions speak for themselves, rather than saying "I want to... I will" and so forth.... I think that's probably something I took from the UK.... I obviously am not going to speak on his [Bashar's] behalf, but he did know from day one that I was a working woman. He knew JP Morgan took up a lot of my time. So he knew that work for me was a big priority and still is.[45]

Bashar and his regime

As discussed previously, Bashar was anxious to maintain the political system his father had established in Syria and not make substantive changes in it. In as much as the transfer of power to him was smooth, with no evidence of significant opposition to him or to the regime, he did not feel the need to take drastic measures to entrench his personal and public status or to build up power bases loyal to him in order to face down a rival camp.

Bashar's confidants

In the perception of many Syrians, Bashar was an unknown quantity, i.e. he was not a product, as was his father, of the military or party system, from which Asad Sr. drew support and recruited a close circle of like-minded associates to help him rule the country. With this, Bashar appeared to have consolidated a personal staff to assist him in promoting his goals and leading Syria toward change, however limited. This staff consisted of young men his age who shared his world view, some of whom, like him, were previously unidentified politically. Three in this group, whom Bashar brought with him from the Syrian Computer Society where they had been involved in disseminating computer and Internet awareness, were appointed to the cabinet, heading the tourism, communications and higher education portfolios. Another member of the Society, 'Imad Zuhayr Mustafa, computers professor at Damascus University, was appointed in January 2004 as Ambassador to Washington, and a further member, Sami al-Khaymi, was appointed Ambassador to London in July 2004. 'Abadallah al-Dardari, who was appointed as the head of the National Authority for Planning and later as a State Minister for Planning, Muhammad Mahir Mujtahid, who was appointed as the Secretary General of the government, Durayd Daghram, the Director General of the Syrian Commercial Bank, and Muhammad Sabuni, the head of the Syrian Communication Authority, were also members of this intimate circle. Other friends and associates brought into this circle were Iyad Ghzzal, appointed head of the Syrian Railway Authority and in January 2005 named as the Governor of Homs, whom Bashar had gotten to know when he served as an aide in the Presidential Palace, and Dhu al-Himma Shalish and Rami Makhluf, both businessmen and relatives of Bashar's. This group, however, was unlikely to be able to assist Bashar in ruling the country, as they lacked power bases of their own and were not influential in governmental circles.[46]

The lack of background of these close associates in managing the affairs of state, and especially in guaranteeing the security of the regime, stood out in marked contrast to the powerful pillars who had supported the regime under Hafiz al-Asad: the Asad and Makhluf clans, the Kalbiyya tribe, numerous highly placed Alawite army officers, and a close circle of politically experienced associates mostly from the majority Sunni community.

Clan, tribe and community

Ostensibly, the element of clan, tribe and communalism continued to play an important role in Bashar's regime. Evidence of this was the presence in his inner circle of his brother Mahir and, even more importantly, his brother-in-law Asaf Shawkat. Additionally, a large number of high-ranking army officers, headed by Bashar's tribesman, Chief of Staff 'Ali Habib, were considered personally loyal to him. However, neither his brother nor his brother-in-law appeared to be involved in managing the affairs of state or in decision making at the highest level. Moreover, the Alawite officers said to be close to Bashar were not depicted as a consolidated group molded by him, or as viewing him as their true leader. Apparently, Bashar had difficulty, or perhaps did not attach sufficient importance to, entrenching his regime on firm clan, tribal and communal foundations, as did his late father.

This difficulty was apparent. The Asad clan avoided taking a firm stance on behalf of the young president. Two of his father's brothers, Rif'at and Jamil, voiced reservations about Bashar's designation as successor to his father, and Rif'at went so far as to challenge the legitimacy of the choice of Bashar as president. While Rif'at was somewhat removed, in exile in Spain, Jamil was close at hand in Syria, elected in March 2003 as a delegate to the People's Assembly from the Ladhiqiyya province. Jamil, however, died in December 2004 and rumors were spread about an attempt on the life of his son, Mundhir, who became a leading figure of Jamil's clan. Rumors also spread in Damascus in late 2004, and were later denied, that Rif'at had become seriously ill. Rif'at had already been forced in early 2004 to wind up his ANN TV network, owing to financial problems.[47] However, Bashar's problems in his immediate family were also public knowledge. Confrontations between the impulsive Mahir and the family's "royal couple," his sister Bushra and her husband Asaf Shawkat, were widely reported. Following Bashar's marriage to Asma, rumors spread in Damascus about the tense relations between her and Anisa, Bashar's mother, and Bushra, his sister.[48] And finally, in mid-2003, Israeli media reported that the head of Bashar's younger brother Mahir's office had initiated contacts with Israeli businessmen in Amman, in an effort to bring about the resumption of peace negotiations between Syria and Israel. Although Syrian sources were quick to deny these reports, it seemed that Bashar had trouble in ruling his own family members.[49] Clearly, neither the clan nor the immediate family constituted a power base or a source of support for him, as they had for Asad Sr. at the start of his rise to power. In February of 2004, Asaf Shawkat was appointed to the powerful post of head of the military security department, eliciting conjecture over whether this step represented a move to reinforce Bashar's status. The head of Israeli intelligence, Aharon Ze'evi, in an interview in April 2005, observed that, "in light of Bashar's weakness, his kinsmen and close associates were seeking a substitute for him, and the names of Asaf Shawkat and Bashar's brother, Mahir, were mentioned in this context."[50]

The trusted leadership nucleus (the jama'a)

Asad Sr. had relied on a governing elite consisting of close associates with a shared viewpoint who helped him maintain his regime and thereby rule the country. This coterie was linked to him through four types of ties: 1) family ties, exemplified by Asad's co-option of his brother Rif'at and a decade later of his sons Basil and later Bashar; 2) tribal or communal ties, i.e. through his reliance on his tribe, the Kalbiyya, and his community, the Alawites; 3) personal friendships, i.e. colleagues who shared his world view and life experiences, and associates and supporters dating back to the 1950s and 1960s – the formative years of his ascent to power; and 4) work ties, i.e. a team of aides and advisors who had worked with him for a long time, or members of the military, the governmental and the semi-governmental elites with whom he had come into contact over time. The majority of this stratum were of Asad's generation, i.e. men in their early seventies. A large proportion, especially those who held high political posts, were Sunnis, including both vice-presidents, 'Abd al-Halim Khaddam and Zuhayr Mashariqa; Minister of Defense Mustafa Talas; and Foreign Minister Faruq al-Shar'.[51]

The elite of Asad's era essentially remained in place during the first years of Bashar's rule. In contrast to Jordan, where King 'Abdallah shook the foundations of the kingdom's military and political elite and within a short time replaced them almost entirely, including those who had orchestrated his succession as king, Bashar avoided introducing dramatic changes in the Syrian leadership and especially in the military/security elite.

The only changes that did occur in the political and military leadership involved promotions of subordinates to leading posts, such as the promotion of Deputy Chief of Staff Hasan Turkmani to the top position, replacing 'Ali Aslan, who reached retirement age in January 2002. In May 2004, following the retirement of the Minister of Defense, Mustafa Talas, Turkmani was named as Minister of Defense and 'Ali Habib replaced him as the Chief of Staff. Notably, Bashar avoided leapfrogging young officers who were close to him into key posts so as to build up power bases in the military and security forces personally loyal to him. Similarly, changes he made in the governmental area – bringing in new faces to the cabinet in December 2001, September 2003 and October 2004 and replacing officials in local government, party bodies and the media – were essentially insignificant, as they generally involved the retirement of veteran bureaucrats, to be replaced by younger ones with the same outlook, devoted to retaining the status quo in the state.

Bashar's father had "anesthetized" the Syrian political, and especially the military/security, leadership, allowing them to reach retirement age in the expectation of continuing on in their posts. He then implemented their legal retirement, a step he viewed as necessary to make room for a younger leadership that would identify with his successor – Bashar. Bashar retained this tactic, legally eliminating the old guard over a period of several years. While this measure was likely to benefit him in the short run, it could not, in itself, build power bases to help him promote needed reforms in the social and economic areas, or assure the long-term survival of his regime.

Bashar thus lacked a loyal circle of supporters with power and status on whom he could rely at critical moments or whom he could involve in the decision-making process. The extant Syrian leadership elite – both the remaining old guard and their successors in government and the military – did not owe any personal allegiance to Bashar beyond the formal loyalty obliged by his office. This absence of a close bond with a leadership circle, combined with the absence in the new president of the kind of defined world view that stems from a coherent personality and formative life experiences, appeared at times to be critical in light of his youth and inexperience. Abroad he was sometimes perceived as being led or managed by others rather than taking charge himself. The decision-making process in Syria in the early years of his rule lacked the balance that could have emanated from the leader's historical memory (i.e. formative life experiences) or, alternatively, from a governmental inner circle that could help him make the difficult decisions that were required. Indeed, in some cases it was the remnants of the old-guard leadership that appeared to function as a needed moderating influence, for example in their reservations over Bashar's encouragement of Hizballah activity in South Lebanon and their efforts to defuse the atmosphere there. Reports in Israel, in this context, cited the long-time "Syrian High Commissioner" in Lebanon, Ghazi Kana'an, as objecting to the escalation of Hizballah activity against Israel, with Bashar's encouragement, in early 2002.[52]

Interesting in this regard was an interview which was given in June 2003 by Bashar to al-'Arabiyya TV channel, where he answered a question about the degree to which the old guard restricted his activities:

> The term old guard is a journalist term, but when they say old do they mean the age, the position of these people or simply the fact that these people belonging to the old guard are simply protecting their interests? I think that they mean that the old guard protects its interests but the young guard confronts them and what is more important is that the two groups are not important. What is important is the general order in the state. We made many personal changes and we determine to replace anyone who lost his value whether he belongs to the old or the young guard.[53]

The Alawite officer class

The Syrian regime which Hafiz al-Asad bequeathed to his son relied on the senior Alawite officer class, i.e. the heads of the security organs and the commanders of the army units, for stability in the state and, by extension, for the very existence of the regime. These officers were partners – some of them visible, most hidden – in the Syrian system of government. Their status and power not only stemmed from the letter and even the spirit of the Syrian constitution, but also reflected the prevailing balance of power in the coalition forces that supported the regime. Notably, although the Alawites constituted a minority of 12 percent of the Syrian population, the overwhelming majority of army commanders and heads of the security bodies – nearly 90 percent – were Alawites.

Several military leaders had a close relationship with Bashar, primarily within the context of their roles, especially former Chief of Staff 'Ali Aslan and Chief of Staff 'Ali Habib. Yet whether the military leadership regarded Bashar as one of their own, as they did his father, is doubtful. Bashar avoided forming close ties or promoting people personally loyal to him, thereby remaining dependent on the formal hierarchical command and perhaps on the tribal and communal solidarity fostered in his father's time, which was sustained by force of inertia. The problem was that a power-based, strong-arm governmental system of the Syrian kind did not tolerate a vacuum or any sign of weakness in the ruling apparatus. A perception of Bashar as weak, therefore, could have invited aggressive intervention by any of the power bases in the state. Conceivably, such a threat could have come from one of the Alawite generals, or from one of the lower-ranking officers who, unimpressed by Bashar and his conduct of the state, might have come to the conclusion that he could do a better job. At a given signal, such an officer might have tried to establish a new ruling elite based on the existing governmental coalition (Alawite generals and their colleagues from the other minorities, the rural population and the Syrian periphery).

In April 2004 Bashar issued an order regulating the duration of service of senior officers of each rank, from regular army service until retirement, and banning them from service in the reserves – an option exploited by many officers in order to retain their post beyond the official retirement age. Whether Bashar truly wanted to regulate military service, or whether he wanted to enhance support for himself by a grateful younger officer class, is difficult to know.[54] At the same time, two of Bashar's close associates were appointed to key posts in the security services: Asaf Shawkat was named head of military security in February 2005, and Bahjat Sulayman was appointed head of the general security directorate in April 2005. It should be mentioned that the two other heads of security organizations had also been appointed by Bashar some years previously: Muhammad Manasra, as head of the political security directorate, and 'Izz al-Din Isma'il, as head of the air force security directorate.[55]

Moreover, since Bashar's ascent to the presidency, a large proportion of the senior officers' corps, which had constituted a loyal base of support for his father, had been retired from the military, including Generals Shafiq Fayyad, Tawfiq Jallul, Ibrahim Safi, Faruq 'Isa and 'Abd al-Rahman Sayyad. Thereafter, Bashar prudently placed the security system in the hands of his close associates. Still, the extent of Bashar's actual control of the Syrian officer cadre remained unclear.[56]

Notably, the Syrian military leadership had been in a somnolent state during Hafiz al-Asad's long rule. Prolonged political stability, signifying the durability of the regime, made the military leadership irrelevant to the ongoing conduct of the state (with the exception of such specific events as the suppression of the Islamic revolt of 1976–82 and Rif'at's revolt against his brother during 1983–84). Presumably, however, the instincts that had led the military to intervene systematically in the affairs of state during the 1950s and 1960s and foment military coups could reawaken.

The civil governmental structure

Formally, the Syrian governmental structure is made up of a series of legislative and executive bodies tasked to conduct the affairs of state – primarily the daily life of its citizens – on an ongoing basis. It is a well-organized hierarchical system based on both the Syrian and the Ba'th Party constitutions. It is made up of the cabinet, the People's Assembly, the presidency of the republic and the Ba'th Party bodies. The importance of the system lies in its availability to the regime for rallying public or legal legitimation of its moves. It also provides the regime with a means of rewarding its supporters. By co-opting them into the system, the regime fulfills their aspirations for accessibility to political power and for economic and social leadership roles. Moreover, the system plays an influential role in the daily life of the people, as reflected in Bashar's attempt to promote social and economic reforms under the aegis of the civic government. Evidently, he attached more importance to fostering a group of colleagues in governmental bodies who would support him in advancing Syria's scientific and technological development than to molding such a support group by his father's time-honored means of focusing on army officers and party activists.

The Syrian government (the cabinet)

Bashar's influence was evident in the formation of the new government in March 2000, three months before the death of his father, the late Hafiz al-Asad. A government reshuffle – the first in a decade – included the replacement of the prime minister, Mahmud al-Zu'bi, who had held the post since 1987, by Mustafa Miru, a veteran Ba'th activist who had served as governor of the provinces of Dar'a, Hasaka and Aleppo, successively, over the preceding 20 years. A group of senior ministers were also replaced, generally by younger ministers described as close to Bashar and his outlook. Prominent among these was 'Isam al-Za'im (b. 1940), of Aleppo, who, as Minister of Planning in the new government, attracted attention by advocating economic reform, albeit limited and under official supervision. Meanwhile, however, Bashar had to accept two key holdover ministers – Muhammad al-'Imadi (Finance) and Muhammad Khalid al-Mahyani (Economics) – as a compromise with the regime's old guard, who opposed making overly dramatic changes in the composition of the government.[57]

The trend of promoting relatively younger technocrats close to Bashar and sharing his outlook was particularly evident in a further cabinet reshuffle on December 13, 2001, which completed the removal of the old guard from the government. The new Minister of Interior, 'Ali Hamud (b. 1944), from Homs, who took over from Muhammad Harba, had headed the General Security Directorate in the past and had taken part in suppressing the Islamic revolt during 1976–82. Another significant shift was the replacement of the veteran Ministers of Finance and Economics, 'Imadi and Mahyani. The finance portfolio was given to Muhammad al-Atrash (b. 1934), from Tartus, who held a doctorate in economics from the University of London and had served in the past as an advisor to the World Bank. Atrash had been Minister of Economics in the early 1980s, but had resigned over differences of opinion with then prime minister Ra'uf al-Kasm. The Ministry of Economics and Foreign Trade was turned over to Ghassan al-Rifa'i (b. 1942), of Homs. Like Atrash, Rifa'i, too, had a Ph.D. (University of Sussex) and had been associated with the World Bank as a deputy to the Director-General of Economic Policy. The reshuffle also included the promotion of 'Isam al-Za'im from Minister of Planning to Minister of Industry.[58]

The most significant of Bashar's moves was the co-option into the cabinet of three of his past assistants in the Syrian Computer Society. In contrast to his father, who brought army colleagues and party comrades into the government, Bashar co-opted partners in the shared vision of the computer and the Internet revolution. Sa'dallah Agha al-Qal'a (b. 1950), of Aleppo, appointed Minister of Tourism, held a doctorate in computer science from the University of Paris and had been in charge of information at the Computer Society. Hasan Risha (b. 1945), from Misyaf, appointed Minister for Higher Education, held a doctorate in engineering from the Leningrad Polytechnic and had headed the scientific committee of the Computer Society. Muhammad Bashir al-Munjid (b. 1947), of Damascus, appointed Minister of Communication, held a doctorate in electronics from the University of Paris and had served as Bashar's deputy in the Computer Society. As mentioned before, the newly appointed Syrian Ambassador to Washington, 'Imad Zuhayr Mustafa, was also an active member of the Computer Society. Mustafa was a professor of computer engineering at the University of Damascus, where he met Bashar, who came to hear one his lectures.[59]

In September 2003, three years after Miru was appointed as prime minister in order to lead Syria into the twenty-first century, his government was defined as a "total failure"[60] and reached its end. Miru was replaced by Naji al-'Atari, born in 1944 in Aleppo. 'Atari was a Ba'th activist with a BA in construction engineering from the University of Aleppo and an MA in urban planning from a Dutch university. He served as the mayor of Aleppo, the head of the engineering union in that city and later head of the national union. He then became the governor of Homs. In the first Miru government he had served as deputy prime minister for services and in March 2003 he was elected as the speaker of the People's Assembly. His appointment as prime minister should be seen as another compromise made by Bashar. After all, reports from Damascus suggested that not 'Atari but a man who had no political background would be appointed as prime minister that time.[61]

Alongside the replacement of Miru by 'Atari there was a wide reshuffle. First the number of ministers was decreased from 35 to 31 and half were new faces. Thus the former Ambassador to Tehran, Ahmad al-Hasan, replaced the Information Minister 'Adnan 'Umran. The spokesperson of the Foreign Ministry and the personal translator of Bashar, Buthayna Sha'ban, was appointed as Minister for Expatriates. Sha'ban was born in 1953 in Homs. She got her Ph.D. in English literature at York University and served as lecturer in poetry and comparative literature at the Department of English Language and Literature in the University of Damascus. Other new faces were Hani Murtada, the president of Damascus University, who was appointed as Minister for Higher Education, 'Adnan 'Ali Sa'd, who had been Dean of the Faculty of Education at Damascus University, who was appointed Minister of Education, 'Amir Lutfi, who was appointed as Minister of the Economy and Foreign Trade, and Muhammad al-Husayn, who was appointed as the Minister of Finance.[62]

Among those removed from the government, Isam al-Za'im had been known till that time as close to Bashar. A few weeks later a decree confiscating all his money was announced. It became clear that he was accused of corruption and bribery for his involvement in the allocation of $19.5 million for the building of a textile factory in Ladhiqiyya. The factory was never established but the money disappeared. He was acquitted from these charges in early 2005.[63]

In October 2004, another reshuffle in the government was announced. Eight new ministers joined the government. Two of the new ministers are worth mentioning: Ghazi Kana'an, former head of the Directorate of Political Security, was named as the Interior Minister, replacing 'Ali Hamud; Mahdi Dakhlallah, former editor of *al-Ba'th*, was named as the new Information Minister, replacing Ahmad al-Hasan.[64]

The task of government in Arab countries is not necessarily to run the country's affairs but to ease pressures on the president or the monarch and protect them from public criticism. This is why many rulers tend to have frequent reshuffles. It seems that Bashar is no exception.

The People's Assembly

The primary legislative body in Syria, the People's Assembly (*majlis al-shab*), was made up of 250 delegates elected regionally every four years. Approximately 60 percent of its members represented the National Progressive Front, an umbrella organization of all the political parties officially permitted to operate in Syria, foremost of them the Ba'th Party. The remaining 40 percent of its members were independents. Essentially, the Assembly was a symbolic body lacking decision-making power or influence regarding regime policy.

The first elections to the Assembly during Bashar's term of office, held on March 23, 2003, ostensibly gave him the opportunity to try to use this body to initiate a process of change, however limited. Yet Bashar avoided taking this step. The number of Assembly delegates remained 250, and the proportion of independent members was also retained (87, constituting 40 percent of the total). Of the 163 delegates from the National Progressive Front, 132 represented the Ba'th Party and 31 represented its satellite parties.[65] Prior to the elections, 10,405 persons submitted their candidacy, most of them for the seats allocated to independent members. These candidates, most of them merchants, businessmen or members of the professions, sought election to the Assembly in order to advance their personal affairs. The campaign turned violent at times, with widespread accusations of vote buying and slander. Reports from Damascus estimated the cost of the campaign for many of the independents at around $1 million or more, indicating the social sector from which they stemmed.[66]

Although the elections resulted in many new faces in the Assembly (178 of the 250 delegates), most of them young, ultimately no change was made to the status of the body within the Syrian political system. Significantly, the elected chairman of the Assembly was Muhammad Naji al-'Atari, a veteran Ba'th politician who had served as deputy prime minister in charge of the service sector. He replaced the outgoing chairman of the Assembly, 'Abd al-Qadir Qaddura, himself a veteran Ba'th activist. In October 2003, 'Atari became prime minister and was replaced by another Ba'th activist, Mahmud al-Abrash.[67]

The Ba'th Party

The Syrian constitution grants the Ba'th Party a preferential status in the country's political life. Article 8 of the constitution states: "The Ba'th Party is the leading party in society and the state and heads the National Progressive Front, which works toward consolidating the power of the masses and harnessing it to serve the aims of the Arab nation."[68] Extensions of the Ba'th Party are to be found throughout the state. These extensions – branches, departments and cells – facilitate the spread of the party's message to all parts of the country. Every four years, the party branches elect delegates to the party congress, which in turn elects the members of the party's two bodies: the Central Committee (*al-Lajna al-Markaziyya*), consisting of 90 members; and the Regional Command (*al-Qiyada al-Qutriyya*), with 21 members. The Regional Command is the party's supreme body and thus the most powerful institution in Syria. This status is reflected in the method by which the president of Syria is elected: the national leadership recommends the presidential candidate, the candidate is then brought to the People's Assembly for approval and, with the granting of approval, a national referendum is held. The party is headed by a secretary-general, a post held today by Bashar al-Asad.

Ever since Hafiz al-Asad took power, and especially in the last two decades of his rule, the Ba'th Party expanded rapidly. According to a report published for the sixth Ba'th Party Congress, held immediately after Hafiz al-Asad's death in June 2000, the membership of the party was 1,409,580, of whom 406,047 were full members (*'Adw 'Amil*) – the highest category of membership (followed by trial member [*Murshshah*] and supportive member [*Nasir*]). In May 2005, on the eve of the coming party congress, it was reported that the number of members had already reached 1.8 million. Notably, in 1971 the membership was 65,398, in 1981 374,332, and in 1992 1,008,243.[69]

The 2000 report cited 67.18 percent of the members as below age 30, and 18.75 percent aged 30–40. Approximately 35.70 percent were students, 16.50 percent farmers and 20.60 percent civil servants. Women constituted 29.14 percent. The army had 27 party branches, 212 sub-branches, and 1,656 cells, with a total of 25,066 members. Additional data pointed to the absolute hegemony of the party in many social sectors. For example, 998 of the 1,307 sitting judges in Syria were members, and apparently most of the intellectuals in the country were at the service of the party: 56 percent of the lecturers at the University of Damascus were party members, as were 54 percent at the University of Aleppo, 79 percent at Tishrin University in Ladhiqiyya, and 81 percent at al-Ba'th University in Homs.[70]

The immense growth of the party did not necessarily indicate the extent of its support or popularity in the population or the attractiveness or relevance of its ideology. Rather, it pointed to pure opportunism on the part of the new members, for whom the party had become a favored and convenient track to social, economic and political advancement. Notably, side by side with the party's vast numerical growth came a loss of its ideological vitality in light of the collapse of the socialist regimes in Eastern Europe along with the collapse of Syria's economy.

Cracks also appeared in the commitment to Arabism and Arab solidarity in the face of the regime's preparedness to advance the peace process with Israel and its dialogue with the West, as well as the development of a statist tendency on the part of the regime's leadership. Lastly, demographic changes in Syria, especially the country's accelerating urbanization, posed a challenge to the party in terms of preserving its relevance for sectors of the population destined to play a decisive role in Syrian life, especially the populations of the poverty-stricken neighborhoods surrounding the large cities.

Thus, despite the impressive numerical growth of the party, fears of a loss of vitality and relevance, and ultimately a loss of influence in Syria's daily life, were aired at the party congress in June 2000 – the first held in 15 years. Bashar, in an address to the delegates, emphasized the need to rejuvenate the party's image. "The Ba'th perceptions and ideologies have not become obsolete," he explained. "Socialism is a flexible perception that cannot be confined to a frozen and definitive compartment, and for this reason it can be developed and promoted." He added: "The continuity of the party depends on its capacity to adjust to today's reality in Syria and to developments in the various areas of life in the state."[71]

Apparently, therefore, Bashar intended to continue using the party as a convenient, accessible and above all irreplaceable vehicle to rally broad public support for himself and his policies throughout the state, especially in such sectors as the farming community and among the workers. As part of this effort, he initiated a process of replacing the leadership of the party, a necessary step since the leadership had not been rejuvenated for decades. He also tried to introduce a trend of limited reform within the party by ordering genuine elections for the leadership of the party cells and branches, with candidates to be drawn from all ranks instead of the entrenched practice of handing down a list of approved candidates from above.

In July 2003, the regional leadership of the Ba'th Party made a historic decision regarding the "separation of authority between the party and the governmental institutions of the state." The decision (No. 408) read:

> The task of the "Leading Party" [the official title of the Ba'th Party] is to plan, supervise, guide, review and necessitate reports. The party electors and institutions must refrain from intervening in the daily working of the governmental institutions and allow the comrades appointed to those institutions to discharge their duties.... Every appointment to managerial and executive positions in the governmental offices will be made on the basis of the suitability of the candidate to his job regardless of his party affiliation.[72]

The decision evoked a stormy public debate, in Syrian terms, between perceptions of it as a first step in the political marginalization of the Ba'th Party in Syria, and implacable opposition, mainly by party activists, to any thought of weakening the party status. Side by side with proposals to dismantle the "National Command" of the party as part of needed radical reform,[73] other opinion, e.g. in the party organ *al-Ba'th*, held that "the existing political system [the Ba'th Party] is capable of renewal and of setting into motion processes of change and development, so that there is no need whatsoever for changing or dismantling it so long as it does not hinder the development of the state."[74] The debate reached a climax when the editor of *al-Ba'th*, Mahdi Dakhlallah, joined the supporters of the process,[75] while Vice-President 'Abd al-Halim Khaddam promptly announced that such a process was out of the question, as it meant a loss of identity and a rejection of the past and thereby of the future as well.[76] Dakhlallah's appointment as Information Minister shortly thereafter indicated Bashar's leanings in this debate. To Dakhlallah's credit, a significant semantic change was instituted in the Syrian press (with the exception of the Ba'th Party organ), namely the cessation of referring to the country's leaders by the title *rafiq* (comrade), signifying their membership in the Ba'th Party.[77] In any event, Bashar ordered the formation of committees to examine the values and principles of the Ba'th Party, including its historic motto "Unity, freedom and socialism."[78]

In any case, it is too early to know whether the prospect of weakening the grip of the party on Syrian politics, which Bashar al-Asad undoubtedly favors, is realistic. Even if he seeks this development, so as to allow additional sectors of society to enter into the country's political life, his capability of bringing it about is doubtful, as his party colleagues will be unlikely to permit it.

Summary

Hafiz al-Asad's regime relied essentially on himself, on an inner circle of loyal colleagues, and on the army and the Ba'th Party. These bodies incorporated, first and foremost, members of his family, his tribe and his community – the Alawites – and only thereafter his coalition partners. Of all these elements, the influence of the Alawite officer class was the greatest, for Asad himself had risen from its ranks, while the day-to-day affairs of state were entrusted to Ba'th Party officials and governmental bureaucrats, most of whom were veteran associates of Asad's from the Sunni community who shared his philosophy and life experience.

Bashar al-Asad avoided introducing significant change in this order, although apparently he hoped to cultivate a coterie of bureaucrats to help him promote what he perceived to be needed reforms in the state. The question was whether he would be able to accomplish this. Could such a group, however unified and committed, be instrumental in implementing a true process of change? Moreover, what would be the response of the Alawite military elite and the Ba'th Party cadres whom Bashar presumably sought to force out and marginalize? Various Syria-watchers predicted that, if Bashar were not wise enough to build bridges with these powerful groups, he would fail in his efforts to advance a process of real reform and, worse, he was likely to lose his ruling status.

PART II

UNFULFILLED HOPES

CHAPTER 4

A false spring in Damascus

Question: You are a young President. You have recently completed your first year in office following the death of your father the late Hafiz al-Asad. In the course of this year, much has been said about reforms, as well as about other changes that are taking place in Syria and even about a "new spring" that Damascus is experiencing. However, recently there seems to have been a deceleration of Syria's progress towards democracy. My question is, then, how do you assess what has happened in Syria in the course of the past year?

Bashar al-Asad: I have noticed that many articles [on Syria] appearing in the Arab and Western press have used the term "spring". However, I am not convinced that spring is indeed the preferred season of the year. While there are those who do prefer the spring, there are also those who prefer the winter or the summer. Aside from that, the term "spring" expresses something temporary since it is a season of the year. Therefore the use of this term [in the context of what is happening in Syria] is, in my opinion, mistaken. After all, the seasons of the year repeat themselves every year and, in any case, the seasons of the year in our time are the same as those thousands and millions of years ago. Thus, the word "spring" totally contradicts the term [which I have chosen to use] in describing what we have done in Syria – "development". We do not wish to stay where we are today. We wish to bring progress and development [to our country]. Therefore, I cannot agree to compare what is happening in Syria today to "spring".

(Bashar al-Asad, in an interview to the
Spanish newspaper *el-Pais*, 1 May 2001)

Most Syrians probably never heard of Mundhir al-Muwassali, a deputy in the People's Assembly representing the Damascus district. Muwassali, who had served in 1964–66 as office director of Syria's strong man then, Amin al-Hafiz, and later worked in the journalism and information fields, was elected to the Assembly in 1998 as an independent delegate, i.e. not representing the ruling Ba'th Party or its satellite parties. Once he was elected, however, and later was appointed to the People's Assembly Committee on Arab and Foreign

Affairs, his involvement in parliamentary affairs was minimal.[1] Still, sometimes even a back-bencher has an opportunity to make history.

Several days after the People's Assembly approved a proposal to amend the Syrian constitution, reducing the minimum age required for a president to be elected from 40 to 34 years, thus paving the way for the election of Bashar al-Asad to the presidency, Muwassali got up during the Assembly session that was broadcast live for the first time over Syrian television and challenged the process of the amendment. While Muwassali did state that he was in complete agreement with Bashar and his path, he argued that the decision taken by the People's Assembly to amend the constitution was clearly illegal. According to Muwassali, this was because, in full contradiction of Article 149 of the constitution, no explanation at all had been made to the members of the Assembly specifying the reasons for the proposed amendment to the constitution.[2]

Anyone who thought that when Muwassali left the Assembly building he would be met by security men who would arrest him for having dared to challenge the process of electing Bashar al-Asad, thus implying some doubt as to the legitimacy of his regime, was in for a surprise. Muwassali left the building a hero accompanied by members of the Assembly who had come to his defense during the discussion. Moreover, it was reported from Damascus that Bashar al-Asad, whose election process had been at the focal point of Muwassali's criticism, had expressed his satisfaction with the open and free discussion held in the People's Assembly on the subject. Bashar was quoted as having said that it was Muwassali's right, and even duty, to say what he said and that what had happened in the Assembly was the actual implementation of the "openness" that he wanted to introduce into Syria.[3]

The principle of "openness," together with the principles of transparency, pluralism and democracy, did indeed hold a central place in Bashar al-Asad's inaugural address on July 17, 2000 before the People's Assembly. In this address Bashar emphasized his total commitment to his late father's path, while at the same time taking pains to present himself as the harbinger of change, albeit limited and gradual, which would not rock the very foundations of the political, social and economic order established by his father in the course of his 30 years in power. This change, he went on to explain, was essential if Syria wished to stride forward, especially in the social and economic spheres, and in the future, he promised his audience, he and his regime might display greater openness, transparency, tolerance and pluralism in comparison to what had previously been acceptable practice.

Bashar went on in his speech stating that:

[In order to achieve our goal] we need analysis and analysis needs studies and results, which in turn need to be based on facts. When we say "reality" it means accurate figures. Figures do not lie and therefore they are genuine and transparent. Dealing with figures requires honesty and transparency. The term "transparency" has been frequently used and discussed lately in dialogues and essays and in other places as well…. Prior to being an economic or political or an administrative case, transparency is a state of culture, values and social habits. This poses a question and a requirement that we should ask ourselves before we address it to others; am I transparent with myself first and with my family second and with the close and distant circle and with my country third?…. This dictates that we should face ourselves and our society bravely and conduct a brave dialogue with both in which we reveal our points of weakness and talk about customs, traditions and concepts which have become a true impediment in the way of any progress…. [What is needed] is the logic of cooperation and openness to others, and it is inseparable from the democratic thinking which has many things in common with it in various places… this [democratic] thinking is based on the principle of accepting the opinion of the other and this is certainly a two-way street.[4]

Bashar's desire to make changes in the social and economic spheres was understandable given the severe economic hardships Syria had suffered in the past decade. These hardships were expressed in negative economic growth rates or the collapse of health, education and welfare services provided by the Syrian state, resulting in a drop in the standard of living of Syrian citizens. All this gave rise to fears for the stability of the Ba'th regime and perhaps for its continued existence. Bashar was undoubtedly aware of this threat. However, it also appears that his steps were the result of his own awareness – a greater awareness than that of his late father – of the benefits of social and economic reforms for the Syrian economy. These reforms, he hoped, might even help extricate Syria from its economic hardships.

However, Bashar did not limit himself to the social and economic spheres. In his speeches and interviews in the early months of his rule, he made it clear that he was also troubled by the political suffocation of the Syrians by the generation-long autocratic regime of his father. It is clear that Bashar was of the opinion that this state of suffocation could block his efforts to bring Syria forward, if only in the social and economic spheres. He may also have assessed that the realities both at home and abroad, i.e. the crossing of borders and globalization, which cannot be ignored, would in any case make it impossible to maintain the regime his father established in Syria, certainly not in the form in which Hafiz al-Asad had maintained it for the 30 years of his rule. Thus, the conclusion that Bashar had to draw was that it was best that the regime initiate the reforms before they were forced upon it by external forces or perhaps by forces within Syrian society itself. Bashar may also have felt that limited and controlled political openness would assist him in improving the image of the Syrian regime both at home and abroad, and would also enable him to gain public support, thus consolidating his standing in Syria vis-à-vis the expected opposition to reforms by the focuses of power and the members of the old guard within the senior echelons of the regime who had remained on from the old era, his father's era.

The reformist camp mounts its path

There were many both inside and outside Syria who assessed at the beginning of Bashar's rule that any attempt that he made to effect even minor changes in the social or economic spheres, but mainly in the political sphere, after three decades of stagnation during which Syria was ruled by the iron fist of a repressive regime, would be like taking the lid off a boiling caldron. Bashar, however, chose to ignore this warning and to pursue his own path – the path of change incorporated into continuity.

The way Bashar rose to power (his being a compromise candidate or even a candidate through lack of choice), his lackluster image as compared to that of his late all-powerful father, and finally the composition of the senior political and military-security echelons in Syria based entirely on people who had been totally indebted to Hafiz al-Asad but not to his son all gave rise to serious doubts as to his ability to fill his father's large shoes and to continue maintaining the regime that the latter had established and led for 30 years. Bashar's own statements on his desire for change and even for openness and democratization only intensified these doubts and even aroused the feeling among many Syrians that, with the demise of the founding father, the Syrian regime was nothing more than a shaky structure that could be totally destroyed with one swift kick to its door.

This feeling prompted many to raise their voices to demand the introduction of greater freedom, far-reaching political reforms and even democracy in Syria. These were mainly intellectuals and a number of businessmen who had done well in the previous decade and now wanted to exploit the economic power base they had created in order to promote their economic and political interests and those of the social stratum to which they belonged. These intellectuals and businessmen emphasized, as Muwassali had, their loyalty to Bashar and even stressed that they were prepared to assist him in promoting the ideas of openness and democracy in Syria, but without a doubt they wanted to use him as a platform for the promotion of their own agenda designed in the final analysis to bring about the collapse of the old regime established in Syria during the rule of Hafiz al-Asad.

Mundhir al-Muwassali was the first to dare to test the limits in the new Bashar al-Asad era, but many followed him. As early as August 31, 2000, about two months after Bashar rose to power, Riyad Sayf (b. 1946), a businessman and People's Assembly member, began holding weekly meetings in his home in the Saydaniyya suburb of Damascus of what he called "The Forum for National Dialogue" (*Muntada al-Hiwar al-Watani*). Sayf did not hide his intentions of transforming the forum into a political-ideological framework called "The Friends of Civil Society" (*Ansar al-Mujtama' 'al-Madani*). Sayf subsequently announced that he also intended setting up a political party, the Social Peace Party (*Hizb al-Salam al-Ijtima'i*), whose objective was to be the "establishment and preservation of social peace" between the various ethnic and religious groups in Syria, between the citizens and the state institutions and finally "social peace" in day-to-day and political life in Syria.[5]

The convening of the forum in Sayf's home was no trivial matter since, according to the emergency laws practiced in Syria since the Ba'th Party rose to power on March 8, 1963, such political meetings or gathering were strictly prohibited without a permit obtained in advance. Moreover, even an innocuous meeting in which more than five people participated could be construed by the authorities as being illegal and could bring in its wake punitive measures against its organizers and participants. This restriction was made explicit to the E.U. Ambassador in Syria, Marc Fiorini, who was requested to pass on to the authorities a copy of an address on "Syria's Image in the European Media" which he was to give at a cultural symposium in July 2002. His undiplomatic response was: "I am not Riyad Sayf or Riyad al-Turk, but the Ambassador of the European Union in Syria."[6]

Yet Sayf's parlor meetings evoked no response from the authorities. On the contrary, the dozens and sometimes hundreds of guests who attended them included personalities identified with the Ba'th Party. Not surprisingly, therefore, similar discussion forums began forming throughout the country. By early 2001, 21 such groups functioned in various locations. In Damascus alone, there were five forums alongside Sayf's forum, including the Cultural Forum for

Human Rights (*al-Muntada al-Thaqafi LiHuquq al-Insan*), established and managed by Khalil Ma'tuq, an attorney known for his close connections with the Communist Party. Forums were also established in Aleppo, Tartus and Ladhiqiyya, and even in provincial towns such as Hasaka, Qamishli, Misyaf and Suwayda.[7] In Qamishli, an area with a large Kurdish population, the forum established in that town, the Jaladat Badrakhan, became a platform for Kurdish spokesmen who demanded that "The authorities recognize about 2 million Kurds living in Syria as a national minority and take steps to end the ongoing violations of their human rights." Parallel to that, other associations and committees were established to protect human rights and even the rights of prisoners of conscience in Syrian prisons, and the proposal was also made to establish a "National Council for Truth, Justice and Reconciliation" like that established in South Africa following the downfall of the apartheid regime in that country.[8]

As already mentioned, the Syrian regime refrained from taking any action against these forums that had been established all over the country, and apparently even encouraged its supporters to participate in them, with the undoubted aim of having them set the tone at their meetings. Faysal Kulthum, the chairman of the Association of Damascus University Faculty, who had become one of the regular participants in the meetings at Sayf's home, explained that his participation in the forum's meetings "is in order to express the commitment of members of the Ba'th Party to the ideas of openness and liberalism," although he warned that "Everyone must know that the way to leading to the point where Syria's citizens will be ready to absorb and internalize the ideas discussed at this forum is a long one."[9] Some time later, in January 2001, the Syrian regime granted permission to Ba'th Party activist and member of the People's Assembly Suhayr al-Ris to set up her own Cultural Forum in Ladhiqiyya,[10] and at the same time extended its aegis over the Tuesday Economic Forum convened by the Association for Science and Economics. Participants in this forum included senior officials, and it became a platform for an open and even scathing discussion on the state of Syria's economy.[11]

The Socialist Arab Democratic Union Party (a Nasserist opposition party which operated with the tacit approval of the Syrian authorities) also established its own forum on January 15, 2000, the eighty-sixth anniversary of the birth of Jamal 'Abd al-Nasir. The forum was named after its late leader, Jamal al-Atasi, and headed by his daughter, Suhayr al-Atasi. The forum's spokesman, Habib 'Isa, explained that: "The forum's objective is the holding of an open dialogue, excluding those things which violate the basic [Syrian] and pan-Arab national principles which the party stands for."[12] The regime refrained from taking any action against the forum even when the forum became the arena for embarrassing and even sharp criticism of it. It preferred to turn a blind eye to the activities of the left-wing *al-Yasar* (the Left) Forum, which was affiliated with the Arab Revolutionary Workers Party (another left-wing opposition party), which began to meet in the home of Munif Milham in the Jarmana suburb of Damascus.[13]

In July 2001, the regime even permitted the Center of Islamic Studies headed by Muhammad al-Habash to set up a cultural forum, which holds meetings and gives lectures on subjects of religion and culture. It should be noted that Habash was the son-in-law of the late Mufti of Syria, Ahmad al-Kaftaru, who was known for his close association with the authorities. Habash himself explained that the forum's aim was "to operate from an innovative Islamic viewpoint." He added that "This forum does not intend dealing with present-day issues, since I believe that everyone should deal with his own affairs and I do not think that it is my task to deal with those issues. Our message is focused on our innovative Islam and we will devote most of our attention and time to that."[14]

As will be recalled, Riyad Sayf's intention was to turn his forum into a political party called the "Social Peace Party." Sayf was followed by another People's Assembly member, Ihsan Sanqar, also a prominent and respected businessman in the Syrian capital, who announced that he intended to establish a liberal party. Towards the end of 2000, Sayf established a political bloc based on 21 independent members of the People's Assembly. These included Mahdi Khayr Bak from Ladhiqiyya and Mamun al-Humsi, a businessman from the Damascus province. The People's Assembly Presidium refused to recognize them as a faction, since political union outside the framework of the National Progressive Front is forbidden in Syria. Nevertheless, the members of the group began coordinating their activities, and were even prominent in their sharp criticism of the regime during People's Assembly discussions, criticism the likes of which had not been heard in Syria for years.[15]

The challenge facing the Syrian regime because of its openness policy went beyond the activities of the cultural forums that rapidly sprang up all over Syria, and the criticism – sharp as it was – by some of the People's Assembly members of the Executive Branch. In September 2000, 99 prominent intellectuals in Syria signed a petition to the regime in which they demanded "the release of all the political prisoners and prisoners of conscience, the return of all the exiles, the establishment of a law-abiding State, the granting of freedoms and the recognition of political and ideological pluralism, the right to organize, freedom of the Press, speech and expression and the release of public life from supervision." The petition went on to say:

> Syria is now entering the twenty-first century and it urgently needs to channel efforts of construction and development toward meeting the challenges of peace, development and openness to the outside world. Reforms – be they economic, administrative or legal – will never achieve security and stability if they are not accompanied to the fullest by political reforms. Only the last mentioned can steer our society to a safe haven.[16]

Among those who signed the petition were Sadiq Jalal al-'Azm, the writer Haydar Haydar and the poet Adonis, as well as Riyad Sayf and the economist 'Arif Dalila.

The petition of the 99 was published in Beirut and not in Damascus, because its initiators refrained from taking the risk involved in publishing it in Damascus. Indeed, for the first time since Bashar rose to power, signs of concern began to appear regarding the increased wave of openness, which he himself had initiated. No mention was made of the petition in the Syrian media. Lebanese newspapers that reported it were confiscated at the border crossings and their distribution in Syria was banned.[17] Moreover, the Syrian media mounted an organized attack on the intellectuals involved. The editor of *al-Ba'th*, Turqi Saqr, wrote: "there are those who are interested in interpreting talk of the stimulation of political life as meaning the elimination of existing realities, replacing them with slogans, shiny on the outside and poisonous on the inside." Saqr asserted that "Security and stability in Syria are the foundation stones of renewal and development."[18] The editor of *Tishrin*, Khalaf Muhammad al-Jarrad, sharply attacked the supporters of civil society for:

> having recently taken up the subject … as if it were a lifeline…. These ideas have to do with a mere minority of symposium stars and seekers of publicity, honors and power, while the vast majority of the public in the Arab homeland are struggling to find bread, shelter and income. Our main objection to this imported concept is … its detachment from its historic and social roots, and its attachment to individual freedom… the idea of separation of the state from civil society is nothing more than an ideological delusion proven false by the history of Western cultures.[19]

Editorials published in the Syrian press were beyond a doubt designed to serve as a warning signal to Syrian intellectuals, who, however, chose to ignore it. It is quite possible that the reactions of the regime, which were in the final analysis hesitant and limited – at least in comparison with the practice in Syria at the time, and were nothing more than the publication of several articles of criticism in the Syrian press – merely served to encourage these intellectuals to persevere in, and even broaden, their activities.

Early in January 2001, a founding document was published in Damascus by the Committees for the Rejuvenation of Civil Society. The document soon became known as the "Petition of the One Thousand," as 1,000 intellectuals from all parts of Syria were said to have signed it. Shortly thereafter, 16 of the signatories, including Riyad Sayf, 'Arif Dalila and Sadiq Jalal al-'Azm, gathered in Damascus and announced that they constituted a "Preliminary Meeting of the Committees for the Rejuvenation of Civil Society," whose goal was "the reinforcement of the coordination and the link between all the committees and forums that have begun to function throughout Syria with the goal of establishing a civil society in Syria in response to the problems of this country."[20]

Notably, the members of the Committees for the Rejuvenation of Civil Society published another document, in April 2001, titled "Toward a National Social Covenant in Syria – General National Principles." The document came as a response to accusations by highly placed Syrian officials that the signatories of the "Petition of the One Thousand" were endangering Syria's national unity and ignoring the issue of the Israeli–Arab conflict, which constituted the cornerstone of the world view of every Arab anywhere and certainly of every Syrian citizen. Replying to this attack, the signatories adopted an apologetic tone, emphasizing their commitment to the Palestinian issue. They expressed full support for "the campaign to liberate our conquered lands [the Golan Heights] as well as the conquered Arab lands in Palestine and Lebanon." They called for the "dedication of all abilities and efforts to fulfill this goal," adding that "peace must not be viewed as putting an end to the conflict between us and the Zionist enemy. We must establish an all-Arab regime, not a regime of the 'New Middle East' or a Mediterranean regime."[21]

On 3 May 2001 the Muslim Brotherhood movement published the draft of the "Covenant of National Honor for Political Activity" (*Mithaq Sharaf Watani Lil-'Amal al-Siyasi*). The publication of the draft by the movement was probably intended to remind everyone of its existence, and even to establish a basis for joint activity with other opposition groups in Syria. It may also have been designed to establish a dialogue with the Syrian regime itself, now that its founder, Hafiz al-Asad, had died. The draft stated that its aim was to:

> arouse a debate that would allow for the formulation of an agreed covenant of national honor to serve as the basis for political

activity in Syria in this sensitive and problematic period and in view of the political changes in the international and domestic arenas…. After all, the time has passed when a single party claimed [ownership of the homeland]. From now on, each political group should be able to have its place on the national map in keeping with its relative strength as expressed in clean and democratic elections.

In the draft document published in London, the Muslim Brotherhood expressed its commitment to maintaining democratic political activity and even voiced strong condemnation of the use of violence. The Brotherhood did, however, state that "any dialogue must be based on a broad national consensus regarding the basic principles on which the existence of the nation, its power and its uniqueness is based."[22]

The Muslim Brotherhood's hope of turning over a new leaf in its relations with the Syrian Ba'th regime with the rise to power of Bashar al-Asad proved futile in view of the regime's strict position and lack of any readiness for compromise in its relations with the organization. On August 23–25, 2002, the Brotherhood held a conference in London designed to draw up an agreed formula for the "National Covenant." They invited people from the entire political spectrum from both inside and outside Syria. However, response to the invitation was insignificant, and most of those who did participate were people close to the Muslim Brotherhood, or at least those who had not returned to Syria in recent years with the permission of the authorities.[23] In any event, the Brotherhood's attempt to get on to the reform bandwagon reflected the inherent danger to the regime in the policy of openness that it encouraged. This danger was focused on the feeling extant both inside and outside Syria that the regime was projecting weakness and the feeling that it could even be challenged.

The wave of openness that swelled to flood proportions presented the senior echelons in the regime with an ever-worsening dilemma, and even gave rise to a sense of losing control. While Bashar did attempt in the early months of his regime to pursue a policy of openness in the hope, which later proved baseless, that the move, limited as it was, would serve to placate the reformist camp and even recruit its support for the Syrian regime and for himself, it soon became clear to him that he would do well to abandon this policy.

The regime mounts a counterattack

If Bashar had expected to build himself up with the political openness he had initiated, it quickly became clear that he had lost control of that move, which turned out to be a threat to the stability of the regime. The problem was apparently not necessarily with the activities of several dozen forums in which a few hundred intellectuals participated, and not with the petitions published by these intellectuals, but rather with the significance of this phenomenon for a state such as Syria, which for years had been used to an iron-fisted, oppressive regime. Thus these forums aroused feelings of loss of control and anarchy. One can readily understand the regime's fear that there would be those in Syria who might wish to exploit the regime's gesture as well as the atmosphere of openness it brought in its wake in Syria, especially the Islamic circles which the regime feared the most.

It is possible that the decision that brought the Damascus Spring to an end was that of Bashar himself; the criticism voiced by these intellectuals had begun to reach his very doorstep, for example in the severe criticism of his late father, who was described as a despot and as an arch-murderer. Evidence of this was visible in an interview that Bashar granted to the London-based newspaper *al-Sharq al-Awsat* in February 2001, which was the opening salvo in the campaign against the reformists in Syria. However, Bashar may have been forced to mount a campaign against the reformists by the conservative camp within the ranks of the Syrian regime, headed by the old guard surrounding him, which was afraid of losing its power and status. It should be borne in mind that this old guard – comprising such figures as Vice-President 'Abd al-Halim Khaddam and Defense Minister Mustafa Talas – did indeed support Bashar's ascendancy to the presidency and was even prepared to pay the price of being shunted to the sidelines, a process which began when Bashar assumed office and which was inevitable considering their age, most of them in their seventies. Nevertheless, when the moment of truth arrived and the old guard understood the danger to its status and even to the very existence of the regime, and perhaps when it realized that Bashar was not determined enough and might not have entirely understood the serious danger confronting him, its members went into action.

As already mentioned, it was in an interview to *al-Sharq al-Awsat* on February 8, 2001 that Bashar fired his opening salvo in the regime's campaign against the reformist camp, a campaign designed to end the "Damascus Spring." In this interview Bashar attacked those intellectuals who raised their voices in demands for reforms and democracy:

I was the first to propose these ideas in my [presidential] inaugural address. I brought them up as a political line, which I was planning to adopt and not merely lip-service slogans. Regarding those petitions [which the intellectuals published from time to time], the president of a state does not have to act in his country on the basis of petitions by private people, especially when they are published outside the homeland and not inside the homeland. He must also not accept the ideas presented by an elite that present itself as speaking in the name of the people. After all, the president's contacts with the people are direct contacts.... Every small group that thinks it is the elite should aim to represent the general [public] and these elitist groups would do well to operate within the consensus reflecting the entire population.... If the elite limit themselves to the narrowest level, they are liable to express limited views.

These intellectuals confuse the civil society with the institutions of the civil society. The civil society is a cultural society that is the essence of many cultures, which have existed for thousands of years. Syria has a past culture that has lasted more than 6,000 years. To say that we want to build a civil society means that we want to do away with all this past and to begin a new history. That is not realistic.... As to the institutions of the civil society, that is another matter, and they do exist in Syria even if not in the ideal form.... What is important is not to view them as the alternative to the institutions of the state. Civil institutions must not precede the state institutions in the building process, but on the contrary, they must follow them, assist them, lean on them and not build upon their ruins.... The development of the institutions of the civil society must come at a later stage.

Thus, his conclusion regarding these intellectuals was: "It seems that there are people who think that the period of [the mandate] or of the repeated revolutions [the 1940s and the 1950s] was preferable to the period of stability that began in 1963 and was strengthened in 1970." Bashar concluded by warning that:

One can pass on to the stage of the political development of the political system in a country only on the basis of existing realities, and on the basis of Syrian history. Already in my inaugural address I said that we are not here to shatter and destroy the system, but rather our aim is to develop it. The meaning of development is that it must be based on existing realities and from there to try and move out of emptiness and vacuum.[24]

In the wake of Bashar's interview, other senior members of the regime joined the all-out campaign against the reform camp in

Syria. As part of the regime's counterattack, the senior members of the party held meetings in the party branches with activists as well as rank-and-file members. Parallel to this, the Syrian media began publishing editorials sharply attacking the supporters of reform, accusing them of harming Syria's national interests, while serving foreign governments at a time when Syria was at the front struggling against Israel. Even the preachers in the mosques were assigned the task of attacking the intellectuals, claiming that those who advocate civil government also advocate civil marriage.[25]

This campaign of the senior echelons of the Syrian regime was undoubtedly designed to lay the groundwork for the blow dealt by the Syrian security services to the reformists and intellectuals. First, in the provincial towns far from the watchful eye of the Western media, which is concentrated mainly on Damascus, action began against intellectuals and founders of forums where reformists met. In Ladhiqiyya, for example, the playwright Nabil Sulayman, who had opened a cultural forum in the town, was attacked and severely beaten up by some unknown persons and had to be admitted to the local hospital. Official sources claimed that the attack on the playwright came in response to erotic scenes in some of his plays. However, it was clear to everyone that his only transgression was the founding and heading of a cultural forum in his home town.[26] Another such incident was reported in Qamishli, where a number of Kurds active in the Jaladat Badrakhan cultural forum were beaten up by the head of political security in the town.[27] The car owned by Suhayr al-Atasi, the leader of the Jamal al-Atasi cultural forum, was stolen from in front of her house, and the lawyer Khalil Ma'tuq, a member of the Communist Party and civil rights activist, was involved in a mysterious car accident in the course of which a Mercedes car bumped into his car trying to force him off the road. Ma'tuq became known in the West for representing Nizar Nayyuf, a Syrian journalist who was in prison for almost eight years and was released during the visit of the Pope to Damascus in May 2001.[28] After his release Nayyuf started attacking the regime, revealing so-called scoops he had found out during his long stay in prison. Thus he told reporters that he had met Ron Arad, the missing Israeli navigator, in a Syrian jail where he was held, and later he reported efforts by the regime to hide the mass graves of victims of the massacre carried out by Syrian security forces in Tadmur jail in 1980. The fact that Nayyuf suffered from mental problems as a result of the long time in prison made it easy for the regime to deny these allegations. Nevertheless, in June 2001 the authorities arrested him for this criticism, but he was released because of Western pressure, since it was shortly before Bashar's visit to Paris.[29]

Second, the leaders of the forums were summoned to supply permits for their activity in accordance with the emergency laws still in force in Syria. They were warned that legal steps would be taken against any forum which did not supply such permits. However, whoever tried to comply with this order encountered bureaucratic obstacles that were virtually impossible to overcome. For example, the exact authority that issued such permits – whether the Ministry of Labor and Welfare, in charge of cultural, sports and welfare forums, or the security authorities – was difficult to ascertain. Riyad Sayf, applying to the Ministry of Labor and Welfare in May 2001 for a permit to operate his forum, received this reply from the minister, Bari'a al-Qudsi:

> After studying the articles of the Law of Private Associations and Institutions No. 93, of 1958, and Order No. 1330 of the President of the Republic, of 1958, which deals with the implementation of this law, I have decided to reject your request for a permit for your forum because the matter does not fall under my ministry's responsibility, and because in any event your request does not satisfy the requirements.[30]

A request by the forum operated by Suhayr al-Atasi was also rejected. The head of the department for social affairs in the Ministry of Labor and Welfare refused the request first by claiming that the officer in charge was on holiday, and later by claiming that the sensitivity of the issue prevented him from issuing such a permit.[31] In the wake of pressures exerted on the organizers of these forums, they began closing down one after the other. In several cases, it was a free decision and in others it was in response to pressure from security forces, which presented themselves at the forums' gates to make sure that they indeed closed down.

Third, the regime began imprisoning intellectuals and public figures who headed the reformist camp. This step was taken in the wake of ongoing harsh criticism leveled at the regime by these people. In August 2001, a deputy of the People's Assembly known for his sharp criticism of the regime, Mamun al-Humsi, was arrested and charged with violation of the constitution and displaying a hostile attitude toward the regime.[32] An article published in *Tishrin* three months later, in November 2001, accused Humsi of tax evasion, injuring several schoolgirls in a hit-and-run accident, car theft, and partnership with "Mr. 5%" (the nickname given to former Minister of the Economy Salim Yasin, known for skimming a 5 percent commission from every matter in which his ministry was involved). The article also compared Humsi to Henri Gouraud, the first French

High Commissioner in the Levant, and accused him of betraying the country's national interests during its war against Israel in Lebanon in 1982.[33] Notably, however, *Tishrin* published a response to these accusations by Humsi's attorney a month later, an unprecedented step in the Syrian press.[34]

On September 1, 2001, Riyad al-Turk, a member of the Communist Party – Political Bureau (a faction of the Syrian Communist Party), was arrested at his summer home in Tartus. Turk, who was released from prison in May 1988 after he had spent 17 years in jail, quickly became one of the Syrian regime's severest critics. On the eve of the referendum on the approval of Bashar al-Asad's candidacy for the presidency, Turk announced that he would not support Bashar's candidacy, since the mentality of the regime of his father, Hafiz al-Asad, had made Syria the private property of the Asad family. In early 2001, he declared that with his release from prison he had ostensibly become a free man, but that in fact what had happened was that he had been freed from a small prison into a large prison (Syria). However, his criticism reached its peak in the summer of 2001, in an address before an audience at the Jamal al-Atasi cultural forum, when he attacked the late President Hafiz al-Asad, accusing him of being a dictator of Stalin's ilk, and said that his rule was characterized by stagnation and corruption and that he was responsible for the massacre at Hama.[35]

Later on, seven other prominent activists in the reformist camp, headed by 'Arif Dalila, former head of the Economics Department at the University of Damascus, were arrested. Others arrested included Habib Salah, a prominent businessman, Turk's close associate Kamal al-Buni, Walid Buzi, a human rights activist, and Habib 'Isa. Finally, on September 6, 2001, Riyad Sayf was also arrested. In mid-February 2001, Riyad Sayf was charged with violating the constitution because of his plans to establish the "Social Peace Movement." These intentions were presented as an attempt to undermine the Ba'th Party's leading position in Syria, as established by the Syrian constitution. The People's Assembly subsequently approved his being divested of his parliamentary immunity because of this charge. Sayf, who is the Adidas representative in Syria, was also accused of tax evasion in the sum of £SY50 million. At first, Sayf gave in to pressure and, on March 21, 2001, he announced that he was closing the forum he had founded. However, in early September 2001 he announced that he was reopening the forum. Several days later he was arrested by the authorities. He was quickly brought to trial, and in April 2002 he was sentenced, with his other colleagues, to five years in prison.[36]

It should be noted, however, that the trials of Sayf and Humsi were held in a relatively free atmosphere, at least in Syrian terms. Their attorneys maintained a media campaign against their arrests and trials and demanded that their clients be released. An Internet site in support of Sayf was even set up, apparently run by Syrians living outside the country. Moreover, Western diplomats were allowed to be present at the court sessions, and the European Union even protested the arrest, and later the sentences of Sayf and his colleagues.[37] The openness displayed by the Syrian regime in its treatment of the affair was attributed to its desire to avoid exacerbating the tension in its relationship with the intellectual community as well as its awareness of existing limitations in its struggle against its enemies. Early in 2002, the regime was reported to be considering pardoning the detainees, lest their trial turn into an arena for attacks against the regime and, by extension, a source of embarrassment for it. These reports, however, proved to be unsubstantiated, for Humsi, Sayf and their colleagues were sentenced to five years' imprisonment. With this, approximately a year thereafter, Riyad al-Turk was released from prison as a gesture of good will to French president Jacques Chirac, who was visiting Damascus then.[38]

The relative ease with which the Syrian regime brought an end to the "Damascus Spring" is rooted first and foremost in the fact that the reformist group that had stood up against it was fragmented and divided and found it difficult to agree on the agenda it wanted to promote. Its members came from different backgrounds. Some of them, like Riyad Sayf or Mamun al-Humsi, were businessmen whose main interest was the creation of a Western-style democracy and a free economy that would serve – economically and politically – the socioeconomic stratum to which they belonged. Others were intellectuals belonging to the Leftist camp and had a Marxist background. Many of them were elderly people in their mid-seventies, some of whom had lived abroad for many years and were to a great extent cut off from the Syrian experience. It is also possible that they enjoyed only limited public support and much of what they said did not touch the hearts of the Syrian public, which was occupied mainly with economic problems. Finally, the early stages of the Reform Movement coincided with the Palestinian Intifada. Popular rage on the Arab street in general and in Syria in particular made it difficult for the reformists, who in essence wanted to promote totally Western ideas, to arouse feelings against a regime whose anti-West and anti-Israel policies were a true reflection of the mood of the Arab man on the street. It is therefore no wonder that one of the Syrian intellectuals was quoted as having said "Bush and Sharon have provided the Syrian conservatives a valuable gift that allowed them to convert 'spring' into 'bitter winter' in Damascus."[39]

It would also appear that most of the Syrian intellectuals have in the end remained mainly party loyalists. Data published in honor of Ba'th Revolution Day in March 2000 reveal that the vast majority of university lecturers are members of the Ba'th Party and are dependent on the party and the regime for their livelihood (56 percent of the lecturers at the University of Damascus, 54 percent of the lecturers at the University of Aleppo, 79 percent of the lecturers at the Tishrin University in Ladhiqiyya and 81 percent of the lecturers at the Ba'th University in Homs).[40] Witness to this is borne out in the strong words hurled at the participants in a meeting at the home of Riyad Sayf, by the Secretary of the Office of Youth and Students of the Ba'th Party Regional Command, Fa'iz 'Izz al-Din, who accused them of wanting only to strike out at members of the Ba'th Party. "You cannot come to me and say that, as one who has been a member of the Ba'th Party for over 40 years, I am worthless, and expect me to take this quietly and with a smile." Husayn al-Zu'bi, a lecturer at the University of Damascus, reminded those present at the meeting that, if it were not for the Ba'th Party, "I could not have studied and become a university lecturer. My father was a simple peasant exploited by feudal lords and the bourgeoisie. Therefore one cannot claim that the regime in power in Syria has done nothing positive."[41]

In November 2001, in a kind of effort to show its self-confidence and commitment to preserving an atmosphere of openness in Syria, the regime released dozens of prisoners, among them senior Islamic leaders such as Khalid al-Shami, who was one of the leaders of the Islamic rebellion against the regime in the early 1980s and had been in prison since 1982.[42] As will be recalled, this gesture was made parallel to the arrests of leaders of the reformist camp in Syria. It is worth recalling just why the regime declared such a bitter war against the intellectuals and the reformist camp in Syria: it was precisely because of its fear of the Islamic circles, which it viewed as the main threat to the stability and very existence of the regime. This fear of a fundamentalist wave that threatened to sweep over the country had many partners, even outside the ranks of the regime, which could explain their support for it or more precisely their reservations about the activities of the reformist camp. As explained by Muhammad 'Aziz Shukri of the University of Damascus:

> The problem is that the leaders of the reformist camp want to achieve everything all at once, but the sudden announcement of elections would create a confrontation between the Ba'th Party

and Islamic circles in Syria, and one must ask what the results would be and what would happen afterwards? I don't want to jump from a reality in which we find ourselves today to the kind of "rotten" situation existing in Algeria in which everyone is trapped between the army and the Islamic circles and no one knows who is killing whom and why.[43]

Summary

With the death of Hafiz al-Asad and the ascent to power of his son Bashar, a change took place in Syria. This change was aptly described by Ibrahim Hamidi, a reporter for *al-Hayat* known for his close relationship with the Syrian regime, who, summarizing Bashar's first year in office, wrote in July 2001 that it was "characterized by cracks in the wall of fear within Syrian public opinion."[44] How significant these cracks were, of course, is debatable. One hint may be found in the fact that, ironically, Hamidi himself was arrested by the Syrian authorities in December 2002 and sent to prison. The arrest occurred after Hamidi had published a report in the paper which embarrassed the authorities, namely that the Syrian government was making preparations to absorb a million refugees from Iraq in anticipation of the invasion of Iraq by the United States. Hamidi was released several months thereafter, just before the fall of Baghdad to the American forces. He resumed writing for his paper and in April 2004 he was formally acquitted of all charges, but his articles showed greater caution than in the past.[45]

Indeed, in every respect, and especially in terms of the expectations aroused when young Asad stepped into his father's shoes, the change that occurred appeared to be surprisingly limited, evoking a widespread sense that ultimately the regime remained as it was, following the same policy despite cosmetic changes. Bashar, in short, was perceived as lacking the strength to initiate a true, substantive process of change in Syria, if he had intended to do so at all.

Although the Damascus Spring had soon turned into a harsh winter, clearly the reality of the old Syria was not likely to return. The era of Hafiz al-Asad had been relegated to history, and restoring it would be difficult if not impossible. The process of change that had begun in the country may have been slow, and at times imperceptible, for it took a zigzag course. Still the process seemed durable, even if its limitations were obvious. The Syrian intellectual Sadiq al-'Azm, warning the regime not to act against the civil society movement, pointed out: "The intellectuals are better at articulating the country's problems than the man in the street, but the problems they raise are the same problems that the man in the street deals with, so that repressing the intellectuals will not be productive." 'Azm urged the regime to learn from the events in the East European states, where the repression of intellectuals by the regime turned them into the spearhead of the struggle against it.[46]

'Azm, focusing on Eastern Europe, might have benefited by studying Syria's neighbor to the east, Iraq. Syrian TV refrained from showing the dismantling of the statue of Saddam Husayn in the main square of Baghdad on April 9, 2003, the day Baghdad fell to the American forces, and instead broadcast a program about Islamic sites in Syria. One Syrian Internet surfer pointed out that there are many statues in Damascus, too (of the founder of the Asad dynasty) that might meet the same fate.[47] The fall of Saddam Husayn's regime, along with the presence of hundreds of thousands of American soldiers along Syria's eastern border, provided a new impetus for the reformist elements in Syria. Some tried to renew their activity, mostly unsuccessfully. It seems that the Syrian public showed an unmistakable aversion to any step that might support or correlate with the American effort to impose a new order in the region. As Haytham al-Mani', a prominent critic of the Syrian regime, put it: "There is no way I will return from my exile to Damascus riding on an American tank."[48] Another sharp critic of the regime, Riyad al-Turk, stated: "The United States must halt its efforts to strike at Syria, for this actually aids the regime in Damascus. Washington must leave the task of regime change to us here in Syria."[49] Nevertheless, many of the reformists believed that in the long run the regime would find it difficult to preserve itself as it had in early 2001 when it brought the brief spring in Damascus to an end.[50]

Indeed, in late 2003 the establishment of the Syrian Reform Party (*Hizb al-Islah al-Suri*) was announced in Washington. The head of the party was a Syrian American businessman, Farid Nahid al-Ghadiri. The party, which enjoyed the blessing of the American administration, held a meeting in Brussels in January 2004 to which all opposition parties that operated outside Syria were invited. It even tried to establish an alliance of the parties – the Alliance for the Democracy (*al-Tahaluf min ajl al-Dimuqratiyya*) – but it seems that it has no real foothold in Syria and its effort to gather around itself opposition elements to the Ba'th regime did not succeed. Indeed, Foreign Minister Faruq al-Shar' reacted to the establishment of this party, adding that its leaders were trying to present themselves as alternative to the regime in Syria but in reality could not run even an elementary school.[51]

However, in light of intensified American pressure on Syria, the party could no longer be dismissed. Its representatives, who were prominent critics of the Syrian regime in Washington and in the capitals of Europe, were invited in March 2005 to a meeting in the U.S. State Department to discuss their position on the chances of forming a democratic system of government in Syria.[52] Shortly beforehand, 'Abd al-Aziz Sahhab Muflat, another American businessman of Syrian origin, announced the formation of an additional Syrian opposition party in Washington, the Democratic Awakening Party (*Hizb al-Nahda al-Watani al-Dimuqrati*).[53]

On March 8, 2004, Syria marked the forty-first anniversary of the Ba'th Party coup that brought the current regime to power. However, the celebrations were deliberately kept low-key in an effort to conceal a sense of growing anxiety and concern about the future.[54] This was not a moment for Syrian self-assurance. Only a year before, the United States had toppled Saddam Husayn's regime, and there was a widespread feeling that Syria might be next on Washington's "hit list."

It was therefore not surprising that, on March 8, 2004, public attention was not focused on Revolution Day ceremonies but rather on a demonstration opposite the parliament building organized by several Syrian human rights activists. The demonstrators demanded the cancellation of the emergency laws in effect since the Ba'th seized power in 1963 and the inauguration of democratic rule. True, security forces quickly broke up the demonstration and arrested some of the demonstrators. But they also quickly released those arrested, largely because of the regime's sensitivity to foreign criticism, especially on the part of Europeans, whose good will Syria wants to cultivate. Those released included a member of the American Embassy who had come to observe. The presence of an American diplomat at the demonstration was a source of particular concern to the authorities and prompted them to claim that Washington was stirring the fires of rebellion and inciting the local population to come out against the regime.[55]

The demonstration in Damascus might have passed as an isolated incident had it not been for the signs of Kurdish rebellion that erupted a few days later on March 12, 2004 in the northern region of Hasaka and especially in the city of Qamishli on the Syrian–Turkish border. There, a fight between fans of Kurdish- and Arab-supported football teams set off a tide of unrest that washed over the entire country. In protest against the deaths of three Kurdish youths at the football stadium and the violence of the police and security forces, Kurds themselves launched a wave of violence that included attacks on government offices and public facilities. The fire then spread to other concentrations of Kurds and even reached the Kurdish quarter of Damascus and the University of Damascus, where Kurdish students denounced violations of Kurdish rights.[56]

The Kurdish protests erupted against a historical background of tensions between Kurds and Arabs in the north, which traditionally had a Kurdish majority but has undergone a process of Arabization in the past few decades. For years, the government has struggled to suppress any expressions of Kurdish national identity and has refused to grant Syrian citizenship to hundreds of thousands of Kurds who, according to it, fled to Syria from Iraq. At the same time, Syria's relatively decent treatment of local Kurds – certainly by the standards of Saddam Husayn's approach to Iraqi Kurds – explains the relative calm that prevailed here until recently.[57]

What upset this balance was the signal of encouragement sent to Kurds in surrounding areas by developments in Iraq itself. American backing for a degree of Kurdish autonomy in Iraq verging on de facto independence has strengthened Kurdish assertiveness against central governments in Syria, Iran and Turkey. That undoubtedly explains the audacity of Syrian Kurds in confronting the regime in Damascus.

In response, the regime tried to conciliate the Kurds and refrained from relying only on an iron fist, as it normally had in the past. It is true that several dozen Kurdish deaths have been reported, but in repressing previous rebellions, such as the 1982 Hama uprising, the regime did not hesitate to kill thousands. In the last analysis, Bashar managed to pacify the Kurds, inter alia by promising to issue Syrian identity cards to hundreds of thousands of Kurds living in Jazira without identity cards, and by releasing all the Kurdish prisoners involved in the Qamishli incidents.[58] In this case, it seemed that, in dealing with a Kurdish challenge in the north, the regime could rely on the support of Arabs, who constituted an overwhelming majority of the population and who reject any expression of Kurdish separatism, especially one relying on possible American support.[59] Nor did the regime need to be overly concerned about the protests of oppositionist organizations and human rights activists. For the time being, they remained a small collection of pro-reform forces lacking any real base in the broader Syrian public. In general, the regime still appeared to enjoy the support of most of the pillars of Syrian society: army officers, economic elites and the small middle class. Those elements understood better than any foreign observer that the alternative to the current regime was not necessarily a liberal democracy as envisaged by the American administration, but rather Islamist fundamentalism of the sort that would make the Ba'th look positively libertarian by contrast.

But even if these events did not represent an immediate existential threat to the regime, longer-term trends are still likely to weaken it and perhaps bring about its eventual demise. After all, recurrent and growing protest will have a cumulative effect, particularly in combination with deepening economic problems and a problematic regional environment in which Syria faces not only its traditional Israeli adversary to the south but also a new American neighbor to the east.

However, domestic developments in Syria had their own dynamic. The Kurdish disturbances were followed by rioting in the Assyrian community in Hasaka, and thereafter local rioting that broke out in the Isma'ili regions of Misyaf and Qadmus.[60] Furthermore, protests and demonstrations by human rights organizations became daily events in Damascus and other cities in Syria, and in 2005 the formation of two new liberal organizations was announced: the Liberal Foundation (*al-Takhaluf al-Libarali*) and the *Sawasiyya* (equality) Organization for Human Rights.[61]

Indeed, the democratic elections held in Iraq in January 2005 and, of course, the eviction of Syria from Lebanon in April 2005 further weakened the Syrian regime not only externally but at home as well. Ironically, it was Bashar himself who had confidently declared, just before the fall of 'Umar Karami's government in Beirut in February 2005 in the wake of the assassination of Lebanese prime minister Rafiq al-Hariri, and the massive demonstrations in the Lebanese capital, that he did not foresee anything similar to what had occurred in Ukraine happening in Beirut. "Lebanon is not Ukraine," he said.[62]

Nevertheless, the terrorist attack in Damascus by a group of fundamentalists in April 2004 continued to demonstrate to the Syrian regime, as to its critics, that a real danger lurked at the door. Indeed, anyone observing what is going on in Syria could get the impression that the end of the road is not necessarily the fulfillment of the reformists' dream, i.e. making Syria into a country with a Western democratic system with an active and vibrant civil society, but perhaps it is rather the fulfillment of the dream of the Islamists waiting patiently for their turn, thriving on and even increasing their strength from the ever-increasing socioeconomic crisis in Syria over the past several years, which is destined to grow worse in the future. In any event, it is clear that many years will pass before it is spring again in Damascus.

CHAPTER 5

Society and economy in the age of globalization

A report on public sector wages in Syria issued by the Ministry of Planning, published in the government-sponsored daily *Tishrin* in April 2000, painted a gloomy picture. Nearly 40 percent of salaried workers earned less than the average wage, which was £SY2,200 (*c.* $44) per month. Approximately 50 percent of salaried workers, comprising a wide range of vocations, from skilled laborers to teachers, engineers and physicians, earned salaries ranging from £SY3,000 to £SY5,000 ($60–$100). Less than 10 percent, consisting primarily of the general-directors of government ministries and senior military officers, earned about £SY8,000 (*c.* $160).[1] Notably, senior government officials and army commanders were likely to have had access to other sources of income, both legal and especially illegal, which allowed them to live in comfort. However, the report showed that the Syrian workforce, from the doorman in a government office to a clerk, a senior bureaucrat or the director of the office himself, constituted a proletariat who earned subsistence wages (ranging from $50 to $150 a month).

Although these data related to the public sector, they are significant in light of the remarkably small size of the private sector in Syria. At the time of publication of the report, the Syrian government employed, by its own account, 1,257,000 persons, to which nearly 500,000 army and security forces must be added. This is an especially high proportion, considering that 30–40 percent of the workforce (nearly 4.5 million persons in early 2000, but almost 5.5 million in early 2005) earn their livelihood in agriculture as small farmers or agricultural laborers, making a below-average wage. Additionally, some 20 percent of the workforce or more is unemployed. The government, therefore, employs about two-thirds or more of the non-agricultural employed workforce.[2]

Since the publication of the report in April 2000, public sector wages rose several times, although previously they had been frozen for nearly six years. On August 25, 2000, shortly after assuming the presidency, Bashar al-Asad announced a salary raise of 25 percent for all government workers, and a 20 percent increase in all government pensions. Less than two years later, on May 24, 2002, he announced another raise of 20 percent for government workers and 15 percent for pensions. And finally, in May 2004, he announced a raise of another 20 percent in salaries and pensions. The goal, according to the authorities in Damascus, was to double salaries by 2005 as compared to their level in 2000.[3] However, this may not have constituted a source of deliverance for most Syrians.

For the benefit of the foreign observer, one way to illuminate the gravity of Syria's economic situation, and the distress of its population in particular, would be to translate earnings into dollars. However, calculating the real value of Syrian wages is complex to the point of impossibility because, until early 2001, the Syrian economy operated with three parallel official conversion rates for the Syrian pound: the official rate of $1 = £SY11.225 for uninitiated tourists at the airport and in the hotels and for the conversion of Syrian pounds to dollars for well-connected Syrians who required foreign currency to import goods officially classified as "priority items"; the "taxation conversion rate" of £SY23.00 for the purpose of financing most of the country's imports; and the "neighboring states rate" of £SY46.50 to compute trade transactions with states such as Jordan and Lebanon, aimed at stimulating this trade. Additionally, there was, and remains, the black market rate of £SY55–£SY60.[4] Most of the trade rates were unified in early 1998 to £SY46.50, but only toward the end of 2001 did the Syrian Commercial Bank announce that from then on it would use a single rate (£SY48.00) to conduct its affairs. Even so, the government did not officially abolish the other currency rates.[5] This situation was an improvement over the one that prevailed during most of the 1980s and 1990s, when there were five different currency rates, as follows: until 1988, there was an official rate of £SY3.935; a "customs rate" of £SY4.00; a foreign tourist rate of £SY8.00; a foreign travel rate for Syrians of £SY10.16 based on a calculation of air fares and foreign currency allocations to Syrian travelers abroad; and the black market rate of £SY9.00.[6] After the devaluation of the Syrian pound from 3.935 to 11.225 in 1988, several of the currency rates were canceled and a new rate was fixed to calculate oil income – an oil rate – which remained in place until the mid-1990s.[7]

Arguably, the purchasing power of the average annual wage in Syria – *c.* £SY10,000 in the early 2000s – is much greater than its dollar equivalent ($200) would be in the U.S. or Europe, especially in the context of the Syrian as compared to the Western standard of

living. However, in an age of unfettered globalization, the translation
of wages, or GNP, into dollars is a recognized tool. This is so because
many products, particularly those that reflect the new technological
revolution, such as fax machines, computers and cellular phones, have
become universally equable and there is little difference in their cost,
whether in China, Syria or the U.S. The labor element, or even the
cost of marketing and distribution of these products, is negligible in
comparison with the products of the traditional economy.

Nevertheless, it would appear that the price of a cellular phone or
a computer is not uppermost in the minds of most Syrians, for whom
these items are luxury goods. Calculating the dollar value of the wage
of most Syrian citizens is unnecessary in order to understand its real
value. Suffice to read Syrian newspaper reports themselves in order
to grasp that such a wage cannot provide a viable standard of living
for the population. A survey published in the government-sponsored
daily *al-Thawra* in May 2002 indicated that 94 percent of a sample of
200 families described their lifestyle as austere, 48 percent reported
that their standard of living had dropped over the previous years, and
42 percent described their economic situation as difficult. According
to official reports published in late 2004, 2.2 million Syrians were
living below the poverty line.[8] One analysis in the press linked the
dire economic situation in the country to the rise in the ages of brides
and grooms, as well as the spread of the practice of municipal-funded
collective weddings for couples who could not afford to finance a
wedding by themselves.[9]

Data issued in November 2002 by the Central Bureau of Statistics
in Damascus showed that the monthly outlay of an average urban
family (five to six persons) was £SY13,334 ($267), and of a similar-
size rural family £SY11,120 ($222).[10] The Bureau also calculated the
average monthly outlay per person in the city at £SY2,095 ($41),
based on food costs of £SY1,253 ($25) and merchandise and serv-
ices expenses of £SY842 ($17). Despite the salary increases of nearly
100 percent in the preceding years, data from the end of 2004 show
that, in dollar terms, the cost of living in Syria rose even more significantly. At the end of 2004, the monthly expenses of an urban family
amounted to £SY22,738 ($375), and of a rural family £SY18,112
($301).[11]

In a meeting held by Vice-President 'Abd al-Halim Khaddam
with faculty and students at the University of Damascus in February
2001, he encountered outspoken criticism of the grave economic
situation in the country. Khaddam's visit to the university was part of
an effort by the regime to rally support from the intellectual community for its anti-reformist campaign. Although the audience at the

event consisted mostly if not entirely of loyal Ba'th Party activists, these stalwarts made it clear that they were much more concerned with the economic situation and their standard of living than with the issue of promoting democracy in the state – the reformists' cause. One lecturer charged:

> My salary is no higher than $200 [a month] and this is an intolerable situation. Even if the Ministers of Finance and the Economy came here, and with them representatives of the International Monetary Fund and the World Bank, they would not be able to convince the audience sitting here that the state cannot improve the living conditions of the lecturers. The cost of fuel and maintenance of the government officials' cars alone would suffice for this purpose.[12]

While most of the Syrian workforce, whether employed by the government or in the private sector, lives from hand to mouth, the other side of the coin is that employment is generally permanent, with no danger of dismissal and, most importantly, with flexible and convenient work conditions. The work day in most government offices and even in the army, for those who bother to appear at work at all (absenteeism is rampant) or who have real work to do (hidden unemployment is widespread), is from 8 a.m. to 2 p.m. Afterward, many workers have second jobs so that they can supplement their income. Commissions and bribes are common in all levels of the bureaucracy. Officials and service providers are likely to charge the public for issuing a document or a permit or connecting a telephone, electricity or water line, even though these services are part of their job. Payment for such services can reach £SY100 to £SY200, but is generally given willingly in recognition of the low wage of the public servant. A less forgiving attitude is shown to high officials and party figures who demand a 5 percent down payment to initiate bureaucratic procedures for economic projects that require their approval, or who embezzle public funds.[13]

A prominent example of such inducement practices was the affair surrounding the sale of Airbus aircraft to Syria, which burst into the media in 2000. Syria had purchased six Airbus 300 passenger planes in the early 1990s at a cost of some $250 million. It later emerged that highly place Syrian officials, including Prime Minister Mahmud al-Zu'bi, Deputy Prime Minister for Economic Affairs Salim Yasin and Transportation Minister 'Abd al-Karim Mufid, had inflated the cost of the transaction to $374 million, which enabled them to acquire handsome commissions. This in itself was not astonishing, as Deputy Prime Minister Yasin, known as "Mr. 5%," was in the habit

of skimming off a 5 percent commission from every transaction under his jurisdiction. The surprising element was the decision by the
regime to expose the affair, apparently as part of the public relations
campaign to project Bashar al-Asad as a "Mr. Clean" who sought to
rid Syria of its aura of corruption. Prime Minister Zu'bi was dismissed in March 2000, followed by a report that he was under criminal
investigation. Two months later he committed suicide by gunshot,
sparing himself the humiliation of a trial and possible imprisonment.
Transportation Minister Mufid and Deputy Prime Minister Yasin, by
contrast, did stand trial and were sentenced to ten years' imprisonment and a fine of £SY470 million (*c*. $715,000) each.[14]

This and other cases of corruption in Syria illuminated the existence of a small sector of persons of means. The exposure of corruption
evidently underlay an order issued by the government in April 2001
banning the employment of foreign domestics and caregivers, especially
from Sri Lanka, Yemen and the Philippines. The order mandated a
$1,000 fine for employers who brought in such workers.[15] The fine,
however, did not deter hundreds of employers from continuing to
bring in foreign domestics, who numbered thousands and possibly
tens of thousands, including Iraqis, Sudanese and others. In a related
development, a report in the Syrian press in the summer of 2002
pointed to a growth of 150 percent in the sale of luxury Mercedes
cars and of 200 percent in the sale of Jaguars. Apparently, poverty and
need were not the province of all Syrians, and especially not those
independent candidates – primarily businessmen and members of
the professions – who spent millions of dollars on electioneering, possibly including vote buying, to ensure their victory in the election to
the People's Assembly in March 2003.[16]

The condition of the rest of the population, however, was characterized by a dearth of cash. The vast majority barely scraped by from
month to month. This explains the absence of a true banking system
in Syria as of early 2005. Most people actually had no need for banks.
With the exception of seven governmental banks, with 268 branches
throughout the country, dealing primarily with loans and mortgages
(the Real Estate Bank, the Agriculture Cooperative Bank, the People's
Savings Bank, the General Savings Agency, and the Postal Authority
Savings Fund, which became a bank in 2002) and with foreign trade
and foreign investment (the Commercial Bank and the Investment
Bank), no banks exist in Syria to serve the ordinary citizen, as in
most countries.[17]

Syrian citizens who manage to save a substantial sum of money
generally prefer to convert it to foreign currency and if possible smuggle it out of the country and deposit it abroad. Holding foreign

currency and, more seriously, trading in foreign currency are crimes according to Syrian law. Law No. 24 (1986), which deals with holding and trading foreign currency, stipulates severe punishments of up to 25 years' imprisonment for smuggling foreign currency, and one to five years' imprisonment for holding foreign currency without a permit. A regulation issued by the government in 2000 relaxed this law somewhat but did not abolish it.[18] Moreover, a series of laws issued after 1986, e.g. Law No. 10 (1991) to encourage investment in the country, allowed foreign or Syrian investors to hold foreign currency. In 2002 the government issued a regulation allowing citizens to open foreign currency accounts in the Syrian Central Bank without having to identify the source of the money. These developments created an atmosphere of uncertainty in the business sector, especially among investors and traders, regarding what was prohibited and permitted in terms of holding and trading foreign currency. Law No. 24 was abolished only in July 2003, and half a year later in February 2004 the Syrian authorities announced the abolishment of the special courts for economic crimes, which were formed in 1963 following the Ba'th revolution.[19]

Ordinary Syrian citizens who sought ways to safeguard their capital in the country and not necessarily smuggle it out generally used moneychangers (*jami'i al-amwal*), who also functioned as private bankers. Hundreds of such moneychangers, many of Armenian origin, operate in Syria. They guarantee a high rate of interest to depositors – about 20 percent – but often do not stand by these generous rates. Furthermore, many moneychangers are periodically arrested and their assets, including money deposited with them, are confiscated. The extent of this phenomenon was observable in a report published by the authorities following a series of arrests in 1997, which included some of the major moneychangers. According to the report, some 133,000 citizens had deposited sums of money with moneychangers totaling approximately £SY15 billion (slightly over $300 million).[20] Another investment channel devised by many Syrians was savings societies in which several dozen or even several hundred friends would invest their money in acquiring a business or small industrial plant and divide up the profits between them. Finally, many Syrians found the Lebanese banking system a safe shelter for their money. According to Lebanese sources some $30 billion were put in banks in Lebanon by Syrian investors during the 1990s.[21]

Yet most Syrians do not have a bank account and do not use checks or credit cards. The Syrian authorities began to permit the use of foreign credit cards in the 1990s, but the number of firms and banks honoring such cards remained minuscule. In 1999, a Lebanese bank was permitted to issue credit cards for Syrian customers, marking a first in the greater Syrian sphere. Thereafter, the Syrian government banks began issuing their own credit cards. The Syrian Trade Bank announced in July 2001 that it was exploring the possibility of the use by dollar-account holders of the American Express card, and the Syrian Real Estate Bank decided to issue 5,500 "Syrian Cards" that year and in early 2005 the number reached 20,000. In March 2003, the Trade Bank announced that it was issuing its own credit card. Until early 2000, there was only one automated cash machine in Syria, located in the luxurious Sheraton Hotel in Damascus. Thereafter, dozens of automated cash machines appeared. As of early 2005, several hundred shops and businesses in Damascus honored credit cards, and an estimated 20,000 residents of the city's population of over 5 million owned credit cards.[22]

This situation prompted Bashar al-Asad to attempt to modernize the country's banking system as a preliminary step to opening the Syrian market to the world economy. However, the bureaucracy was slow to adapt, especially conceptually, and ultimately defeated the attempt. *Tishrin* wrote, typically, in July 2001: "Syria has no need for private banks which would enable Israeli capital to flow into Syria, and through which figures such as George Soros would be able to try to undermine the economic stability prevailing in the state."[23]

As a first step, at Bashar's insistence, the government eased the enabling of foreign bank branches opening in Syria. In May 2000, the Economy Minister, Muhammad al-'Imadi, issued an order defining the parameters of the functioning of foreign banks in Syria, including limiting their activity to free trade zones in various parts of the country. In October 2000, a Lebanese bank, the European-Lebanese Bank of the Middle East (SGLER), was granted the first permit to open a branch in a free trade zone near Damascus. The bank was opened to the public ceremoniously in March 2001, although reports from Syria a year later indicated that the bank stood empty for lack of customers.[24]

At Bashar's instigation once again, the regional command of the Ba'th Party voted in December 2000 to permit the establishment of private banks in Syria, a step explained in the Syrian press as aimed at "advancing Syria toward new horizons in development and modernization, and encouraging investors in the private and public sector."[25] In accordance with Law No. 23 of March 2002, a Council for Currency and Credit was set up to supervise the establishment and ongoing management of private banks, while a banking confidentiality law was also passed.[26] In the wake of this legislation, the authorities announced in April 2002 that applications could be submitted for the establishment of branches of private banks throughout Syria. However, even though nearly 30 such applications were promptly submitted to the government, mostly from banks and investment companies in the Gulf states and Lebanon, by early 2004 only one private bank had actually opened. This was the Syrian and the Diaspora Bank (*Bank Suriyya wal-Mahjar*), whose chairman was no other then Ratib al-Shallah, the head of the Damascus Commerce Bureau. Another two banks were opened in 2004, and some others were expected to be opened in 2005.[27] Evidently, in this case too, Bashar preferred not to confront the governmental bureaucracy and the party leadership head on. Conceivably, he himself had second thoughts about the issue. Early in 2002 he was quoted as saying that "consideration must be given to the prospect that the opening of private banks in Syria is liable to harm the national economy."[28]

Moreover, a stock market had not been opened in Syria, although the government had decided to do so in February 2001 in the wake of a decision to this effect by the Ba'th Party Regional Command in December 2000. In June 2004, the Syrian government decided to follow the Regional Command's decision, but only in February 2005 was a governmental authority for stocks and bonds established. A senior Syrian official admitted that the Syrian market did not just-ify or even have the prerequisites for the establishment of a stock market. Industry Minister 'Isam al-Za'im, who had been known for his close ties with Bashar (until he was charged in late 2003 with corruption) and who had promoted economic reform himself, albeit to a limited extent and under the control and supervision of the authorities, explained that "Syria's distinctiveness, in comparison with other Arab states, lies in its geographic proximity to Palestine and the duty imposed on it to deal with the Israeli occupation of part of its land. So long as this reality continues, a 'neutral economy' cannot exist in Syria." Za'im added: "Should a stock market be established in Syria, undesirable monies would flow into it, especially Israeli capital, and therefore the economic openness advocated by the Syrian government must be limited and measured."[29]

The Syrian economy during Hafiz al-Asad's era

Syria's economic problems were hardly confined to the absence of a modern, progressive banking system, although this lacuna may be viewed as a symptom of the much graver fundamental problems that beset the Syrian economy. Ultimately, it was an economy under the centralized control of the government, still guided by rigid socialist principles. It had a large, inefficient public sector that nominally employed over 40 percent of the country's workforce but in practice, discounting small farmers, agricultural laborers and the unemployed, employed approximately two-thirds of the workforce.

This discouraging reality contradicted the impression the authorities sought to entrench in the population, namely that the Syrian economy was stable and strong. The statistics released by the authorities managed to confuse even some of the experts, who had the impression, especially as eyewitnesses, that Syria did not have poverty of the same scope as Egypt or other Third World countries. The impression gotten was that ultimately the Syrian regime was able to keep the economy going, and especially to maintain an economic infrastructure and a system of education, health and welfare services broad enough to fill the needs of the population.

On the occasion of national holidays like the Day of the Corrective Movement (the day Asad took power in Syria on November 16, 1970) or the Ba'th Revolution Day on March 8, 1963, the Syrian press published impressive statistics which indicated the unprecedented progress achieved in Syria under the leadership of Hafiz al-Asad. Deputy Prime Minister Muhammad al-Husayn chose, for example, on the occasion of the thirty-second anniversary of the Corrective Movement to refer to the following data as representing the dramatic progress made in Syria since November 1970: the number of industrial buildings rose from 31,300 to 90,000; the use of land fit for cultivation grew from 37 percent to 77 percent; crops of wheat rose from 635,000 tons to 3.105 million tons; cotton production rose from 383,000 tons to 1.032 million tons; production of citrus fruits rose from 80,000 tons to around 800,000 tons; production of olives rose from 8,600 tons to 866,000 tons; and, finally, production of apples rose from 18,000 tons to 287,000 tons. Husayn reported also that the number of students in schools rose from 1,126,383 to 3,730,000 and the number of students in the universities rose from 37,000 to 155,137, that the number of beds in hospitals rose from 6,126 to 19,669, that houses connected to the electricity grid rose from 43 percent to 97 percent and that houses connected to running water rose from 43 percent to 84.2 percent.[30]

There is no doubt that, in absolute terms, in those years the Syrian state made significant progress. And still, even in these data one can find evidence for the backwardness of the Syrian state compared with other countries in the world. After all, up-to-date economic reports put Syria at the bottom of the world's list as far as economic growth and human development are concerned. Syria is no better then countries like Sudan, Yemen or even Botswana. Such reports show that in 22 percent of the villages in Syria there is no running water in the houses and many of them are not connected to the electricity grid. In the country there is one dentist to 3,333 citizens and one GP to 1,221 citizens. In hospitals in Damascus there is one bed for every 304 citizens but in the province of Idlib in the north of Syria the average is one bed for every 1,824 citizens and in the province of Hasaka it is one bed for 2,134 citizens. The reports show that, in recent years, illiteracy among the population has been increasing. According to UNESCO, the rate of illiteracy is 10 percent, but according to unofficial Syrian sources it is around 30 percent. It is mainly found among the rural population, where 25 percent of girls between the ages of 15 and 24 are illiterate and 5 percent of the boys. According to these reports, while 90 percent of children attend elementary schools, only 43 percent attend middle school and only 12 percent attend high school.[31] It seems that this unpleasant picture has gotten even worse in recent years as a result of population growth and the difficulty of the governmental system in dealing with this growth.

With this, Syria's rulers, including Asad himself, viewed the country as poor but not bankrupt. They were prepared to acknowledge its relative backwardness in comparison with the rest of the world, but reiterated and emphasized four main achievements in the socio-economic realm that had been attained during Hafiz al-Asad's rule:

1. Syria managed to take care of its needs over this entire period, especially in the areas of energy, water and food, without developing dangerous or problematic dependencies on outside sources. Syria is an oil exporter, primarily to Western Europe, while also selling food surpluses worth hundreds of millions of dollars to its neighbors – Jordan, Iraq and Lebanon. Indeed, side by side with the development of an oil industry, Syria made great strides in agriculture. Areas brought under cultivation were expanded significantly, the agricultural water supply system was improved, and a series of governmental institutions and organizations were set up to provide economic and other support for farmers.

2. Asad's regime managed to deal successfully with population growth, especially in rural areas, preventing the migration of the surplus population in these regions to the major cities. Up until the early 1990s, the Ba'th regime implemented a policy of population dispersal that prevented a disruption of the balance between the periphery and the cities. The measures used were agricultural development and soil improvement along with incentives for migration

to new settlement areas, primarily the Jazira region in the north and the Ghab region near Aleppo. These inducements enabled the regime to regulate and direct surplus populations from rural areas in the center of the country to new settlement areas, a program that made a distinct contribution to preserving political and socio-economic stability in the country.

3. The regime prudently established a welfare system that provided services, albeit limited and basic, to the vast majority of the population. Data published by the government periodically point to a dramatic growth in education, health and welfare services from 1963 to the early 1990s, especially in the periphery. The regime's ability to continue investing in and, by extension, developing these regions enabled it to retain the support of the population there. Significantly, it was from these regions that the ruling political leadership of the country sprang over a period of four decades.[32]

4. Side by side, and sometimes at the expense of other national needs, the regime allocated significant resources to security. Syria's considerable military strength constituted a heavy burden for the state, as Information Minister 'Adanan 'Umran pointed out when he described Syria as "building with one hand and defending itself with the other."[33] This strength contributed to the political stability of the state over decades and to its ability to deal with external threats to its existence, first and foremost the Israeli threat.

Upon his ascent to power, Hafiz al-Asad had inherited a devastated economy, the product of a radical, rigid socialist policy implemented by the neo-Ba'th regime that preceded him (and in which he had been a major player). Once in power, he moderated this policy and initiated a series of reforms aimed at achieving greater economic openness and stimulating private sector activity. This policy, however, was not consistent, and was subject periodically to domestic and foreign political constraints.[34] Ultimately, Asad advanced Syria to a certain extent, but whether a different policy would have advanced it further, as was the case, for example, in Egypt under Sadat, is a question worth considering. Arguably, Asad's legacy in the economic realm amounted to a total regression of two-thirds of the national per capita income, from $1,400–$1,600 at the start of the 1980s to *c.* $1,030 in 1995 and *c.* $700 in the early 2000s.[35] Notably, the economy was a low-priority issue for him, ranking far below national security and foreign policy. Moreover, rather than conducting economic policy with an eye toward the future, he treated it circumstantially and with a good measure of reliance on luck.

The Syrian economy in the 1990s – a matter of luck

The economic prosperity of the Lebanese economy was often explained by the disasters in the countries around. After all, the war in Palestine in 1948, the free officers' revolution in Egypt in July 1952, the revolution in Iraq in July 1958 and finally the Ba'th Revolution in Syria in March 1963 all brought about the collapse of competing economic centers and led to a loss of revenues from these countries to Beirut, where they were put in Lebanese banks. Thus, the stability in the Arab world since the 1970s is one of the explanations for the Lebanese predicament and the breakdown of the Lebanese state in 1975.

As in the case of Lebanon, so in the case of Syria there are many explanations for the country's economic situation which have nothing to do with academic analysis. These explanations focus on one word: luck. Indeed, as in other fields of activity, in the economic sphere Hafiz al-Asad seemed to be someone who had luck whenever it seemed that the Syrian economy was on the brink of collapse.

The 1990s stood as a good example of the good luck of the Syrian regime. Indeed, in the mid-1980s the Syrian economy faced serious distress because of the increase in military expenditures as a direct result of Hafiz al-Asad's decision to adopt the policy of strategic parity with Israel. The increase in military expenditure led by the end of the 1980s to the dropping of foreign currency reserves to a few dozen millions of dollars, to the absence of basic goods in the markets and to an annual decrease of almost 10 percent in GDP and an annual inflation rate of 60 percent.[36] But then Syria's luck changed: in the late 1980s oil fields were discovered in eastern Syria, and in early 1990 Syria started producing oil. Oil exports became a source of blessing yielding Syria annual revenues of about $4 billion. Moreover, as a result of the Gulf Crisis in early 1991 Syria received financial aid from the Gulf states in the sum of around $2 billion to $2.5 billion. It should be mentioned that during the 1980s it was Iran that gave Syria financial support of $1 billion in return for Syria's supporting Iran during the Iraq–Iran war. Finally, after a few years of drought Syria witnessed heavy rains in the early 1990s. This improved agricultural production, which contributes one-third of GNP.

This luck enabled the Syrian regime to get out of the economic crisis. It also helped it to cope with the political difficulties it underwent as a result of the collapse of the socialist regimes in Eastern Europe. Indeed the new revenues enabled the regime to take measures aimed at increasing economic activity and creating new jobs. These measures were aimed at attracting the support of political sectors that the regime needed, mainly the Sunni urban economic elite. In addition the regime invested huge amounts in improving the economic infrastructure as well as the services that the state provides its citizens such as electricity supply, communication, transportation, education, health and welfare.

The luck returned towards the end of the 1990s after a few bad years of drought and low oil prices. In 1998 oil prices decreased significantly and the revenues from oil dropped by around 30 percent. In 1999 Syria witnessed one of the worst droughts since 1958. This drought led to a decrease in the agricultural production of wheat from 4.2 million tons in 1996 to 3.2 million tons in 1997 and in cotton from 1.5 million tons to 1 million tons.[37] Drought in Syria is significant. After all, one of the explanations for the secession of Syria from the union with Egypt was the drought in 1961 that led to economic distress. Bad rains increased dissatisfaction in the late 1960s with the neo-Ba'th regime under Salah Jadid and made it easier for Hafiz al-Asad to take power.

But in 1999 the Syrians learned of the increase or even the doubling in oil prices. These unexpected revenues were used by Asad to buy new military equipment from the Russians. He used the money in a similar way to that in which he had used the money he received from the Gulf states at the end of the first Gulf War. Then he bought advanced surface-to-surface missiles from North Korea. Growth was also marked in agricultural production. In addition, trade with Iraq flourished, and Syrians started selling smuggled oil from Iraq.

Bashar al-Asad's economic challenge

With the death of Hafiz al-Asad and the transfer of power to Bashar, the solutions of the past were shown to be insufficient to meet the challenges facing the country at the turn of the twenty-first century. Syria found itself at the start of a renewed economic crisis more acute than in the past, distinguishable even before Asad's death but ignored by him.

The demographic crisis

Syria's socioeconomic problems centered on the long-term demographic challenge which it faced. The country held the doubtful distinction, during the 1970s and 1980s, of having one of the highest rates of natural increase in the world: 3.3–3.5 percent. Its population at the start of 2003 was estimated at 18.660 million and was predicted to pass the 20 million point around the end of 2005. By comparison, its population in 1946, the year Syria gained independence, was

3 million, rising to 4.5 million in 1960 and 6 million when Asad took over the government in 1970.[38]

Updated data published by the Central Bureau of Statistics in Damascus in October 2000 regarding population growth during 1994–99[39] showed a drop in the rate of increase to 2.7 percent (as compared to 3.3 percent during 1981–94) and a further decrease to 2.45 percent by mid-2000. This decline apparently resulted from a rise in urban population density, with a typically concomitant lower birthrate than in rural populations. However, Syria's rate of natural increase continued to be high in the periphery. Such regions as Raqqa and Hasaka had a 5.4 percent rate, and Dar'a 4.5 percent, in the latter half of the 1990s, as compared to 1.9 percent in Damascus. Women's fertility rates also declined steeply, from an average of 8.5 children in the 1970s to 6.1 in 1980, 4.7 in 1994 and 2.99 in 2000. In a parallel development, the average women's age at marriage rose from 21.4 in 1980 to 25.1 in 1994, and men's from 25.7 to 28.9.

These encouraging statistics, however, emerged after a long period of soaring rates of natural increase. Syria's problem, therefore, centers on the results of this high rate, i.e. the population born during the 1970s and 1980s, which has now reached adulthood. Moreover, despite the decline in the total rate of natural increase in the country, Syria's rural areas, where nearly half the population still resides, will evidently be a contributing factor to the high rate of natural increase in the future as well.

Family planning: too little and too late

Starting in the early 1990s, the regime began promoting a family planning policy, albeit cautiously and gradually, a reflection of its growing awareness of the consequences of uncontrolled population growth for the future of the country. At first the focus was on disseminating information aimed at heightening awareness of the need for family planning and birth control. In this context, planning centers were set up in peripheral areas, and sex education classes were introduced in school curricula.[40]

In May 2002, a first step was taken toward enforcing family planning rather than simply raising awareness. Bashar al-Asad announced an order reapportioning child subsidies and maternity leave with the goal of lowering the birthrate. The order stipulated a monthly subsidy for the first child (born to a man's first wife only) of £SY300 ($6); second child £SY200 ($4); third child £SY100 ($2); and additional children £SY25 ($0.50) each. Moreover, in the event of the death of one of the first three children, the subsidy was not transferable to the other children within the family. Lastly, maternity leave for a first baby would be 120 days, for a second 90 and for a third 75 days.[41] The significance of the order was clear, aptly described by the Ba'th Party organ, *al-Ba'th*, as "the first practical step on the road to Syrian family planning based on a modern approach." If in the past, the newspaper wrote, "the state encouraged population increase with an eye toward growth and development, there is an increased awareness now of the negative aspects of such unprecedented growth in population size, necessitating a change in the authorities' approach to this issue."[42]

The first indications of an economic and social crisis as a consequence of the demographic problem began to show up in the late 1990s in the form of a freeze and then a drop in economic growth rates. The result was a regression in the scope of government services available to the citizen; pressure on the already overloaded infrastructure, causing water and electricity stoppages; a sharp rise in unemployment, especially among entry-level workers; an increase in illiteracy; and unprecedented signs of poverty on the city streets. The fact that Syria was a Third World country with a backward infrastructure to begin with, and that it was still ruled by a regime committed to a world view copied from the defunct socialist regimes of Eastern Europe, undoubtedly impeded any attempt to deal with this emerging crisis.

Negative economic growth

The harsh economic reality in which Syria found itself was reflected, first, in data indicating a significant slowdown and an actual regression in the economy from 1999 onward, in contrast to high growth rates in the early 1990s. A regression of approximately 2 percent in GDP was recorded in 1999, although growth rates of 0.6 percent and 1.7 percent were recorded for 2000 and 2001 respectively. However, considering the population growth for that two-year period, estimated at approximately 2.7 percent or more, the real growth rate for those years was negative as well. Estimates posited for 2002 were a growth of 1.6 percent in GDP, and 3.2 percent for 2003, 2.2 percent for 2004, only 1.9 percent for 2005 and 1.8 percent for 2006, yet even so the anticipated real growth rate, taking into account the high rate of natural increase of the population, would be negative. Notably, skyrocketing inflation in Syria in the late 1980s, reaching about 59.5 percent in 1988 and 60 percent in 1989, was eliminated largely by an acute recession thereafter, lasting to the present day, with inflation at 1–3 percent in the early 2000s. Syria's foreign debt, estimated in early 2004 at approximately $21 billion to $22 billion, also constitutes a heavy burden on its economy. Of this, $12 billion is owed to the former Soviet Union, a debt denied by Syria on the grounds that, since Russia is not the sole inheritor of the Soviet Union, Syria has no obligation to pay these debts to it. Indeed, during Bashar al-Asad's visit to Russia in January 2005, the two countries reached an agreement according to which almost 80 percent of the Syrian debts to Russia were written off and the other part was to be covered during a period of ten years through Russian investment and purchasing in Syria.[43]

Reflecting the slowdown in economic growth, Syria's foreign trade remained static or even declined. Estimated export value in 1990 was $3,009 billion, and imports $2,080 billion, or a positive trade balance of $929 million, while in 1998 the figures were $3,142 billion and $3,320 billion respectively, or a negative trade balance of $178 million. In 2001, exports were estimated at $4,984 billion and imports at $4,201 billion, or a positive trade balance of $783 million, and in 2004 exports were estimated at $6,400 billion and imports at 5,090 billion, or a positive trade balance of $1,310 billion.[44] These data are partial and do not include Syria's military expenditure of billions of dollars on armaments during this period, especially on imports from North Korea, Iran, Russia and other East European countries.

Most importantly, over the last decade to the present, the bulk of Syria's exports – about two-thirds – consisted of oil and oil products. Estimated oil exports for 2001 were *c.* $3,169 billion (of total exports of $4,984 billion).[45] The problem was that Syria's oil reserves were limited and were expected to be depleted within a decade, according to estimates by experts. Furthermore, its oil production was shrinking by 5 percent annually owing to outdated equipment and production techniques, as well as underskilled workers. Production dropped to *c.* 510,000 barrels/day during 2002, and to 500,000 barrels/day in early 2005 as compared to its peak production of *c.* 620,000 barrels/day in the mid-1990s. This decline would have been much graver if it had not been for the flow of oil from Iraq to Syria at a rate of 150,000–200,000 barrels/day, enabling Syria to maintain its rate of oil export. Otherwise, this rate would have slipped to some 400,000–450,000 barrels/day.[46] As part of this secret agreement, Iraq sold oil to Syria at a reduced price, which the Syrians used for domestic needs, allowing them to earmark domestically produced oil for export abroad. The flowing of Iraqi oil to Syria was stopped by the Americans after they occupied Iraq in April 2003.

For years, Syria denied the prospect of the depletion of its oil sources. Senior oil industry officials predicted that the discovery of new oil fields in the eastern part of the country and the introduction of modern production methods would help Syria maintain its production rates. Since the early 2000s, however, decision makers in Damascus showed an awareness of the possibility of depletion. Thus, for example, Industry Minister 'Isam al–Za'im admitted, in July 2001, that Syria must develop its human resources and rely on them as a replacement for oil income, and the Minister for Oil and Mineral Resources, Ibrahim Haddad, noted in April 2004 that by 2020 the Syrian production of oil would be less then 300,000 barrels/day.[47]

Notably, Syria's other export branches are negligible in comparison with oil. According to data updated for 2005, they included fruit and vegetables, valued at $259 million; textile products, $317 million; and cotton, $196 million. Export destinations were Europe, 61.7 percent; the Middle East, especially Iraq, which from 1997 was a favored destination for Syrian products or for products in transit, 17.7 percent; Turkey, 8 percent; and the U.S., 3.1 percent. Imports came mainly from Europe, 34.2 percent; the Far East, 22.7 percent; Russia, 8.3 percent; and the Middle East, 8 percent.[48]

The collapse of economic infrastructures and welfare service systems

Although the regime allocated significant resources in the early 1990s to improve the standard of living of the population, this investment was dissipated by the huge population increase. Reports in the early 2000s described water and electricity shortages in Damascus once again. As *al-Ba'th* put it: "The noise of the generators used by the population during the prolonged blackouts dictated by the shortage of electricity once again causes the city to shudder."[49] The water supply, too, was sporadic, and in the summer the regime rationed the supply to the extent of cutting it off for up to 16 hours consecutively. The Syrian press reported that in some neighborhoods in Damascus the water supply was cut off for weeks, quite aside from the many slum neighborhoods built without permits which had no access to running water at all. Syrian sources estimated the monthly water requirement for Damascus at 670,000 cubits, while the actual supply was 400,000 cubits.[50]

This depressing reality of a crumbling infrastructure was reflected in the collapse on June 4, 2002, of the Zayzun dam, the fourth largest in Syria, inaugurated in 1996 by the leaders of the regime in an impressive ceremony. The collapse of the dam occurred following the appearance of cracks in it over time, which were left untreated by the authorities. As a result of the collapse, vast expanses of land in the al-Ghab region north of Hama were flooded, 27 persons were killed and nearly 80,000 were made homeless.[51] At first, the regime tried to turn the disaster into the cornerstone of its campaign to improve the efficiency of the civil service. Apparently, this underlay the arrest of former Irrigation Minister 'Abd al-Rahman al-Madani and several senior officials in his ministry. However, fearing that the public would not be satisfied with this retribution, the regime changed direction and explained that the disaster was attributable to an error by junior officials, and that: "the entire regime ought not to be blamed for the mistake of a single clerk."

The trial of the person responsible for the collapse of the Zayzun dam continued for almost a year. Only in July 2003 was it announced that the Irrigation Minister and some of his aides were cleared for lack of evidence but that the contractor who had built the dam had been convicted and tried for the use of unauthorized equipment. He and other low-ranking officials were sentenced to 8–15 years in prison and to fines.[52]

Accelerated urbanization

An accelerated trend of migration to the major cities, and the dramatic rise in the urban populations, loomed as one of Syria's most pressing problems in the first decade of the twenty-first century. Conceivably, the government's population dispersal policy had gone as far as it could, and the new settlement areas targeted for population absorption in the past were no longer attractive. A review of the statistics shows that the proportion of urban residents in the total population rose from 37 percent in 1960 to 43 percent in the 1970s and 55 percent in 2000. Considering that the cities expanded geographically, incorporating rural areas, which were later still cited as rural for official statistical purposes, the proportion of urban residents was probably considerably larger than the data indicated. Clearly, the regime was having difficulty dealing with this accelerated urbanization, and especially with the growth of impoverished neighborhoods that sprang up around the cities. Research about Damascus published in May 2002 showed that it had a population of 5.5 million, as compared to 528,862 in 1960. Of the 5.5 million, an estimated 3.9 million had migrated from rural areas during the preceding two decades. Another 1.1 million entered the city daily for work. The population density in the poor neighborhoods, where housing was generally constructed illegally, reached 70,000 per kilometer, with families living 10–12 persons to a dwelling, or three to four persons to a room.[53]

Not surprisingly, the residents of these deprived neighborhoods were unable to find secure employment and consequently were essentially excluded from the education, health and welfare systems. As a result, they were detached from any association with the regime, and the regime, in turn, could not rally them for support. Undoubtedly, this issue was destined to occupy a prominent place in the Syrian agenda and affect the country's political and socioeconomic stability.

Reports from Syria cited frequent clashes between the authorities and the residents of the depressed urban neighborhoods in the early 2000s. Thousands of citizens took part in a protest in April 2001 in Saydaniyya, to oppose the announced demolition of their homes. In September 2002 a confrontation erupted in the Kabas neighborhood of Damascus between the residents and the authorities in protest against the demolition of hundreds of illegally built houses for the purpose of paving a new road. The authorities were forced to back down. In October 2002 the country was in turmoil over the deaths of nearly 40 persons when six illegally constructed buildings in the al-Kalasa neighborhood of Aleppo collapsed during a storm. The authorities had ignored the fact that the buildings had been put up over an area of caves, and in effect had approved them retroactively when it connected them to the electric, water and telephone systems.[54]

Rising unemployment

Another pronounced sign of Syria's economic crisis was rising un-employment. Official data published by Damascus in 2005 indicated that unemployment had reached 11.5 percent that year, up from 9 percent in 1999, i.e. 800,000 additional jobless persons, with un-employment expected to continue rising by 150,000–200,000 persons annually. Official spokesmen admitted, moreover, that the actual num-ber of unemployed was even greater, encompassing almost 20 percent of the standing workforce of 5.5 million. The data showed partic-ularly high unemployment rates in the Alawite coastal region, in the Jazira region to the east, and in southern Syria, reaching 20.5 percent in Tartus and 15.7 percent in Suwayda. By contrast, the large urban areas, e.g. Damascus, showed a relatively low unemployment rate, estimated at 7.5 percent. Additionally, 71 percent of the unemployed were ages 15–24, with 51 percent residing in rural areas. The data also pointed to the lack of employment opportunities for university graduates. Apparently, however, the gravest problem was that of un-educated young people: 43 percent of elementary school dropouts and approximately 23 percent of high school dropouts were unem-ployed, while only 10–15 percent of university graduates could not find work.[55]

These data accounted for the phenomenon of the steady flow of Syrian workers to Lebanon, where the wage paid for unskilled labor was incomparably higher than in Syria. An unskilled Syrian worker in Lebanon could earn $300–$500 monthly in construction, domestic work or waiting on tables, while a respectable clerk in a government office in Damascus earned $40–$50 monthly. Although the number of Syrian workers in Lebanon is in dispute, it is undoubtedly in the hundreds of thousands.[56] The significance of this situation is that the dramatic changes in the political reality of Lebanon in early 2005, which led to the flight of thousands of Syrian workers from Lebanon back to Syria, could have disastrous repercussions for the Syrian economy. Additionally, hundreds of thousands of Syrians work in the Gulf states, and many thousands are to be found in Jordan as well.

In light of the dramatic rise in unemployment in Syria, the government approved a Five-Year Plan, after Bashar assumed office, aimed at creating 432,000 jobs by 2005. However, the budget for the plan – £SY50 billion (*c.* $1 billion) – was to come from foreign investment or private Syrian investment, neither of which seemed to be attracted to backing the Syrian government.[57] Notably, according to the official budget, the government of Syria creates 50,000–60,000 jobs annually, but these are bureaucratic posts in government offices and not necessarily substantive or productive jobs.

In July 2002, a demonstration by the unemployed broke out in Damascus, a first in Syria. Approximately a thousand jobless persons waiting in vain outside the social insurance office in the Abu Rumana quarter to receive documentary approval entitling them to an unemployment allowance erupted in a spontaneous protest, calling on Bashar to help them solve their problems. A similar demonstration broke out some weeks later outside the central post office in the city, where only a single clerk was assigned to grant approvals to thousands of unemployed persons waiting in line, some of whom had spent the previous night guarding their place in the line. The demonstrations signaled the hidden danger to domestic stability posed by rising unemployment.[58]

The hopelessness of this situation was demonstrated by the dismissal of Tawfiq al-'Ammash, appointed in 2001 to head the National Authority to Combat Unemployment. 'Ammash was dismissed by Prime Minister 'Atari in January 2005 after he criticized the government's policy on unemployment.[59] Student demonstrations had broken out already in February 2004 in the engineering faculties at the universities of Aleppo and Damascus following an announcement by the government that, because of a surplus of engineers, it would no longer guarantee work to all engineering graduates, as had been the practice in Syria ever since the Ba'th regime came into power. Dozens of students were arrested during the protests.[60]

Bashar's first economic steps

Responding to the harsh economic reality in Syria, Bashar's government focused on an effort to promote change and reform in this area, albeit to a limited extent. As Bashar pointed out, people with empty stomachs could not be of any use in promoting needed reforms and revolutions in other areas.[61]

This line had been adopted by the new government headed by Mustafa Miru in March 2000, and was reinforced upon Bashar's assumption of the presidency in July. A profusion of orders were issued in this context, aimed at updating and amending existing laws in the social and economic realms that had long since become irrelevant. The orders ranged from updating the investment law, to approving the personal import of cars, and allowing the private import of films after 35 years of import through government companies only. (Damascus had only nine movie theaters serving a population of 5.5 million, and the entire country had only 23 movie theaters for a total population of 18.6 million.) The housing rental law was updated for the first time since 1949. Government salaries and pensions were raised, and orders for the development of a modern banking system were issued.[62]

Two weeks after taking the oath of allegiance as president, on July 30, 2000, Bashar al-Asad issued Order No. 11 regarding exemptions from military service for Syrian citizens living abroad. The order allowed Syrians living abroad for over 15 years who were past age 40, or Syrians living abroad over ten years who were interested in investing in Syria, to obtain an exemption from military service in exchange for a payment of $10,000–$15,000. The order was welcomed by the emigrant Syrian communities throughout the world, as it gave them the opportunity to visit Syria without being charged with evasion of military service. According to government estimates, expatriate Syrian capital amounted to $80 billion to $120 billion.[63] Another order issued in 2005 required every male born in an Arab country of Syrian parents, who wished to return to Syria, to pay an indemnity of $7,000 in lieu of military service, while males who had left Syria before age 11 and had spent 15 years outside Syria would have to pay an indemnity of $15,000 in order to return.[64]

The new winds blowing through Syria upon Bashar's ascent to power were also evident in the government's handling of the state budget. In the past, Syrian governments had favored a strategy of foot-dragging, generally presenting the budget toward the end of the fiscal year in question, and sometimes after it had ended. The 1999 budget, for example, had been approved only in January 2000. That budget encompassed a total of £SY255.3 billion, allocating £SY121.8 billion for investment and £SY133.5 billion for current expenditure. The delay in preparing the budget was attributed to fluctuations in oil prices which hindered a precise estimation of the scope of anticipated income.

The formation of Miru's government in March 2000 promised a change in approach. Indeed, within a month, a budget for 2000, encompassing £SY275.4 billion, was submitted to the People's Assembly for approval. The budget allocated £SY132 billion for investment, £SY108.4 billion for current expenditure and £SY35 billion for debt repayment, price stabilization and export stimulus. It was also committed to create 92,322 jobs. In December 2000 the People's Assembly voted to increase the budget by £SY66 billion to finance public companies' debts. The proposed budget for 2001 was submitted at the end of 2000, marking a first in many years. The 2001 budget, encompassing £SY322.2 billion, included an allocation of £SY161 billion for investment and £SY161 billion for current expenditure. It was to create 65,000 jobs. The budget for 2002 was submitted toward the end of 2001. It encompassed £SY356.389 billion, allocating £SY172.4 billion to current expenditure (including £SY40.5 billion to covering the public debt) and £SY184 billion to investment. The government was to create 69,773 new jobs. An additional £SY48 billion was attached for debt repayment. The 2003 budget, approved toward the end of 2002, encompassed £SY420 billion, with £SY209 billion allocated to current expenditure and £SY211 billion to investment. The 2004 budget encompassed £SY449.5 billion, and the 2005 budget encompassed £SY460 billion.[65]

One of the first economic issues that Miru's government set out to promote was stimulating investment. Sharp criticism in Syria had been leveled at the investment law (Law No. 10) of May 1991, the flagship of the Syrian economy. These principles, the critics asserted, no longer met the country's needs and had lost all relevance to the economic reality in Syria and in the world. In response, Hafiz al-Asad had announced Order No. 7 on May 13, 2000, aimed at amending Law No. 10 by easing investment restrictions in the areas of holding and trading foreign currency, taxation, land rental and protection against nationalization.[66] According to data issued by the Central Bureau of Statistics in Damascus in late 2002, 3,085 projects amounting to £SY406.2 billion (*c.* $8 billion) had been approved by the government up to that time. These projects ostensibly contributed to the creation of 100,000 jobs, although Syrian sources admitted that some three-quarters of the projects had not materialized.[67]

Whether the measures taken by the regime offered real or comprehensive solutions to the grave problems facing Syria, especially its demographic issue, seems doubtful. The outcome of this problem could prove disastrous for the economy and ultimately for the political stability of the country. This threat explains the intense public debate over economic and social policy taking place in Syria in recent years. Indeed in September 2003 Prime Minister Miru was removed from office and was replaced by Naji al-'Atari for what was described in Damascus as "serious economic failures of his government."[68]

A central issue, linked to the development of banking services, has been opening up the Syrian economy to the world market. Syria's failure to deal with this issue is reflected in the nature of its contacts with the E.U. since 1998 with the aim of gaining an association status. These contacts had not proven productive, owing to the exacting preconditions presented by the Europeans. As Industry Minister 'Isam al-Za'im explained in 2001, "Syria will not be able to meet the conditions stipulated by the Europeans regarding opening up its markets to free trade. Syria will need a particularly long transitional period for this purpose."[69] Following the occupation of Iraq by the U.S., Syria was ready to show more flexibility on economic as well as political issues in its negotiations with the E.U., and in October 2004 the association agreement was signed in initials. However, the deterioration in French–Syrian relations in early 2005, against the background of French efforts to get Syria out of Lebanon, deferred any chance for the implementation of the agreement in the foreseeable future. The Syrians also continue to toy with the idea of setting up an Arab common market in the hope of easing their isolation and possibly helping integrate Syria in the world economy. This was the intent of remarks by Prime Minister Miru in September 2002 about the importance of promoting economic, social and cultural integration between the Arab states by establishing a large Arab free trade zone, i.e. an Arab common market, because this would allow the Arab states to deal with the dangers lurking in the international economic blocs and the challenge posed by economic globalization.[70] However, the likelihood of establishing such a market is virtually nil, both for political and for economic reasons. Trade between the Arab states constitutes a negligible proportion of their total foreign trade, most of which is linked to Europe, the U.S. and East Asia. Another idea, which seemed to be easier for the Syrians to implement, was to turn Lebanon into an economic buffer zone, as Hong Kong is for China, which would ease Syria's integration into the world economy. However, after the withdrawal of Syrian forces from Lebanon in April 2005, this idea too seems to be unrealistic.

Reportedly, Finance Minister Muhammad al-Husayn declared in late 2004 that, for all intents and purposes, the Syrian economy had become a market economy.[71] In practice, this description appeared to be far from the reality. Yet in one respect the Finance Minister was correct, namely the impact that world events had on Syria. Syria's political isolation in the international and the regional arenas was exacerbated in the spring of 2003 when the Americans captured Baghdad, which had such a negative effect on the Syrian economic situation that it threatened to wipe out all the efforts made by the Syrian government to improve the country's economy. The results of the war in Iraq led to a loss of billions of dollars for Syria because of the loss of the trade markets with Iraq. Moreover, the sanctions imposed on Syria by the American administration in May 2004 had a negative psychological effect on economic activity in Syria. The eviction of the Syrians from Lebanon in April 2005, too, was likely to have negative consequences for Syria's economy.

PART III

SYRIAN FOREIGN POLICY UNDER BASHAR

Bashar al-Asad in the international arena – the al-Aqsa Intifada, the September 11, 2001 events, and the war in Iraq

Bashar al-Asad's 36th birthday, which fell on September 11, 2001, held an unanticipated surprise for him. Early that evening, the first reports of terror attacks against New York and Washington began coming into Damascus from the United States. Bashar's reaction to the reports is unknown, but Syrian TV, while refraining from interrupting its broadcasting schedule with a special report, as did other Arab TV channels, nevertheless devoted a large part of its regular news broadcast that evening to the events in the U.S., signifying Syria's acknowledgment, however constrained and equivocal, in the style typical of Damascus, that something had happened in the outside world.[1]

Still, scenes of the fall of Baghdad a year and a half later were not shown by Syrian TV. When all the other TV channels – Arab as well as international – showed crowds of Iraqis (with the help of American soldiers) dismantling the statue of Saddam Husayn in the main square in Baghdad, Firdus Square, on April 9, 2003, Syrian TV chose to broadcast a documentary about Islamic sites in Syria.[2] Not only did this reflect Syria's difficulty in reading the new map in the region and internalizing the changes taking place there, especially upon the occupation of Iraq by the U.S., but it revealed Syria's true opinion of these changes – hostility and resentment. Notably, the scenes of masses of young Lebanese demonstrating in Beirut's Martyrs Square in February 2005, demanding that the Syrians leave Lebanon, were not shown on Syrian TV, nor was the joy in the Lebanese street when the Syrians pulled out of Lebanon in April 2005.[3] Indeed, the story of Syrian foreign policy in the Bashar era was ultimately the story of the country's failure to deal with three major events in the history of the world and of the region: the events of September 11, 2001, the war in Iraq and the Lebanese crisis.

Indeed, there is no doubt that the terrorist attacks by Usama bin Ladin's al-Qa'ida organization on New York and Washington on September 11, 2001 brought about a sharp change in global and Middle Eastern realities, leading to the formulation of a new global and regional agenda. There were even those who compared the attacks to the collapse of the Soviet Union and the Iraqi invasion of Kuwait in its wake. These events, of about a decade before, had had similar fateful implications for the entire world and for the Middle East and Syria in particular. It is therefore no wonder that the U.S., having emerged from the terrorist attacks on it even more determined than ever to strike at its enemies, was quick to present Syria even more determinedly with the dilemma of a decade before: Are you with us or against us?

Syria's reaction was apparently identical to that which Damascus had presented to George Bush Sr. in the early 1990s: with you, but, more precisely, with you and against you. Thus, Syria adopted an elusive policy, desiring to both have its cake and eat it. On the one hand it took steps to prevent a frontal and direct confrontation with Washington. To that end, it was prepared to cooperate with the U.S. in its struggle against the al-Qa'ida organization. On the other hand, Damascus continued to adhere to its world view and to courses of action that stood in total contradiction to Washington's policies. These courses of action had the potential of obstructing America's regional interests. American interests jeopardized by Syria's actions included the promotion of the Arab–Israeli, and certainly the Israeli–Palestinian, peace process; the overthrow of the Saddam Husayn regime in Iraq; the isolation of Iran and possibly the overthrow of the regime of the ayatollahs there; and the destruction of Hizballah in Lebanon.

Apparently, the difference between Syria in the era of George Bush Sr. and the Syria which his son, George Bush Jr., faced did not necessarily lie in the measure of American assertiveness (or the absence of assertiveness, and the cordiality) which the Americans tended to show at first toward Damascus. It was especially attributable to the fact that the ruler who sat in the Syrian presidential palace was no longer the experienced and admired Hafiz al-Asad, but rather his young son Bashar, who showed himself to be an inexperienced amateur in conducting Syrian foreign policy, at least in the early stage of his rule.

The conquest of Iraq by the United States in April 2003 was a significant event in the history of the Middle East. Alongside Iraq itself, it would appear that Syria was the Middle Eastern country most affected by this event, mostly adversely. The conquest of Iraq by the U.S. dealt a serious blow not only to the Syrian economy and to Syria's regional and international standing but also to the image of the Syrian Ba'th regime, clearly undermining its standing at home.

However, more than anything else, the conquest of Iraq by the U.S., which made it Syria's neighbor to the east, created a new focus of friction, or even an open and bleeding wound, in relations between Damascus and Washington. This wound has over the past few years significantly contributed to the deterioration of relations between the two countries, relations which from the outset had not been characterized as close or overflowing with good will. Syrian–American relations have not reached their absolute nadir, but this is liable to occur sooner than might have been expected. Witness to this is borne out by the voices which were being raised in Washington in late 2004, mainly in the Pentagon, calling for a military strike against Syria in order to get it to fall into line with U.S. polices.[4]

Indeed, Syria chose to place itself at the head of the Arab camp opposing the war, and was prominent in its sharp and even belligerent criticism of Washington's decision to go to war. However, Syria not only supported Iraq rhetorically, but when the war actually broke out Syria, to the surprise of many, continued to turn a blind eye to the smuggling of weapons into Iraq via Syria and, moreover, allowed Arab and mainly Syrian volunteers to cross the Syrian border into Iraq. Syria's behavior during the war led Washington to adopt a threatening tone, unprecedented in its severity, toward Damascus. The accusations leveled against Syria by the United States bear witness to the potential for disaster inherent in the path along which relations between the two countries have been moving in recent years. While Bashar, like his father, did demonstrate his awareness of the fabric of constraints facing Syria and did try to prevent Syrian–American confrontation, he was less cautious and thus crossed red lines which ultimately brought him to the brink of a confrontation with Washington.

Syrian foreign policy in the 1990s – between East and West

The policy of Syria in the last decade of Hafiz al-Asad's life was aimed at the effort of dealing with the consequences of the collapse of Soviet Union in 1991. The collapse of the Soviet Union led to the collapse of Syria's security concept, which had two principles. First was the effort to achieve strategic parity with Israel. Second was the reliance on the Soviet umbrella in the event of Syria being attacked by Israel or the U.S. The collapse of the Soviet Union led to the emergence of a new world order and even new regional order where the U.S.A. was in the lead. This was clearly manifest in early 1991, when an American-led coalition defeated Iraq and forced it to leave Kuwait. At the end of that year the U.S. led in convening the Madrid conference and in beginning the peace negotiation between Israel and its Arab neighbors.[5]

These developments weakened Syria, pushed it into a corner and posed a threat to the stability of the Syrian regime. In Damascus there was a fear that it would deprive Syria of its strategic aim of regaining the Golan Heights and securing its presence in and hegemony over Lebanon. Fateful as these events appeared to be for the Syrian state and the regime at its helm, many months passed before President Asad shared with his fellow citizens his assessment of the events. He finally told his people what he thought the regional turmoil held in store for Syria's future at his swearing-in ceremony as president for a fourth term in March 1992. This address was one of few that decade to the Syrian nation.

In his remarks, Asad addressed the difficulties facing Syria under the new regional and international circumstances. It was a sober, even sorrowful, speech; his concern and uncertainty over the future were evident. However, Asad did not leave his audience without hope. He expressed his conviction that the future would prove correct the course he had steered his people on since rising to power, and that it would lead Syria safely to shore. In his speech, Asad said:

> Something has happened in the world and we must not ignore it. Stability reigned in the world for a long period, during which a clear system of equilibrium existed. But significant changes took place in this equilibrium…. The world today is turbulent and it is not clear where it is heading or what its last stop will be. However, even if we do not know how long the tempest in our world will continue or how it will conclude, it is clear that it will quiet down, and the world will stabilize, at least for a time…. The history of mankind teaches us that the duration of such stability differs from period to period, and that means the growth of systems of equilibrium and treaties different from those that were and those that are now. Therefore, it is important at this time to be alert to the dangers that threaten us until tranquility and stability are achieved in our world.[6]

These remarks illustrate the two basic assumptions that lay at the foundation of Syrian foreign policy throughout the 1990s. The first was that the regional and international circumstances facing Syria posed an immediate danger to its interests and, indeed, to its very security and territorial integrity (and thus to the stability and future of the regime). However, circumstances are never incontrovertible. Syria thus faced a transition period characterized by upheavals and a lack of stability, but this period would one day pass, after which circumstances in the region were likely again to favor it. The second basic assumption to guide Syrian foreign policy was that Syria must – in cooperation with other Arab states – prepare itself to confront these threatening circumstances and wage a battle of survival that would at least ensure the preservation of the status quo in the region. To this end, certain changes were required in its policy that would restore to it the capacity to maneuver that it had lost with the disintegration of the Soviet Union. At the same time, Syria would not need to overhaul its policy dramatically or back away from its fundamental concepts. On the contrary, such a reversal would probably prove catastrophic in that it would cause damage much more serious than that engendered by prevailing circumstances.

Thus, the notion that Syria's condition was difficult but not hopeless was Asad's point of departure. Feeling a need for change, but not upheaval, Asad charted a new course, one that he traveled through most of the 1990s. It bore the marks of contradictory impulses. One was Damascus's readiness and desire to guarantee Syria a place in the new regional order that was taking shape under U.S. leadership. In this framework, Syria took action to improve its relations with the U.S., aiming to imbue them with a certain measure of depth and intimacy. The Syrians were at the same time careful to preserve maneuverability and freedom of action vis-à-vis Washington, and thereby to avoid undue dependence on the U.S. This was by way of establishing an all-Arab front around the Egyptian–Syrian–Saudi Arabian axis and, in tandem, by fostering contacts with Western Europe. The second impulse to guide Syria's new path seemed completely at odds with the first. Essentially, it bade Damascus to try to curb the American–Israeli effort to establish a new regional order in the Middle East. Success therein would preserve the status quo that had existed in the region until that time. To this end, Syria acted to maintain and improve its ties with Iran, to rebuild a close relationship with Russia and, from the start of 1997, to make headway in its relations with Iraq under Saddam Husayn. The Syrian regime was also careful to adhere, at least publicly, to its ideological commitment to the patently anti-West world view that had served as its guiding principle since seizing power in Damascus at the start of the 1960s.

Under such conditions, it comes as no surprise that Syria failed to make real progress in its relations with the U.S. Bilateral relations with the countries of Western Europe and with the Arab states did not gain any ground either. Syrian caution, hesitation and duality of purpose (as evinced by Damascus's simultaneous efforts to improve relations with Iran and the West) raised repeatedly the question of Syrian foreign policy aims. What was the Syrian desideratum in the early 1990s – to foster ties with the East, or with the West?

Syria's strategic isolation, not to say weakness, the clear result of the difficulty in deciding on its orientation, was exposed and seen in late 1998 following the deterioration in its relations with Turkey. Ankara decided to force Syria to make up its mind and stop supporting the Kurdish P.K.K. movement. The clear-cut Turkish ultimatum, which included a clear threat to start a war, forced Syria to settle its conflict with Ankara and to give in to all Turkish demands.[7]

Bashar al-Asad – first steps

Against the background of Syria's poor relations with most of the countries of the world and the sense of socioeconomic stagnation and suffocation at home which most likely infiltrated the halls of the Foreign Ministry as well, Bashar al-Asad's rise to power was received as a welcome breeze. There were many inside and outside Syria who hoped that Bashar would bring with him the opening of a new era in Syria's relations with the world. This hope was focused both on the style (a new and open style that would replace the feeling of isolation, suspicion and suffocation that characterized the rule and policies of Hafiz al-Asad) and on the change in content (a new foreign policy which would recognize the new regional and international realities, opening itself up to substantial changes and the adoption of an unequivocal pro-Western orientation).

It is important to mention the positive impression that Bashar made on quite a number of Western leaders as well as journalists who had met him before he rose to power. They described him as a young, open-minded, very intelligent man, well versed in details and quite in control of facts. He appeared not to need his aides or previously prepared notes in order to lead a fluent, matter-of-fact discussion on any subject with those he met.[8] Bashar's deep familiarity with Western ideas and the openness which he displayed, even declaring that he was a jazz fan, and, of course, his penchant for frequently surfing the Internet, only strengthened that impression.[9]

There appeared to be good reason why many chose to view him as an undoubted representative of the younger generation of Arab leaders destined to take the helm in the Arab world. Among those mentioned together with Bashar were King 'Abdallah II of Jordan, King Muhammad V of Morocco and, of course, the ruler of Qatar and the crown princes of a number of the Gulf emirates. These young leaders frequently met with Bashar even before he rose to power, and these meetings provided Bashar with some experience in the sphere of foreign policy and also granted a measure of legitimacy to his rise to the presidency, since his friends the monarchs appeared to be willing, and even enthusiastic, to make him one of their own.

Nevertheless, there still remained some doubt as to whether Bashar actually belonged to the group of young monarchs who had, until they rose to power, spent most of their lives, and certainly their formative years, in Western educational institutions and a Western environment. King 'Abdallah II frequently and staunchly claimed that Bashar, like him, belonged to the Internet generation.[10] However, the passage of time, especially after he rose to power, revealed that Bashar did not really belong to that group and that the differences between him and the other young monarchs were greater than the similarities. It seems even that Bashar felt himself closer to Hasan Nasrallah, the leader of Hizballah, also one of the younger faces in the Arab world, than he was to Kings 'Abdallah II and Muhammad V. Indeed, contacts between Bashar and the young monarchs, which had apparently been against the background of personal interests, ended as soon as the members of this young group rose to power and faced stormy domestic, regional and inter-Arab realities.

Bashar also embarked on an extensive series of visits to Arab countries and beyond at a pace unknown in Syrian till then. The number of foreign visits he made during his first years in office may have exceeded those his father made during his entire rule. Bashar visited every Arab state, excluding Iraq, more than once – essentially annually or more – including Lebanon, marking the first visit by a Syrian president to that country since the outbreak of the civil war there in 1975. He also visited the capitals of Western Europe and other capitals frequently, including Madrid (May 2001 and June 2004), Paris (June 2001), Berlin (July 2001), Rome (February 2002), London (December 2002), Athens (December 2003), Ankara (January 2004), Peking (June 2004) and Moscow (January 2005). Bashar attached great importance to these visits in that they provided him with the opportunity to meet Arab and Western leaders personally and acquire first-hand impressions of them. He made a practice of taking along delegations of Syrian businessmen on these visits with the aim of promoting economic ties between Syria and the host countries. Prior to each visit, he arranged to be interviewed by the major media of the host country, during which he generally came across as open and curious, interested in listening and not only in being heard, and anxious to use his visit to promote what he himself termed "inter-cultural dialogue."[11]

Bashar's policies, at least in the early stages of his rule, reflected the continuation of those of his father, i.e. continued cautious maneuvering between East and West while attempting to straddle the fence. On the one hand, attempts were made to promote a political dialogue with the countries of Western Europe and the moderate Arab countries and even with the United States. On the other hand, there was the desire to preserve close ties with Iran and promote relations with Iraq. In addition, there were clear attempts on Bashar's part to exploit the change in rule in Damascus in order to turn over a new leaf in his country's relations with the world at large while shaking off the residue of the past, especially personal residues that had frequently beclouded Syria's relations with its neighbors. Particularly prominent in these attempts were those designed to improve relations with Jordan and Turkey and to a certain degree with Iraq, with which Syria had been in serious conflict for several decades.

However, it quickly became clear that realities were stronger than Bashar and that smiles and good will cannot erase with one sweep of the hand substantive differences of opinion on key issues or the residues of the past which had for so long overshadowed Syria's relations with its neighbors. Moreover, when he was faced with his first crisis, Bashar's balanced, placating statements and his smile on more than one occasion hid immature positions and policies and the folly of youth. Since Bashar lacked practical experience in the sphere of foreign policy and apparently also a comprehensive view of Syria's place and role in the regional and international arenas, it is not surprising that he was motivated to adopt radical policies, not only in the Israeli–Arab context, which considerably damaged Syria's foreign relations without promoting any Syrian interests.

In the first year of Bashar's rule in Syria, two crises broke out that were to impact on his regime from then onwards. The first was the outbreak of the al-Aqsa Intifada in October 2000 followed by the renewed activities of the Hizballah against Israel's northern border. The Palestinian Intifada as well as the renewed Hizballah activity against Israel could potentially have created a regional conflagration or at least an Israeli–Syrian confrontation. The second was the war on terrorism declared by the United States in the wake of the attacks on New York and Washington on September 11, 2001. As part of this, the United States first brought down the Taliban regime in Afghanistan and then in spring 2003 took over Iraq. At the same time, Washington became increasingly critical of Syria, not only for not severing its ties with the "Evil Axis" but for in effect promoting its relations with the elements composing it: Iran, Iraq, Hizballah at the time and North Korea as well. After the war in Iraq, U.S.

criticism of Syria increased significantly and relations between the two countries almost reached their absolute nadir.

Bashar, the United States and the war against terror, and the war in Iraq

The September 11 terror attacks on New York and Washington by Usama bin Ladin's al-Qa'ida organization opened a new era in the Syrian–American relationship, ostensibly leading both countries toward a confrontational course. Although neither Damascus nor Washington appeared to be interested in such a confrontation, whether they were prepared to do everything possible to prevent it was unclear.

A primary element underlying the hostility between the U.S. and Syria even before the terrorist attacks of September 2001 was the burgeoning relationship between Damascus and Baghdad. The Iraqis began exporting oil to Syria in the fall of 2000 through the Kirkuk–Banyas pipeline, which had been shut down by the Syrians in 1982 because of their dispute with Iraq regarding Syrian support for Tehran during the Iran–Iraq War. With the thawing of relations between the two from 1997 onward, the Iraqis began pressing for the reopening of the line and proposed laying an additional line to increase the quantity of oil that Iraq could export via Syria. Once the Syrians agreed to reopen the old line, in 2000, 150,000–200,000 barrels of oil per day began to flow to Syria. This oil, sold to Syria by Iraq at a reduced rate, was diverted to the local Syrian market, allowing Damascus to expand its own oil production for export.[12] Notably, data regarding the growth of Syria's oil exports from the fall of 2000 – a period when domestic oil production in Syria actually declined – were public knowledge and could be accounted for only by the flow of oil from Iraq into Syria. Washington promptly protested to Syria over this blatant violation of the sanctions against Iraq, whereupon Bashar informed Secretary of State Powell, and later President Bush himself, that the inflow of oil from Iraq was only for the purpose of testing the pipeline, which had been shut down for nearly two decades, and that when the tests were completed the flow of oil would cease.[13]

An additional element of the Syrian–American confrontation was Damascus's support of Palestinian terrorism and its encouragement and aid for Hizballah. Significantly, the U.S. had refrained from censuring Israel for its attacks on Syrian radar installations in Lebanon in April and July 2001, in retaliation for a Hizballah attack on Israeli army positions in the Shab'a farms area. Instead, Washington laid the blame for the deteriorating situation along the Israeli–Lebanese border on Syria in light of its refusal to halt Hizballah activity.[14] The U.S. State Department also promptly denounced Bashar's anti-Semitic remarks during his welcome of the Pope in Damascus in May 2001, when he referred to the traitorous mentality of the Jews. A State Department spokesman depicted the comments as "erroneous and unacceptable," and expressed the hope that the United States would be able to maintain working relations with Syria's young president. In response, the American Ambassador in Damascus was summoned to the Syrian Foreign Ministry and was handed a Syrian protest against "the faulty interpretation given by the Americans to President Bashar's remarks, an interpretation that stemmed from ignorance and lack of knowledge of the facts, for Bashar al-Asad never mentioned the Jews in his speech, but attacked Israel."[15]

However, it was the terrorist attacks by Usama bin Ladin's al-Qa'ida organization against American cities on September 11, 2001 that signaled a new era in Syrian–American relations, setting the two countries on a confrontation course. This reality was not altered by the Syrians' perfunctory denunciation of the attacks, or the condolence letter sent by Bashar al-Asad to President Bush, in which he called for "international cooperation to uproot terror at its base, and determined activity to protect the human right to live in peace and security."[16]

For many Syrians, the events of September 11, 2001 were reminiscent of the collapse of the Soviet Union in the early 1990s, a development that posed a real threat to the Syrian regime at the time. Nevertheless, the combination of Foreign Minister Faruq al-Shar' (who was highly experienced in evasive maneuvering regarding the U.S. throughout the 1990s, learned from Asad Sr.) and the present Syrian president, Bashar (who lacked any experience whatsoever in the foreign policy realm and therefore tended to display a daring attitude toward the U.S.), initially resulted in an approach by Damascus that sought to minimize the significance of the September 11 events. By extension, this approach also disregarded every demand by Washington that Syria alter its foreign policy toward Iraq and curb Palestinian and Hizballah terror against Israel.

Bashar himself referred to the September 11 events when he addressed the summit of Arab leaders in Beirut in March 2002, explaining that:

> As a result of the September 11 events, fear prevailed everywhere and the Arabs were not immune to this though without any justification. Some of them tried to get out of their skin and said that "if it was up to me I would have changed my identity and my religion and even my name." Some started to call for making con-

cessions about some of the rights with the pretext that they wanted to get out of the way of the storm, thinking that by doing so they would be able to bend to the storm. But they did not differentiate between bending to the storm and being uprooted even before the storm arrives. When your roots are uprooted any light wind will take you to the unknown. When there is a storm the need is greater to cling to the roots. No matter how long the storm might last it is going to stop and when you try to stand up after the storm you will not be able to unless you have roots.

If the concepts and principles are lost, you won't be able to restore them, whereas storms are changeable because interests bring them. We are ideological people, which means that we stick to our principles and constants and we cannot live by the temporary values the others live by.... [The Americans] have asked us to commit ourselves to combat terrorism. We did it and so did all the Arabs in general. But it seems that all our experience in combating and all the statements issued before and after September 11 are not enough to prove that Arabs are against terrorism and that they are the first people to combat terrorism.... The [Americans] forgot that they were the ones who prepared the ground of terrorism. That they opened the way for financial transactions which were going to the terrorists, and that they gave the terrorists media facilities which poisoned the minds of others. They definitely know that terrorists did not start in our region but rather in other regions. But shock sometimes leads to wrong conclusions and this is something we understand because it leads people to lose their control and consequently understanding. Perhaps it is difficult for them to believe that the Arabs, in this issue, were wiser and more far-sighted than they were. But now they start to decide who is the terrorist among us, and which is the terrorist state. They decide for us and we have to keep silent and abide and convince ourselves with what they say. They even seem to think that they know us better than we know ourselves.[17]

Nevertheless, Bashar understood the need to minimize the possible damage to Syria from bin Ladin's terror attacks against Washington and New York. Not only did he decide to distance himself from them and denounce them, but he also offered to assist the United States in its efforts to trace bin Ladin operatives in Syria or in contact with Syrian citizens. Indeed, American agents arrived in Syria early in 2002 to investigate these possibilities. Inter alia, the name of Muhammad 'Ata, mastermind of the September 11 attacks, came up, as did that of Mamun al-Darakzali, a Syrian-born member of al-Qa'ida who was involved in handling its finances. Later, the Syrians also arrested Muhammad Haydr Zamar, a Syrian-born German citizen who apparently had recruited Muhammad 'Ata into al-Qa'ida.[18]

The Americans were grateful to the Syrians for this assistance, and President Bush telephoned President Asad to thank him for it. High-ranking American officials were quoted as implying that the information delivered by Syria enabled the deterrence of attacks against American targets and thus saved many American lives.[19] However, Syria appeared to conceal more than it revealed. While the Syrians seemed to have no desire or interest in promoting bin Ladin's affairs (significantly, they refrained from broadcasting the video-cassettes he disseminated throughout the world via al-Jazira TV after the September 11 attacks), their restraint stemmed from a fear of arousing latent Islamic sentiment in Syria which could erupt against the regime itself.[20] At the same time, the Syrians chose to ignore the presence in Syria of bin Ladin operatives, and possibly other Islamic activists involved in terrorism, over a long period. Indeed, bin Ladin's wife Najwa, who was of Syrian origin, and the couple's son 'Umar, as well as other relatives of the leader of al-Qa'ida who may have been active in the organization, resided in Ladhiqiyya, Syria up until September 2001 and possibly thereafter. Notably, a report published in Israel indicated that the Syrians had permitted approximately 150 al-Qa'ida activists to settle in refugee camps in Lebanon after the fall of Afghanistan to the U.S., information which the Syrians denied.[21]

In addition to that, Syria continued to devote efforts to promoting its relations with other members of the "Evil Axis," as George W. Bush defined them, North Korea, Iran and the Hizballah as well as Iraq. Indeed, one of the prominent names in the F.B.I.'s list of 22 most wanted terrorists is that of 'Imad Mughaniyya, a Hizballah member who had been involved in attacks on American targets in Lebanon, as well as the names of two more of the organization's activists. As is known, these people operate openly in Lebanon under the Syrians' watchful eye. Incidentally, when American Under Secretary of State William Burns presented this list to Bashar, the Syrians were quick to deny having any information on Mughaniyyah and his colleagues.[22]

It is no wonder that the Chairman of the Senate Intelligence Committee, Bill Graham, who had visited Syria in the winter of 2002 and even met with Bashar, said on his return to Washington that, while Syria had cooperated with the United States in the war on terrorism, it could not be denied that it was the source of several problems in the sphere of terrorism facing the United States. Graham was also quoted, to the surprise and disappointment of the Syrians, as having recommended that Hizballah and other terrorist bases in Lebanon be attacked if necessary.[23] Threats against Syria were also voiced by Under Secretary of State Richard Armitage, who said that he did not discount the possibility of the use of force against Syria because of its support for terrorism.[24] Armitage subsequently even defined Hizballah as the "A team" of the terrorist organizations, and as an element against which the United States had an open account that it hoped to settle sooner or later.[25]

Syria continued to occupy a leading place in the annual reports on world terrorism issued by the U.S. State Department, which indicated repeatedly that Syria offered assistance and refuge to terrorist organizations. The Syrians, in response, claimed that all they were doing was assisting the legitimate resistance of the Palestinians to the Israeli occupation, and that Damascus was in no way involved in terrorist acts.[26] Bashar personally explained:

> This report is a political report which has no relation to terrorism. Several years ago I asked one of the American leaders who visited us whether he thought that Syria is a terrorist state, and he answered no. When I then asked him why Syria is included in the report on terrorism published by the State Department, he attributed this to domestic American political considerations.[27]

Side by side with the American focus on Syrian assistance to the terrorist organizations, high-ranking figures in the United States began attacking Syria for arming itself with advanced non-conventional weapons, especially chemical and biological weapons. Defense Secretary Donald Rumsfeld has publicly warned Syria over and over during the last few years against continuing to develop such means of warfare.[28] Reports published in Washington in October 2002 pointed to Syrian–Russian cooperation in the nuclear sphere. These reports were denied vehemently both in Moscow and in Damascus, with the Syrians labeling them as an attempt by the U.S., at Israel's instigation, to lay the groundwork for an attack against Syria in the future.[29] Testifying before the Senate Foreign Relations Committee just before the war in Iraq, Secretary of State Colin Powell declared:

> We are keeping an eye on Syria's interest in weapons of mass destruction and we are following the support it is giving to Hizballah. Its cooperation in the war against terrorism does not mean that we are retracting our criticism of it for supporting terrorist organizations. They assisted us and we appreciate it, but this will not prevent us from arguing with and criticizing them.[30]

It seemed, however, that there were differences of opinion within the American administration regarding the line to be adopted toward

Syria. This was mainly because Bashar had denounced the September 11 attacks and even instructed his people to assist the U.S. in its struggle against Usama bin Ladin's al-Qa'ida organization. The Defense Department held a firm anti-Syria stand, and its spokesperson frequently brought up the possibility of a military move against Syria. On the other hand, the State Department preached a more moderate line designed to placate the Syrians and win them over instead of subjecting them to heavy pressures.[31] Congress, for its part, continued to pursue the firmer line on Syria. In the summer of 2002, in response to pressure from AIPAC and from the anti-Syrian Lebanese lobby active in the U.S., Congress brought up for discussion the "Syrian Accountability" draft law. This included broadening the sanctions already in force against Syria because of its support for terrorism and because of the continued Syrian military presence in Lebanon. The draft law prohibits academic contacts with Syrian educational and cultural institutions, and limits the entry of Syrian citizens into the U.S., even of those coming for academic studies and research.[32] The administration quickly expressed its opposition to the draft law and, in a letter sent to a number of members of the House of Representatives, explained that, despite the serious differences of opinion between Washington and Damascus, the administration felt that it must act with discretion and examine which of the options at its disposal would best serve American interests. President Bush added that he was afraid the draft law would limit the ability of the U.S. to deal with the difficult and complicated situation in which it found itself in the Middle East.[33] Only in summer 2003, following the war in Iraq, did the administration change its mind and give a green light to Congress to pass the law. The law was approved by Congress in October 2003 and was signed by President Bush in December that year.[34]

American preparations to strike at Saddam Husayn created tension in relations between Syria and Washington, with Syria quickly taking the side of Iraq, conspicuously hosting Iraqis in the Presidential Palace in Damascus. Syria also joined the efforts to thwart Washington's efforts to recruit international broad support. Nevertheless, on November 8, 2002, Syria gave its blessing to Security Council Resolution 1441, which included a strong demand that Iraq agree to the renewing of the activities of the international inspectors in Iraqi territory or else suffer the consequences. The Syrians tried to present its vote as a "Syrian diplomatic victory" or alternatively as in response to the Arab consensus that Syria is called upon to represent in the Security Council. They even bragged that their vote had succeeded in foiling, or at least postponing, the American attack on Iraq.[35]

Together with its attempts to foil Washington's efforts in the international arena, Syria adopted a staunch anti-American stance – strongly opposing the United States' moves, accusing Washington of having a "hidden agenda" whose objective was the establishment of a new American order in the Middle East for itself and on behalf of Israel. For example, Syrian Vice-President 'Abd al-Halim Khaddam warned that:

> The American attack on Iraq is designed to bring about the partition of that country, which is a strategic objective of Israel's; in fact it is part of the long-standing Zionist aim of breaking up the national fabric of the countries of the region.... We are defending Iraq, which is an Arab country, and the fate of all the Arabs is bound up with its fate. We are not Finland and therefore we cannot relate to Iraq's fate with equanimity. Iraq is a strategic hinterland for Syria in its conflict with Israel. We supported Kuwait when Iraq invaded its territory, but today Iraq is under attack and therefore we are standing at its side.[36]

Syrian Minister of Information 'Adnan 'Umran fell into line with Khaddam, explaining:

> The excuse that the Americans are providing for the expected attack on Iraq is ludicrous. The entire Arab world is in fact a target for threats by the United States. The involvement of the Americans in the internal affairs of the Arab states recalls the colonial period, and there is no doubt that if Washington could it would take all of us back to that period.[37]

The hostile attitude among the Syrian public towards the U.S. had already started in early 2002, following Israeli operation Defensive Shield. Actively encouraged by the regime, this hostility took the form of street demonstrations near the American Embassy in Damascus, and later in organized boycotts of American goods, personalities and even cultural symbols. A popular committee was established in Damascus for the purpose of the boycott of American products. It is no wonder that signs appeared in the windows of restaurants reading "No entry to Americans,"[38] and the American Consul in Damascus was ceremoniously escorted out of the Ocsigen Restaurant in Bab Tuma, the Christian quarter of Damascus. The owners of the restaurant became heroes for more than a day in Damascus.[39]

On the eve of the outbreak of the war, Syria adopted an even harsher tone in its protest against the U.S. Bashar said that the United States "is interested only in gaining control over Iraqi oil and redrawing the map of the region in keeping with its world view." He added: "In the past we did not sense the danger closing in on us in the face of fateful developments including the Sykes–Picot Agreement, the Balfour Declaration, the establishment of the State of Israel, but the danger to the Arabs inherent in the war in Iraq is no less than any over those."[40] He warned the Arabs about the United States' friendship, which is "more fatal than its hostility."[41] In another place he compared the United States to:

> a car speeding towards a concrete wall, but even if the power of an American car will allow it to penetrate a concrete wall, it is liable to discover that on the other side of the wall there would be no bed of roses either, but it would lead to an abyss... since Bush does not understand that for the Arabs honor is more important that anything else, even food.[42]

From the moment the war broke out, Syria was totally mobilized, even if mainly verbally, against the U.S. This reached one of its pinnacles in the statement by Syrian Foreign Minister Faruq al-Shar', before the Foreign Affairs Committee of the People's Assembly, "We want Iraq's victory."[43] Shar' subsequently even compared the United States to the Third Reich and President Bush to Adolf Hitler.[44] Bashar granted an interview to the Lebanese newspaper *Al-Safir* in which he warned that Syria might become the next target for the U.S., adding that, in view of Washington's moves, "Syria does not intend sitting idly by."[45] The Syrian authorities also allowed, and even encouraged, thousands of demonstrators to go out on to the streets of Damascus and other cities all over Syria and protest against the American attack on Iraq. The Syrian media mounted their own campaign against the United States. Radio Damascus said, for example, that the American–British attack violated the most basic of human values and human rights and was also a crass violation of international law. "Our experience proves that the interests of Israel are controlling American policy and not the interests of the United States; after all it was the supporters of the Likud among the Zionists in the corridors of the American administration who led to the attack on Iraq."[46] In another place Radio Damascus said: "The forces of evil in the world have conspired to gain control over the wealth and resources of the Arab nation. The superpower in the world is acting today in a biased way in order to achieve its aims and its satanic arms bring harm to peaceful peace-loving peoples."[47]

The United States, especially Defense Secretary Donald Rumsfeld, quickly responded, accusing Syria of granting assistance to Iraq by smuggling night-vision binoculars and other equipment into that country. The Americans also accused the Syrians of allowing Arab volunteers to reach Iraq via Syria, and later one senior American official also accused Syria of allowing Iraqi leaders to escape from Iraq via its territory. Secretary of State Colin Powell threatened to impose sanctions against Syria, and President Bush, in a strong message to the Syrians, accused them of developing chemical weapons, which was troubling for the United States and would force it to take action against Syria.[48]

Undoubtedly, Bashar had difficulty comprehending Washington's moves, which accounted for his problematic conduct toward the Americans. Presumably, the situation became clear only when the U.S. became Syria's neighbor to the east. Indeed, in light of this new regional reality, the verbal attacks against the U.S. ceased and, instead, the Syrian leadership and its spokesmen vied with each other in declarations of friendship toward the American people and their president. Syria also hastened to seal its border with Iraq, turned over high-ranking Iraqi officials who had fled to Syria to the Americans, and softened its opposition to Washington's efforts to promote the Israeli–Palestinian peace process. Visiting Damascus in May 2003, Colin Powell received a promise from Bashar that Syria would shut down the offices of the Palestinian organizations operating in its territory – a promise that was not fully kept.[49] Powell left behind a long list of American demands at the conclusion of his visit, including disarming Hizballah, ending the Syrian military presence in Lebanon and refraining from any activity that could hinder the Israeli–Palestinian peace process.

Clearly, however, the Syrian regime was conducting a defensive battle and did not intend to embrace the U.S. Bashar had apparently made up his mind to play for time in the hope that the Americans would become bogged down in Iraq, thereby weakening Washington's resolve to act against Syria. At the same time, Bashar displayed interest in the involvement of Syria in a political process under American leadership in the event of a breakthrough in the Israeli–Palestinian talks. Washington, however, favored progressing on the Israeli–Palestinian track over dealing with a regime that for the U.S. was problematic, unsympathetic and in effect a replica of that of Saddam Husayn.

The American entanglement in Iraq in late 2003 restored the Syrians' self-confidence. Refraining from complying with Washington's demands, they later sharpened the anti-American tone of their statements. Foreign Minister Shar' announced that Damascus would be willing to comply with Washington's demands only if they were "logical and balanced."[50] Prime Minister Mustafa Miru declared that Iraq under U.S. rule was a worse neighbor for the countries around it than Iraq under the rule of Saddam Husayn.[51]

Washington, meanwhile, reiterated its demands of Syria and added the demand that Syria close its border with Iraq, on the grounds that most of the terrorist acts against the American forces in Iraq were attributable to non-Iraqi infiltrators entering Iraq from Syria. American officials also charged that, before his fall from power, Saddam Husayn had deposited billions of dollars in Syrian banks.[52] Washington's displeasure with the Syrians' behavior was reflected in American backing for Israel after it attacked a Palestinian training camp outside Damascus in October 2003. A complaint lodged by Syria with the Security Council over the attack elicited the response by the U.S. Ambassador to the U.N. that Syria has positioned itself on the wrong side in the war against terror.[53] This evoked suspicion in Damascus that the Israeli act had been carried out with Washington's knowledge or encouragement, and that it was the first step in an overall American move to bring down the Syrian government. The fact that at the same time the American administration promoted the legislation in Congress of the Syrian Accountability Act only heightened this suspicion. Syria adopted a two-pronged policy. On the one hand, it continued trying to pacify the U.S., permitting American investigators to come to Damascus and examine the Syrian banking system for deposits by Saddam Husayn and his agents. It also supported a decision by the Security Council in October 2003 to accept an American request for cooperation in the rehabilitation of Iraq.[54] On the other hand, however, Damascus continued denouncing the American presence in Iraq and expressed support, albeit low-key, for terror acts against the American forces there. As Syrian Chief of Staff Hasan Turkmani explained, "We must stand up against the enemies of occupation in Palestine and in Iraq, who are part of an attempt to create a new American order in the region."[55]

The capture of Saddam Husayn in December 2003, and the policy about-face by Libyan ruler Mu'ammar Qadhdafi, who divested himself of his long-time hostility toward the U.S. and the West, side by side with continued terrorism against the Americans in Iraq further heightened pressure on the Syrian regime by Washington. On December 12, 2003, President George Bush signed into law the Syrian Accountability and Lebanese Sovereignty Restoration Act of 2003 following its passage in both Houses of Congress by a majority. Senior American officials, most prominently Secretary of State Colin Powell, announced that the U.S. was determined to implement this law and was considering imposing sanctions against Syria, as stipulated in it.[56] Notably, the obvious disregard by the Americans of Bashar's signals early in 2004 that he sought a renewal of talks with Israel demonstrated a loss of faith in Syria by Washington decision makers.

Bashar, however, continued to display confidence that the Americans would ultimately stop short at taking action against him. Undoubtedly, his perception was supported by conflicting messages emanating from Washington. On the very day President Bush signed the Syrian Accountability Act, the newly appointed Syrian Minister for Syrian Expatriates, Buthayna Sha'ban, a confidante of Bashar, was meeting at the State Department in Washington, while the appointment of a new American Ambassador to Damascus, Margaret Skobie, was also announced at that time.[57] These events constituted clear evidence for Bashar that the Americans sought dialogue with Damascus, even with the intent of criticism, and not confrontation. Significantly, during a visit in Athens in December 2003, Bashar expressed certainty that Syria would not be attacked by the U.S., stressing: "Syria is not Iraq."[58] Interviewed by *al-Sharq al-Awsat* in late 2003, he elaborated:

> Although our argument with the United States is liable to cause a storm for Syria, we hope this will not happen. There are differences of opinion in the American administration about Syria, and in general it is clear that the United States does not have a fixed and clear-cut outlook regarding events in the Middle East, and its policy is influenced by its support for Israel. As Foreign Minister Shar' put it: "The United States Congress is even more closely duty bound to Israel than is the Knesset."[59]

The Syrians were ready, however, to make some cosmetic moves designed to avoid bringing Washington's wrath down on them. Syria announced that it was going to increase its forces along the Syrian–Iraqi border and also reported on the construction of an earthenwork embankment designed to foil the passage of smugglers and terrorists between the two countries. It also announced, following the visit of American officials to Damascus to examine Syria's banking system and to determine whether Saddam Husayn had indeed invested money there, that it was ready to return $3.5 million out of the $261 million that, according to Syrian findings, had been deposited in Syrian banks.[60] Damascus was also ready to cooperate with the temporary Iraqi administration which was established by the U.S. As Bashar said, "While we do recognize the temporary Ruling Council in Iraq because it is an established fact, we have made it clear to them [and to the Americans] that this does not mean that we have granted it legitimacy, since legitimacy must come from the people."[61]

Nevertheless, the Syrians reiterated the denial of their involvement in terrorist activities against the Americans in Iraq and added that they were doing everything they could to prevent such acts but that the border between the two countries was very long and it was impossible to prevent passage across it. In early January 2005, Bashar explained:

> The Americans have to understand that guarding the border with Iraq cannot be our responsibility. The border between Syria and Iraq is exactly the same as the border between the U.S. and Mexico and the fact is that the U.S., despite all its efforts, cannot exercise control all along the border to prevent the smuggling of goods and even people across it.[62]

The Syrian Minister of Information, Mahdi Dakhlallah, supported Bashar's statement, adding that "The border between Syria and Iraq is exceptionally long and over the years, even at the time that rivalry existed between Syria and Iraq under the leadership of Saddam Husayn, we found it difficult to guard it and close it off to terrorists who infiltrated from Iraq in order to carry out acts of sabotage against Syria."[63]

However, realities in Iraq had a dynamic of their own. As the attacks against U.S. troops grew more frequent, the U.S.'s anger at Syria increased. One of the turning points was the American assault in early November 2004 on the town of Faluja in northern Iraq that was a major center of activity for forces operating against the U.S. led by Mus'ib al-Zarqawi. According to American sources, documents were seized in this action which bore witness, albeit not always direct, to Syrian connections to terrorist activities in Iraq. For example, it transpired that some of the anti-American terrorists had come from Syria, that former Iraqi Ba'th leaders were in Syria coordinating the struggle against the U.S. and, finally, that Syria allowed or at least ignored the establishment of training camps for terrorists.[64] In addition to these reports, Iraqi officials for the first time accused Syria of being involved in terrorist attacks in Iraq. The chief of police in the city of Najaf reported, following a big terrorist attack there in December 2004, that one of the perpetrators of the attack who was captured by his men admitted that he had trained in Syria.[65] Iraqi Prime Minister Iyad al-'Alawi stated that, during his visit to Damascus in mid-2004, he had given Bashar information on some of Saddam Husayn's associates who had fled to Syria, among them the former chief of military intelligence, Saddam Husayn's former deputy 'Izjat Ibrahim al-Duri and others.[66]

Although it appeared that the U.S.'s reactions in view of Syria's policies regarding Iraq appeared at first to be slow and hesitant, one must remember that reference is to a heavy and cumbersome system that needs time in order to change policy and the direction of its activities. It should also be borne in mind that presidential elections were held in the U.S. in November 2004, and the election campaign also held back the decision-making process in Washington and delayed the adoption of a sharper tone and even the adoption of more severe steps by the U.S. against Damascus. Of note is the fact that the Syrians had hoped with all their hearts that the Democratic candidate, John Kerry, would defeat George W. Bush, since they viewed the latter's remaining in office as a danger to Syria, and Syrian sources did not hide their trepidation regarding the future of the Arabs when it became clear who had won re-election.[67]

Indeed, throughout 2004, especially towards the end of the year, there were signs of a clear worsening in relations between the U.S. and Syria. First, in May 2004 the Syrian Accountability Law came into effect. Although the administration used only a small portion of the possibility and sanctions that the law allowed it, the psychological effect of the law was greater than either Washington or Damascus had expected. For example, the sanctions leveled against the Syrian Trade Bank, the largest and most important of Syria's banks, made it difficult for Syria to carry out financial transactions with the international banking systems and drove investors away. Moreover, the Syrian Accountability Law was not a one-time move but rather an ongoing process, since it provided a mechanism according to which, every few months, the degree of Syria's acceding to Washington's demands is examined and, in the light of its results, the administration has the option of increasing its sanctions against Damascus.[68]

Second, the tone of American media rhetoric against the Syrians worsened, with more than one writer attacking the administration in Washington, especially the State Department, for its weak policy towards Damascus. The American press was also full of reports about military plans being prepared in the Pentagon to strike a military blow against Syria. Border incidents in which American forces fired at Syrian forces were also widely reported in the American newspapers.[69]

Particularly noteworthy was the increasingly antagonistic tone on the part of senior American officials. President Bush, in late 2004, described Bashar as a weak leader and therefore unreliable,[70] later likening his attitude toward Bashar to his attitude toward 'Arafat and stating that he had no intention of dealing with him.[71] Bush's new Secretary of State, Condoleezza Rice, was even more pointed, describing Syria's conduct as turning that country into an obstacle to progress in the Israeli–Arab peace process and in the reforms that the U.S. sought to bring about in the Middle East, and responsible for causing serious damage to relations between the two countries.[72] Implicitly, Rice portrayed Syria as an obstacle to all that the U.S. held dear. These sharp statements elicited conjecture that the American administration had decided to bring about the collapse of the Syrian regime sooner or later.[73]

The Syrians tended to attribute the rupture in their relationship with the U.S. to Israel's influence or, alternatively, to a malicious anti-Syrian mindset on the part of the Americans, so that, no matter what Syria did, the Americans would be dissatisfied with Syria and would keep up pressure on it. Bashar explained that he greatly feared the Americans and was not interested in a "second Iraq," although Syria had to prepare for this eventuality. He predicted, however, that "the Americans would ultimately understand that we [Syria] are the key to the solution. We are vital to the renewal of the peace process [and] to the future of Iraq, and one day you will see that they will come knocking on our door."[74]

Evidently, the Syrians had difficulty comprehending the American system, as reflected in Bashar's seeming naivety, or perhaps genuine surprise, in an interview with Turkish TV, when he wondered: "Why do the Americans call me a dictator? I did not take control in a military coup or by force."[75] Moreover, the Syrians were unable to understand the rules of the game set by President Bush's administration, by which Syria had to respond to Washington's demands immediately, without any expectation of reward, with no negotiations beforehand. In a typical statement, Syrian Ambassador to the U.S. 'Imad Mustafa explained: "Relations between any two countries always involve give and take, and it is therefore impossible to accept the U.S. demand to conduct relations involving giving with no recompense."[76] In a similar vein, Syrian commentator Fawzi Shu'aybi asserted that "Syria is not a charitable organization that gives something without receiving in return."[77] Questioned as to why Syria did not follow in Libya's footsteps when it improved its relations with Washington immeasurably in mid-2004, Syria's then Information Minister, Ahmad al-Hasan, replied that Syria was not Libya, in that Libya was distant from the front with Israel.[78] One way or another, Washington refused to play Syria's game and the results turned out accordingly.

Indeed, a clear expression of the disastrous result for Damascus from the worsening of Syria's relations with the U.S. was seen at the end of 2004 with regard to Lebanon. The U.S. joined up with France, its sworn rival in the international scene, and together the two countries led a move that would pose a threat to the future of Syria's presence in Lebanon. The arena was Lebanon, but Syria was called upon to pay a price in Lebanon, for its acts, or rather its failure to act, in Iraq.

It seems, thus, that the future of Syrian–American relations will be determined not in Damascus by Bashar al-Asad but in Washington by a president whose lack of patience toward Syria has become well known during the last few years. In any event, even if the Syrian regime survives the American pressures and threats and in the future even possible strikes, Syria will pay a heavy price for its failure to come to terms with the Bush administration.

CHAPTER 7

Syria and Israel in Bashar's era

On December 8, 1999, U.S. President Bill Clinton announced the resumption of peace talks between Israel and Syria, with the participation, for the first time, of Israeli Prime Minister Ehud Barak and Syrian Foreign Minister Faruq al-Sharʻ. The resumption of the talks at so senior a level, and in effect for the first time at the political level (in the past, only diplomats and technical or military experts were involved), aroused a wave of optimism for prospects of a breakthrough in the negotiations, even the possibility of reaching an Israeli–Syrian peace accord within a few months.[1]

However, no such breakthrough occurred. The renewed negotiations in Washington, and the talks subsequently held in the town of Shepherdstown, Virginia produced no results. The talks ended shortly after they had begun, leaving Israeli–Syrian negotiations at an impasse.[2] In fact, it appeared that the psychological barriers between the two countries – barriers of suspicion, distrust and animosity – grew even higher after the failure of the talks. The burial of the peace process on the Syrian and Lebanese tracks – at least for the foreseeable future – was announced in Israel and the United States after the failed Geneva summit between President Clinton and the late President Hafiz al-Asad on March 26, 2000. Indeed, within the first five minutes of the Asad–Clinton summit, it was clear that difficulties had arisen. Asad refused to listen to the compromise proposal presented on behalf of Ehud Barak, and declared that Syria demanded the northeastern shore of the Sea of Galilee, and thus water rights in the sea. Asad also told Clinton that the northeastern shore had been in Syrian hands prior to the Six Day War, and that he himself had swum in the waters of the sea and had fished and eaten its fish. Asad also reminded Clinton that, even in the period of Salah al-Din, the Sea of Galilee had been Arab and Muslim.[3]

The failure of the attempt to attain an Israeli–Syrian peace agreement at the start of 2000 was to mark the end of the Israeli–Syrian talks, at least in the format in which they were conducted during the

1990s. Although both sides had reached the threshold of attaining a bilateral agreement, they did not achieve the long-awaited goal. This failure was not yet another of the ups and downs in the obstacle course that had become familiar to both countries on the road to peace. This particular juncture represented the moment of truth when Israel and Syria were required to make the final effort for peace. It became evident that such an effort was beyond their ability, and that the goal was unobtainable by the parties.

The failure of the negotiations was attributed to differences of opinion by the two sides over their future border line, i.e. their inability to resolve the conflict over several dozen or at most several hundred meters along the northeastern shore of the Sea of Galilee. Assuming that this was the case, and that achieving a peace agreement remained a priority for both Syria and Israel, a reasonable prediction would have been that sooner or later both countries would reconsider and work toward bridging this gap – undoubtedly a negligible barrier in comparison with the differences that both countries had managed to surmount since the start of the talks in October 1991.

However, this reasoned approach tended to ignore what the failure of the talks finally revealed: an absence of readiness by both sides – the leadership and the public in Syria and in Israel alike – to pay the price for peace. The Syrians refused to adopt a "peace policy," i.e. to convey a message of peace to the Israeli public as a necessary precondition to rally broad public support for the painful concessions demanded of Israel in order to attain an agreement. For its part, the Israeli government avoided responding to the Syrians' demand for a full withdrawal to the June 4, 1967 lines, apparently because of public opposition to this prospect. Such a withdrawal would mean, in effect, the return of the Syrians to the northeastern shore of the Sea of Galilee. Not surprisingly, the widespread assessment in the wake of the failure to attain an Israeli–Syrian peace in early 2000, in light of the fundamental gaps in perception that remained between the sides, was that this time it would take more than an American mediation effort consisting of one or another semantic formulation acceptable to both sides in order to renew the talks. Only a dramatic turn-around in Israel or Syria could create the circumstances that might extract the negotiations from the impasse they had reached.

Ostensibly, the death of Hafiz al-Asad in June 2000 constituted such a turning point. Asad Sr. was widely perceived in Israel and in the West as an obstacle to peace by his personality, his world view and, most importantly, his immutable identification with a generation of the past – the generation of the 1950s and 1960s, which was totally committed to a struggle to the finish against Israel. By contrast, Bashar al-Asad was perceived as young, modern and having a deep awareness of the Western lifestyle and way of thinking. The fact that Bashar made a point of projecting himself as seeking to advance Syria into the twenty-first century and integrate it into the world politically, socially and economically supported this image. Some Israelis also pointed to the fact that Bashar, born in 1965, was only 2 years old at the time of the Six Day War, when Israel conquered the Golan Heights. Conceivably, he was not burdened by the residue of this history or by the suspicion, hostility and desire for revenge that molded his father's attitude toward Israel. Indeed, it appeared that while Asad Sr., in his world view, had reflected the heated nationalist mood of the Arab street of the 1950s and 1960s – and by extension an anti-Western and anti-Israeli mindset – Bashar embodied a change in the Arab street, i.e. a diminishment of Arab nationalism and a moderation in the anti-Western and anti-Israel sentiment that had typified the past.[4]

In the wake of the outbreak of the al-Aqsa Intifada

Hopes for the eventual renewal of the Israeli–Syrian talks, and the bridging of the remaining gaps between the sides, faded in early October 2000 with the outbreak of the second Palestinian Intifada and in its wake renewed military activity against Israel by the Hizballah in the Shab'a farms area on Israel's northeastern border with Lebanon. The al-Aqsa Intifada quickly escalated into a violent and bloody conflict between Israel and the Palestinians which stirred up the Arab street against Israel. This agitation was fanned by the Arab media, especially by such satellite TV channels as al-Jazira, Abu-Dhabi and MBC, which covered the events in the killing fields live, thereby making a contribution by means of the communications revolution and globalization to deepening the breach between Israel and the Arab world.

The outbreak of the al-Aqsa Intifada came as a surprise to Damascus, and it is probable that the renewed attacks against Israel by Hizballah at the start of October 2000 were not initiated by the Syrians. At most, the Syrians may have been informed by Hizballah about its general intentions – a sign of the new equation in the power relationship between Damascus and the Hizballah that had evolved since Asad's death. Nevertheless, from the moment of the outbreak of the Intifada, Bashar sought to capitalize on the new reality emerging in the region to promote both his own status and Syria's regional prestige. Ultimately, this reality presented a golden opportunity for him to entrench his status as leader of the Arab rejectionist camp, or at least of a camp that took a tough, uncompromising stand toward Israel. Undoubtedly, the mood in the Damascus street, as in the other Arab capitals, also contributed to the hardening of his policy toward Israel, since he portrayed himself as attentive and responsive to the feelings of the people. In early October and again in late November 2000, violent demonstrations broke out in Damascus, and more particularly in the Palestinian refugee camps around it, such as the Yarmuk camp, with dozens of protesters wounded and extensive damage to property before the police subdued them.[5]

However, Bashar's policy regarding the crisis in the region also revealed something besides his desire to capitalize on the Palestinian Intifada in order to prove his leadership at home and abroad. In the view of many observers in Israel and in the West, it revealed the Syrian leader to be emotional, impulsive and rash, not to mention lacking in maturity and experience, leading him in directions he may not have anticipated. Additionally, a hostile, uncompromising attitude toward Israel was evident in his reactions to the events in the region, traceable to his upbringing in his father's home. This attitude had receded during the peace talks between Israel and Syria in the anticipation, or even hope, of peace between the two countries, but re-emerged as a central element in Bashar's strategic thinking. The animosity toward Israel in some of his comments were reminiscent of his father's remarks in the early years of his rule when Hafiz al-Asad was deeply immersed in the confrontation with Israel. Yet Asad Sr. had matured in time and had learned to distinguish between his vision and world view, which rejected Israel's existence out of hand, and the constraints of reality, which obliged him to adopt a balanced and pragmatic policy and led him to the verge of signing a peace agreement with his sworn enemy. This common-sense view was the product of Hafiz al-Asad's long experience with Israel, beginning with his crushing defeat by Israel during the Six Day War, continuing with the October 1973 War (which may be considered an achievement for the Syrians but certainly no victory) and ending with the start of the Lebanese war of 1982, when the Syrians endured a harsh blow by Israel.

Time had moderated Hafiz al-Asad's style, which at first had been infused with anti-Semitism. Bashar, however, lacked his father's experience, and appeared to choose, or perhaps to have been pushed by the outbreak of the Intifada, to begin his role as leader at the same point at which his father had been at the start of his rule, rather than at the point his father had come to at the end of his life, as would have been expected or hoped for.

Undoubtedly, Bashar viewed Israel as a fact, and avoided using the rhetoric that had been widespread in the Arab world during the

1950s and 1960s, replete with exhortations to wipe Israel off the face of the earth and throw its people into the sea. In certain circumstances (although following the outbreak of the Intifada these appeared entirely theoretical), he even seemed to be prepared to reach a peace agreement with Israel. However, his pragmatic strategy toward Israel, including his recognition of the fact of its existence and possibly even of the historic necessity eventually to reach a political settlement with it, obscured several other components of his perception of Israel and the conflict with it, namely:

1. *A rejection of Israel's legitimacy.* Statements by Bashar clearly suggest that, although he was prepared to recognize Israel as an existing fact, basically he continued to reject the legitimacy of its existence in the Middle East, viewing it as an artificial and alien entity in the region, lacking historical roots. The territory on which Israel was established, Bashar claimed, was stolen from the original inhabitants of Palestine, who were dispossessed of their land and driven out of their homes.

   An echo of this perception, which is deeply rooted in Syrian thinking, resonates in the words of the Syrian commentator Fawzi al-Shu'aybi, who explained the Syrian peace policy in Hafiz al-Asad's time, to which Bashar remained committed, thus:

   > As I understand it, the late Asad put his trust in the assumption that in a relatively short time, in 2005 at the latest, the number of Palestinians living in the 1948 territories [the state of Israel prior to the Six Day War] will reach over 50 percent of the population of [Israel] and this will force Israel to see its true face. For the Israeli model is determined by a historical situation that does not promise continuity but rather functions by dint of inertia, on the condition that it does not encounter effective opposition.[6]

   In a similar vein, Majid Shaddud, a member of the regional command of the Ba'th Party, explained in an interview in 2002:

   > There is no possibility of normalization in relations with the Zionist colonialist–settlement entity. For normalization exists between two normal sides, but the Zionist entity, which stole [Palestine] and settled foreigners in place of the original residents of the land, is not a normal entity. This is an irregular situation, such as existed only in South Africa, where the apartheid regime finally collapsed.[7]

2. *Casting doubt on the extent of Israel's desire for and commitment to making peace with the Arabs.* Bashar repeatedly questioned the Israeli gov-

ernment's as well as Israeli society's commitment to peace. In his perception, Israel was an aggressive, expansionist entity with which peace was difficult if not impossible to attain. Notably, Asad Sr. too had perceived Israel in these terms, especially as a result of the lasting imprint of the events of the Six Day War of 1967 and the Lebanese war of 1982. Bashar, for his part, was fixated by the events of the second Intifada and even more so by the results of the Israeli elections in February 2001, which installed Ariel Sharon as prime minister, followed by the elections of January 2003, which left him in place. This was clearly expressed by Bashar, who said in an interview he gave to *al-Safir* in March 2003 during the war in Iraq:

> No one among us trusts Israel, not us in Syria, and not any of our Arab brothers. We expect an attack by Israel anytime; even if it does not threaten to attack us right now, we have to understand that Israel's way is a way of treason, a mentality it has followed ever since it was established. Its existence itself is threatening to us. This is a continuous threat. This is deeply rooted in its actions and nature and, after all, the West formed it so it will be a continuous threat for us.[8]

3. *A recognition of Israel's military superiority and the futility of mounting an all-out war against it, but a belief that the Arabs have the capacity to face down Israel's superiority in this realm by carrying on a limited armed struggle against it, as the Hizballah and the Palestinians successfully demonstrated.* This limited struggle, Bashar maintained, would block Israel from using its full strength, strike at its Achilles heel – its inability to tolerate losses or absorb sustained damage to its inhabitants' standard of living – and therefore force Israel to accept the Arabs' peace dictates.

From Israel's point of view, what was worrisome about this policy was that it was not being conducted, as in the past, by a shrewd and experienced leader, which is what Hafiz al-Asad was, but rather by his son, a young man perceived in Israel and abroad as inexperienced. His generation's experience with Israel was defined by the Hizballah's struggle against it in South Lebanon during the 1980s, during which that organization ultimately routed the Israeli army; and the Palestinians' struggle against Israel during the first Intifada (1987–91). Bashar was thus part of a generation that had not experienced defeat by Israel. Many of these younger Syrians tended to doubt the fundamental assumptions that had guided their parents' generation and led it to the peace process, a process underlain by the preparedness for a historic reconciliation with Israel. Bashar indeed seemed to lack the fear bordering on obsession that characterized his father's attitude to Israel, a fear rooted in the traumas of 1967, 1973 and 1982. Although far from belittling Israel's military strength, Bashar was less agitated than his father about it.

With this, he is to be credited with reading the regional picture more accurately than was assumed in Israel, and especially with a readiness to learn from his errors. For example, he apparently grasped the change undergone by Israeli society following the outbreak of the al-Aqsa Intifada, namely a preparedness and even a determination by Israel to counterattack – a response backed by the Bush administration, especially after the events of September 11, 2001 and the war in Iraq. Indeed, Bashar wisely refrained from involving Syria in a confrontation with Israel during this period.

Bashar's first opportunity to promote his perception of the conflict with Israel came at the Arab leaders' summit of October 2000 in Cairo, convened in the wake of the outbreak of the al-Aqsa Intifada in order to discuss aid to the Palestinians in their struggle with Israel. Vague as it was, Bashar's speech outlined his view, combining a recognition that an overall confrontation with Israel was not in the Arabs' best interest with an explicit appeal to his colleagues to support a limited and indirect confrontation along the lines of the struggles waged by Hizballah and the Palestinians. This, he believed, would enable the Arabs to force the perception of the "peace of the strong" on Israel.

> [After the break of the Intifada] we were asked to be realistic. But let us define realism. What does it mean? There is a person who subdues to reality and there is another one who reads reality accurately; there is another person who changes reality. We call for reading reality accurately and clearly and then for changing this reality. I am not speaking from a theoretical point of view. There is an old–modern experience.
>
> It is the experience of Lebanon… it is no longer a Lebanese experience. It is rather an Arab experience which every one of us has the right to speak about and to be proud of. Israel occupied South Lebanon for 22 years with the objective of expelling the Palestinian resistance from the south or from Lebanon or expelling them in the first stage from north Palestine. In 1982, the Israeli forces invaded Beirut. Then the Palestinian forces went out of Lebanon and later Syria left Beirut. Israel withdrew in retreat. It first went out of Beirut and then from Mount Lebanon. The multinational forces came in and they were driven out by resistance. Meanwhile, the Israeli retreat continued day after day. These calls always told all the people and the resistance in the first place:

What are you doing? This action is unrealistic. The action will yield nothing. You will not be able to affect Israel. You are always scratching, etc. The result was an Israeli defeat in May. It was an achievement which had not been made since the 1973 war... in 1973, the Arab forces reached the depth of the occupied territories. Then they retreated to a certain line as a result of the Israeli counterattack. For the time being, Israel is massing its troops against Lebanon, but I think what happened in May was a real deterrent and that Israel will not repeat this experience once again.

The question is: How did the resistance score this victory in May? Did they reach it by armed force? What had been achieved was not done by weapons but by the power of will and the power of faith. They achieved it by determination to change this reality. They said, let us change reality and then liberate the land. They did not only say, we want to fight. And I believe that what is now happening in Palestine is a message from our brothers: the Palestinians inside the West Bank and inside the 1948 lands of Palestine. It is a message that we got the lesson and that we will work for changing the reality. Therefore, we the Arabs at this summit cannot be in between, either with the killer or with the killed, and we have to define our position.

We can briefly talk about some reasons which produced the situation we have reached.... The word "strategic peace option" is one of the reasons which has led us to the situation we are now in. It is true that we opted for a strategic peace, but this option was not clear cut. The "strategic peace option" means there are other different notions and does not mean only the war or peace options.

There are for example the options for strategic peace, strategic war, strategic force, strategic deterrence and other socioeconomic options. This is not a call for a war but a simple and general analysis. When we opted for a strategic peace, the option was an alternative for the war option we thought of earlier, to liberate our lands. This is true but does peace option mean, a first point, giving up the defense option? The second point is that peace needs force and deterrence. I am not talking about the military element. The force or deterrence has different and various elements. Arab solidarity is the force and deterrence option that can be expressed in terms of a national project.

Hence, we are before different options. The best option is peace with force, i.e. the peace of the strong. Then comes the option for war with force, i.e. the war of the strong. I do not say what we want. The easiest thing is peace with weakness or war with weakness. If we opted for peace let this peace be the peace of the strong. But if we are weak, we cannot say there is an option but rather here is something imposed on us from abroad.[9]

Bashar thus remained committed to his father's legacy of preparedness to hold talks and even reach a peace agreement with Israel, but, in contrast to the past, he insisted that such an agreement be based on Arab power. This represented a clear retreat from the perception of the "peace of the brave" referred to by his father at the conclusion of his summit meeting with President Bill Clinton in Geneva in January 1994, namely:

> Syria wants a just and comprehensive peace with Israel. This desire reflects a strategic choice [by Syria] intended to guarantee the rights of the Arabs and the end of the Israeli occupation, so that the nations in the region will be able to live in peace, in security and in dignity.... We fought with honor, we are conducting negotiations with honor, and we will establish peace with honor.... We are interested in an honorable peace for our people and for the hundreds of thousands who sacrificed their lives to defend the homeland, the nation and Arab rights. There is hardly a home in Syria without sacrifices in the defense of the homeland, the nation and Arab rights. For the sake of all of them, and for their children and families, we want a peace of the brave, a true peace, which will exist and ensure the interests of all, but will also grant each person his right.... If Israel's leaders summon up the courage needed to respond to this peace, a new dawn will burst forth in the region, security and stability will be assured, and we will establish normal peaceful relations between all the nations of the region.[10]

Bashar's hostile statements to Israel continued and even intensified with the escalation of the Intifada, as he repeatedly articulated his view that the problem did not lie in the personality of the Israeli prime minister, Ariel Sharon, or any other prime minister, but in the nature of Israeli society, which was racist, aggressive and expansionist. These statements seemed to reach a climax with the visit of Pope John Paul II to Damascus in May 2001, when Bashar, in his welcoming remarks, pointed to a direct link between the Jews' betrayal of Jesus, their attempts to betray Muhammad, and their current deeds, which, he asserted, proved that the Jewish mentality was that of betrayal:

> We see our brothers in Palestine being killed and tortured and we see that justice is being violated. There are conquered lands in Lebanon, in the Golan and in Palestine. We see them [the Israelis]

acting against the principle of equality and violating it by claiming that Allah distinguished their nation from all others. We also witness that they damage the places holy to Islam and to Christianity in Palestine. They damage the sanctity of the al-Aqsa Mosque, the sanctity of the Church of the Holy Sepulcher, and the Church of the Nativity in Bethlehem. They try to obliterate all the principles of the monotheistic religions with the same mentality by which they betrayed Jesus and tortured him, and in accordance with the same mentality that prompted them to betray the Prophet Muhammad. The meaning of the principle of equality to which we cling is to treat all the other nations not through the prism of emotional complexes or by claiming to be superior; while the meaning of the principle of justice is the restoration of rights to their possessors, the restoration of the land to its owners in Lebanon, Syria and Palestine, as well as the restoration of the refugees' homes to their owners; and lastly the meaning of the principle of love is to stop killing everyone who is an Arab out of a motivation of hatred and to begin to teach the young generation not to hate the other. The meaning of the principle of justice is also to cease falsifying the facts – the facts of our lives today as well as historical facts – and to stop laying claim to rights to a history that has no basis.[11]

Notably, Bashar's address evoked an international storm. The French and American governments promptly denounced his remarks and delivered an official protest to the Syrian government. The Syrians, for their part, expressed surprise at this reaction, which was based, they said, on "a mistaken and erroneous interpretation of Bashar's remarks, ignorance, and a lack of knowledge of the details." According to a Radio Damascus commentator, "President Bashar did not mention Jews in his comments and did not intend to denigrate the followers of the monotheistic religions, but all he sought was to put an end to Israel's aggressiveness."[12] Apparently, Bashar himself, while not retracting his remarks or apologizing for them, took care to moderate his style thereafter in encounters with Western personalities and interviews with the Western media. Questioned during an encounter with French parliamentarians while visiting Paris in June 2001, regarding whether he still stood by his remarks to the Pope, Bashar replied:

In your press, the Western press, I was reported as attacking the Jews. This is mystifying. What do my remarks regarding the torments of Jesus have to do with an attack on the Jews? I speak of Israel, which tortures the Palestinians. I did not mention the word

Jews in my speech. There are Jews in Syria. We have had a Jewish community living in Syria for thousands of years. They are Syrians in every respect. Moreover, we Muslims recognize the Jewish religion because its origin is in one God, exactly like Islam and Christianity, and therefore it is illogical that we would oppose it. I spoke about the torments that people have suffered throughout human history and about the torments that people are suffering today. I was asked whether in my remarks about Jesus I didn't mean the Jews, and I replied that I did not. Are the Germans of today responsible for what their forebears did? If someone commits a crime in some state, does this signify that his sons are responsible for his deed? We do not have this kind of logic, and we in Syria, or anywhere else in the Arab world, do not operate according to such logic. We live in a region known for tolerance displayed by its inhabitants for thousands of years, in which people of all ethnic groups and religions live. Thus, there was nothing abusive about Jews in my speech.[13]

By contrast, in addressing the Syrian or the wider Arab public, not only did Bashar show no moderation on this issue, but he appeared intent on utilizing every opportunity to air extreme anti-Israel sentiment for maximal political and propaganda effect. Furthermore, his addresses to this public reflected the sentiments of the Arab street. If he sought to follow in his father's footsteps, replicating Hafiz al-Asad's vaunted skill at articulating the mood of the Arab street better than any other Arab leader, Bashar achieved his first success.

A further exacerbation of his tone was evident in his address at the Arab summit in Beirut in March 2002. The conference marked the adoption of a Saudi-sponsored peace initiative, while Bashar's speech stood out in its militancy and its justification of the suicide terror attacks in Israeli cities on the grounds that all Israelis are armed, and an attack against any of them constitutes legitimate resistance to the occupation:

> The war of words and idioms [following the September 11, 2001 events] has been a real war and we heard one example today in one of the speeches by one of the guests about the idiom of striking at innocent civilians... this idiom of not striking at innocent civilians is good but not in this case. We are talking about occupation. When you have two warring countries with military battle that is one thing, and when there is occupation that is another thing. The issue here is not an issue of who is a civilian and who is a military. At any rate, the military is a man who has honor but the one who occupies other people's territories cannot be classified as

civil or military; the one who occupies other people's territories is either armed or not armed. This is in general, but in the case of Israel everyone is armed: the settlers are armed as the Israeli army is armed and they took part in killing the Palestinians. They participated in expelling the Palestinian people and in everything also. All the settlements are built as military bases for war, which means that their lives revolve around war and killing.... At any rate the term we adopt is resistance, which is a legal right against occupation. Every occupier is an occupier, and we should not differentiate between armed and non-armed occupier, and resistance is a legitimate right.[14]

Syria and the Hizballah–Israeli confrontation

Hizballah military activity against Israel in the Shab'a farms area along Israel's northern border became a central issue on the Israeli–Syrian agenda from late 2000 onward. Hizballah renewed attacks against Israel on October 7, 2000, after a period of quiet that began with the withdrawal of the Israeli army from South Lebanon in May 2000. On October 7, Hizballah kidnapped three Israeli soldiers, who, it was learned much later, were killed during the kidnapping. Thereafter, the organization mounted attacks against Israel in the Shab'a area once every few weeks throughout 2001, resulting in the killing and wounding of Israeli soldiers.

Israel refrained from responding to these attacks. However, following the change of administration in the country with the election of Ariel Sharon as prime minister, a new policy was adopted. On April 16, 2001, in response to an attack on Israeli army posts in the Shab'a area, during which an Israeli soldier was killed, Israeli aircraft attacked and destroyed a Syrian radar station in the Dahr al-Baydar area of Mount Lebanon, killing four Syrian soldiers at the station. The Israeli retaliation evoked fears of an armed confrontation between Israel and Syria, as the widespread assumption was that Syria, or Hizballah, would counterattack, leading to a possible escalation of the situation to a regional war.[15]

This was the first frontal military confrontation between Israel and Syria since November 1985, when a Syrian fighter plane that mistakenly approached an Israeli fighter plane carrying out surveillance over Lebanon was downed north of Damascus by the Israeli air force. The last time Israel had attacked Syrian military targets in Lebanon was in June 1982 during the Peace for Galilee War.

Responding to another Hizballah attack on Israeli army posts in the Shab'a area, Israel attacked a second Syrian radar station, at Riyaq in the Lebanese Biqa', on July 1, 2001. This move once again evoked concern that Bashar would feel compelled to retaliate. Indeed, reports from Syria cited pressure on Bashar from his army to do exactly that. However, it was Hizballah that responded with an attack on Israeli posts in the Shab'a area, sparing the Syrians the need to react. The Syrians meanwhile contented themselves with defiant pronouncements that Israel had erred badly and would pay dearly for it, that Syria retained the right to respond at a time and place of its choosing and that it would not sit idly by for long in light of Israel's aggression.[16]

In any event, immediately after the Israeli army's withdrawal in May 2000 from the security zone it had created in Lebanon, Hizballah had taken control of the entire Lebanese–Israeli border area militarily, politically and administratively, effectively blocking the deployment of Lebanese military and police forces there. All this took place with Syrian backing and with a resigned silence on the part of the Lebanese government, for lack of any alternative. Under the aegis of the period of calm that followed, primarily because Israel did not want to give the Hizballah any pretext to renew its aggression, that organization built up an impressive military presence along the border, which included reconnaissance and surveillance backed by military forces deployed throughout South Lebanon. The most worrisome aspect of this development, from Israel's point of view, was the positioning of katyusha missiles and advanced Iranian-produced Al-Fajr rockets with a range of up to 75 kilometers, capable of reaching all of northern Israel as far south as the outskirts of Hadera.

Bashar, for his part, avoided restraining Hizballah moves against Israel, explaining repeatedly:

> It is not the Syrian army's task to prevent [Hizballah from acting against Israel]. Fundamentally, Syria is convinced that Hizballah is doing the right thing and that it constitutes resistance aimed at bringing about the restoration of the occupied lands. With this, we keep explaining that we do not direct or control Hizballah activity, and make no decisions whatsoever in these matters. It is Hizballah that makes this type of decision, which also means that we have no responsibility for any activity it carries out. Hizballah is a Lebanese resistance organization, although we stand by it politically and morally, and in any event it is not in need of material assistance from us.[17]

Hizballah escalated its anti-Israel activity during March and April 2002 in light of Operation Defensive Shield mounted by the Israelis in the West Bank. The escalation evoked renewed fear of a flareup along Israel's northern border that would involve Syria too. According to Israeli sources, Israel planned to bombard Syrian military targets in Lebanon and in Syria itself, but the attack was not implemented for lack of broad support for it in the government.[18] Following several tense weeks, relative calm was restored along the Israeli–Lebanese border, although not necessarily of Syria's doing. Rather, it was Iran, and possibly Hizballah itself. Indeed, despite claims by some analysts that Bashar used his full weight to persuade Hizballah to rein in its anti-Israel activity, Israeli sources reported that the Syrians transferred advanced long-range (20-kilometer) missiles to Hizballah in order to improve the organization's military capacity vis-à-vis Israel. Bashar's motivation for this step is unclear, although analysts agreed that by transforming this advanced equipment the Syrians sent to the Hizballah a message of encouragement to keep up the organization's anti-Israel harassment.[19] Bashar's pattern of conduct seemed to replicate his disregard of, or perhaps encouragement of, Saddam Husayn when the Iraqi ruler dispatched expeditionary forces to the Syrian–Iraqi border in late 2000 as part of an attempt to send a threatening message to Israel. Conceivably, Bashar viewed that Iraqi move as potentially reinforcing Syria vis-à-vis Israel, although he evidently ignored the long-term implications of it for Syrian–Iraqi relations or for his relations with the Gulf states, with Israel and with the U.S.[20]

To many Israelis, the situation in the Middle East in the wake of the second Palestinian Intifada, and following the renewal of Hizballah aggression along the northern border, was reminiscent of that on the eve of the Six Day War. In 1967, it had been the Syrians who declared a "people's liberation war" against Israel, and in this context dispatched Fath forces under the leadership of Yasir 'Arafat to Israeli territory to perpetrate acts of terror. The widespread perception in the Arab world then was that Israel was struggling unsuccessfully with this terrorist challenge. This perception led to an image of Israel's deterrent capability as weakened, ultimately resulting in the Six Day War – a war that no one foresaw and no one wanted, even the Syrians themselves. The fear in Israel in late 2000 and thereafter was that Bashar was trying to take the same road (or might find himself on it unwittingly) which Syria's rulers, including his father, had taken 30 years earlier.

A point that bears emphasizing in this context is that, for the first time in the history of the Israeli–Arab conflict, the Arabs had created a "balance of fear" with the Israelis by virtue of the nonconventional weapons capability of several of the Arab states. These included Syria, which had chemical and biological weapons along with ground-to-ground missiles with a range that reached most of Israel's territory, as well as chemical and biological weapons, and Iran, which was gradually nearing nuclear armament capability. Moreover, Hizballah was supplied by Iran with missiles thought by Israeli sources to have a range that covered all of northern Israel, as discussed above. Apparently, these new capabilities also contributed to Bashar's indifference when he was requested by Israel in late 2000 to restrain Hizballah. Reportedly, Bashar replied that Syria was not afraid of Israel and that it could deal with Israel inter alia by means of the missiles in its possession.[21]

The disappointment in Israel with Bashar in terms of his inflammatory anti-Israel rhetoric, his unwillingness to soften Syria's stance in its negotiations with Israel, and his readiness to tolerate and even encourage Hizballah activity against Israel evoked a shift in the Israeli approach to him. The initial praise for the smooth transfer of rule to Bashar and his rapid integration in the governmental sphere was replaced by derision about his inexperience, impulsiveness and immaturity. The title "The Imaginary Doctor" which headlined an article about him in the Israeli press, hinting that some in the Israeli intelligence community doubted the authenticity of Bashar's medical title, and reports that he had no control whatsoever over events in Syria and devoted most of his time to computer games in his palace,[22] indicated this change.

Still, despite his verbal aggressiveness, in practice Bashar took care to avoid taking any step against Israel, a policy his father had followed faithfully. Another possible contributing factor to this policy was the retention of his father's political and military old guard during his first years in office. Conceivably, Bashar himself had arrived at the conclusion that he had best tread cautiously in regard to Israel, especially after the events of September 11, 2001. Indeed, he refrained from any response to the Israeli attacks on Syrian installations in Lebanon in 2001, despite threats by senior Syrian officials, including Bashar himself, to take revenge on Israel at the time and place of Syria's choosing.

Moreover, Syria refrained from closing the door entirely on the peace talks with Israel, reiterating, albeit primarily to Western audiences, that peace remained the favored option, and that its implementation depended on Israel's preparedness to respond to accept Syria's territorial claims. The attainment of a peace agreement, Bashar explained, was possible even with Ariel Sharon. In fact, just before Sharon took office in March 2001, Bashar related in an interview, the newly elected Israeli prime minister sent a special envoy to Damascus with a proposal to begin secret talks with the aim of advancing the peace process on the Syrian track. Bashar said he informed the envoy that Syria rejected Sharon's proposal, for its aim was only to maneuver between the Syrian and Palestinian tracks. He emphasized that he opposed all efforts by Israel to jeopardize the Palestinian track, and that Syria would not agree to resolve the problem of the Golan Heights before the problem of Palestine, including the issue of Jerusalem, was resolved.[23]

The events of September 11, 2001 forced Syria into a defensive position regionally and internationally. The Syrians' primary fear was the negative fallout aimed at Damascus in light of accusations by Washington that it aided and hosted Palestinian terrorist organizations. Syria behaved cautiously in early 2002, as reflected in a series of reports from Damascus ostensibly showing that Syria was prepared to lessen its support for the Palestinian rejectionist organizations. Syrian Foreign Minister Faruk al-Shar' told reporters that "the resistance should take a break from time to time,"[24] a hint that Syria would restrain the activity of those organizations operating in its territory. Later on, however, the Syrians permitted Hizballah to escalate the situation along Israel's border, while at the same time acquiescing to the Saudi peace initiative of March 2002, led by Saudi Crown Prince 'Abdallah. This initiative presented a problem for Bashar, for the Syrians suspected that it was a move intended to promote the Israeli–Palestinian peace talks at the expense of Syria, prompting a reworded version to pacify Damascus. Syria's support for the initiative was often described by Western analysts as subdued and unenthusiastic.

Moreover, during his visit to Britain in December 2002, Bashar stated in a closed meeting with British academics:

> I have a message for the Israelis. We are interested in peace. The Israelis must choose [in their forthcoming elections] between a candidate interested in peace and another who wants war. Some people try to explain and justify [Israel's acts] as stemming from fear. But this explanation is unacceptable. The Israelis are not children and they must decide which path they want to take. We, for our part, are interested in reaching a solution to the certainty that people are killed there every day.... The Arab peace plan is clear. It proposes peace and normal relations (*'alakat tabi'iyya*) to Israel on condition that it [Israel] withdraws to the 1967 border.[25]

A point that bears emphasizing is that side by side with Bashar's declared readiness to renew the talks with Israel at any time was a perceptible hardening of the Syrian position on two key issues. One was a tightening of the link between the Syrian track and the Palestinian track, making any progress on the Syrian track conditional on the termination of the Intifada – clear evidence of the imprint of the Intifada on the Syrian public. The second issue was Syria's demand to reassess the political process before renewing it, so as to initiate a new process that would yield results and not end in disillusionment like its predecessor after a decade of sterile discussions.

The conquest of Iraq by the United States elicited a measure of change in Syria's posture in recognition of the new reality in the region. This was reflected in such statements by Bashar as:

> We know that Israel is supported by the United States and that all its arsenals are open to [Israel]. This occurs at a time when the Soviet Union is no longer at our side. The world power balance has changed. Therefore, [a strategic military balance between us and Israel] is no longer on the agenda.... We must strive for an [Arab–Israeli] balance of power. No single Arab country can establish a balance of power, however limited, with Israel. Additionally, the problem is not military. I believe that the graver problem is the question of a balance of power in its broad sense: economic, technological, social and other. We must strive for this kind of balance of power with Israel, and of course Syria cannot attain it alone.[26]

Responding to the threat conveyed by the Americans to Damascus through their policy on the Iraqi issue, the Syrians at first moderated their stance on the conflict with Israel and signaled their willingness to renew the stalled peace talks. Moreover, while at the beginning of 2003 Syria did not hide its pronounced opposition to the "road map" drawn up by Washington with several partners, this opposition soon turned into silent agreement or, as Syrian President Bashar al-Asad put it: "We neither support nor oppose the road map, but what we do not understand is why a road map has not been drawn up [that includes] Syria and Lebanon [in the peace process] as well."[27] Israel reported receiving Syrian signals conveyed by the president's brother Mahir that Damascus wanted to resume talks with it, a report promptly denied by Syria.[28] Washington, however, refrained from including Syria in the road map it presented in June 2003, making it clear that only when real progress was attained in the Israeli–Palestinian talks would the prospect of including Syria in the process be discussed, and even then on condition that Damascus fulfill Washington's demands in a long list of areas.

In the event, the American entanglement in Iraq, alongside difficulties in making progress with the road map, restored the Syrians' self-confidence and stiffened their stance on Israel. Relations between Syria and Israel deteriorated further toward the end of 2003. In August of that year, Israel air force planes overflew Bashar al-

Asad's palace at the seaside city of Ladhiqiyya to convey a warning to the Syrian president to rein in Hizballah attacks along the Israeli–Lebanese border.[29] More significantly, Israeli air force planes attacked a training camp used by several Palestinian militant factions near the 'Ayn Sahab refugee camp a few miles north of Damascus. The Israeli attack – the first on Syrian soil since the end of the Yom Kippur War over 30 years previously – was a response to a suicide bombing in Haifa by the Islamic Jihad, in which 22 Israelis were killed. According to Israeli sources, the attack was meant to send a message to Damascus, where the headquarters of the Islamic Jihad and of its leader, Ramadan Shallah, was located, to halt its support of the Palestinian terrorist organizations. These sources pointed out that, following Israel's decision in principle in September 2003 to expel Yasir 'Arafat, thereby deterring his organization, the Fath, from carrying out terrorist attacks against Israel, and after a balance of fear had been achieved between Israel and Hamas in light of Israel's attempts to eliminate the leaders of that organization, Israel was trying to attain a similar balance of fear with the Islamic Jihad.[30]

Syria, however, perceived the attack as part of an overall Israeli–American move to destabilize and possibly bring down the regime in Damascus. The Syrians promptly lodged a complaint with the U.N. Security Council over the Israeli attack, but came up against a firm American refusal to censure Israel for the move, while blaming Damascus for the deteriorating situation in the region. In response, Hizballah mounted an attack against Israeli forces, during which an Israeli soldier was killed. This failed to ease the situation of the Syrian regime, which apparently was criticized sharply at home for its helplessness against Israel.[31]

For the first time, threats emanated from Damascus that, should Syria be attacked by Israel again, it would respond and not sit idly by as in the past. Foreign Minister Shar' warned: "The Syrian people are not prepared to disregard further attacks against Syria, and the government of Syria is usually attentive to the feelings of the public in the country. Syria holds many retaliatory cards, such as [attacking] the settlements spread out in the Golan Heights."[32] Although Information Minister Ahmad al-Hasan issued a clarification of Shar's remarks, which, he said, were "part of an informal interview [and were] taken out of context," Shar's comments, like other statements heard in Damascus, reflected the regime decision to respond to any future Israeli attack against Syria.[33]

Syria's problematic situation prompted Damascus to try to renew the peace talks with Israel toward the end of 2003 in an effort to improve its image in the West and especially in Washington. Granting an interview to the *New York Times* in December 2003, Bashar al-Asad announced his wish to resume the talks and his preparedness to establish normal relations with Israel. Notably, his father, Hafiz al-Asad, had consistently refrained from using the term "normalization," which was widely associated with the Israeli–Egyptian peace agreement he had criticized so vociferously. Bashar, replying to a question about his perception of the kind of relationship he envisioned should a peace agreement be concluded between both countries, stated benignly:

> I mean normal relations. This word ["normalization"] has no limit. Normalization means like the relations between Syria and the United States. One day is good. The other day is bad. It is like the relations between Syria and France; and like the relations between Syria and other countries with whom it is not at war. In the 1980s we had some problems with the UK and we cut our relations. So when you talk about normalization, it is very wide. You may have warm or cold relations.
>
> [As for the relation between the people] that takes time. It will happen but it takes time. This is the difference. Between the governments it is a matter of signatures on some procedure. But between the peoples it takes time and it depends on the will. Let me talk about the Syrians and I can talk on behalf of the others. As a Syrian who lives among the Syrians and represents them, I can tell you that the Syrians always look for peace in different circumstances. Now we are in the worst situation regarding peace but they still look for peace. If you don't have hatred, there is no problem. That is why I can say I am always optimistic about peace even if there is no indication of peace like I told you at the beginning. But this is the only option that everybody in this region has. I am very optimistic after the peace is signed. If it is a just and comprehensive peace there will be no problem. Everything you are asking about will be real.[34]

This announcement evoked a debate in Israel between those who viewed it as a reflection of Bashar's readiness to make peace with Israel, even if this stemmed from his desire to survive in power in light of his problematic situation, and those who viewed his remarks as a tactical public relations move aimed primarily at the American administration, lacking any real substance. The Syrians, for their part, did not ease the position of advocates of the "Syrian option" in Israeli public opinion, and typically refrained from any show of public diplomacy, a lacuna that in the past was a contributing factor to the failure of efforts to create a climate for an Israeli–Syrian peace. The messages directed by the Syrians at Israel continued to be aggressive, mainly in their insistence on an Israeli withdrawal to the June 4, 1967 lines as a precondition for the resumption of the peace talks. Moreover, an invitation by Israeli President Moshe Katzav to Bashar al-Asad to visit Jerusalem, as Anwar al-Sadat had done in his day, was flatly rejected.[35] In the event, Israeli Prime Minister Ariel Sharon, too, appeared far from enthusiastic about renewing talks with Syria. According to his close aides, he was unprepared to pay the price of withdrawal from the Golan Heights for peace with Syria. Israeli reports also indicated that, side by side with Syrian hints at peace, the Syrians continued to aid the arming of Hizballah, using the same aircraft they sent to Tehran to deliver supplies to the victims of the earthquake in Iran in January 2004 to bring back advanced weaponry for Hizballah.[36]

Thus, since early 2004, against the background of the worsening of relations between Syria and the U.S., Bashar al-Asad began sending signals of his readiness to renew peace negotiations with Israel with no preconditions. These signals were sent mostly through various emissaries who visited Bashar's palace, for example Martin Indyk, who visited Damascus in September 2004, and Terje Roed-Larssen, who met Bashar in November 2004.[37] However, these signals elicited shrugged shoulders both in Jerusalem and in Washington. Nor was any attention paid to a historic decision adopted by the command of the National Progressive Front in Syria, headed by the Ba'th Party, deleting from its platform Article no. 6, which stated that there would be no peace or negotiations with the Zionist entity, replacing it with a much softer formula calling for the liberation of the Arab territories occupied by Israel in June 1967.[38]

In Israel it was pointed out that, alongside their peace signals, mostly inarticulate and hesitant, Syria continued granting assistance to the Palestinian terror organizations operating out of Damascus as well as to Hizballah. In the summer of 2004, Israel even made an attempt on the life of the senior Hamas figure in Damascus, 'Izz al-din Khalil, an event which once more directed the spotlight on Syria's involvement in terror.[39] Israeli sources also indicated that the instruction for Islamic Jihad activists to launch an attack in Tel Aviv in February 2005, after a cease-fire was declared between Israel and the Palestinian organizations, came from the headquarters of the organization in Damascus. The headquarters had been closed long ago by the Syrians, at least according to Syrian sources.[40]

Thus, Bashar's overtures were seen in Israel as insufficient in depth and courage. Even when Israeli President Moshe Katzav shook hands with Bashar for the first time in history, when the two attended the funeral of Pope John Paul II in Rome in April 2005, the Syrians were quick to deny the handshake, and later dismissed it as a routine procedure during such a funeral, hinting that Bashar did not recognize Katzav at all.[41]

One way or the other, the unwillingness in Jerusalem, and even more so in Washington, to throw Bashar a life-line, and simultaneously the unwillingness in Damascus to initiate a substantive negotiation process, resulted in the demise of the Syrian initiative, if indeed there was one, to renew talks with Israel.

Summary

Six years after the passing of Hafiz al-Asad and the ascent of his son Bashar to power, and approximately five years after the outbreak of the al-Aqsa Intifada, Syria still appeared to be committed to the peace process as the preferred route to achieve its goals. Moreover, the gaps between the positions of the sides – Syria and Israel – had not widened and in fact remained surprisingly narrow, i.e. focused on the Syrian demand for an Israeli withdrawal to the June 4, 1967 lines. Nevertheless, it appeared that both states, and especially their leaders, still had a long road to travel, with many stations along the way, before they could renew the talks between them, for the following reasons:

1. *Bashar's need to secure his status as his country's ruler.* So long as Bashar did not feel his rule to be stable, his ability to promote a concrete process with Israel, let alone sign a peace agreement, was doubtful. The Israeli–Arab peace process had never been a source of support or popularity for those Arab leaders who promoted it for personal or political reasons despite negative public opinion in their countries. Bashar, therefore, was likely to respond to American pressure to renew the talks with Israel and thereby project a moderate attitude toward Israel, but the prospect of his reaching the moment of decision before he felt his own status to be secure was doubtful.

2. *Bashar's personal maturity as a leader – a necessary condition to promoting the Israeli–Syrian talks.* Bashar's moves, and especially his pronouncements, during the first years of his rule did not signal an ability to adopt a realistic or pragmatic policy unaffected by emotion or youthful impulsiveness. His late father, too, required a similar maturation process before he was ready to embark on peace talks with Israel.

3. *The attainment of regional calm, and especially the renewal of the Palestinian–Israeli talks, so as to end the violence and neutralize the poisoned atmosphere in the region.* The resumption of these talks could grant

Syria the needed legitimation to renew its own talks with Israel and perhaps even reach a separate peace agreement with it, thereby breaking up the Arab rejectionist front that Syria itself sought to establish.

Notably, the Oslo Accords had served as a pretext for Asad Sr. to explain his readiness (which had actually evolved previously) to move toward peace with Israel. Bashar, too, had undergone a similar transformation. Asked in an interview with a Spanish newspaper in early 2001 whether he thought that the refusal by the Arab world to accept the U.N. decision to partition Palestine in 1947 wasn't a mistake, he replied:

> You cannot determine that it was a mistake at that time. The world partitioned Palestine without seeking the opinion of the Arabs. The world believed that it could force a fait accompli on the Arabs. But we are talking about what is happening now, and not about the past, that is, the period that started in the wake of the peace process begun in Madrid. For from the start of the peace process, everyone agrees − that is, we and the international community − on a certain perception of how this process will be conducted. There is no point in returning to the past, for dealing with the past is a difficult matter for all of us.[42]

With this, the fact that Bashar repeatedly expressed a deeply felt commitment to the idea of the Syrian territorial state might indicate that he had the capability, as Asad had in his time, of initiating a "Syria first" policy with the goal of promoting Syrian state interests even at the expense of pan-Arab ones.

4. *An Israeli dialogue partner prepared to accept the Syrian demand for a complete withdrawal from the Golan Heights back to the June 4, 1967 lines (i.e. back to the eastern shore of the Sea of Galilee).* This demand became a sine qua non for Damascus, with the Syrians' determination to achieve it undoubtedly reinforced by the responsiveness of a series of Israeli leaders in the past, however indirectly and noncommittally, to consider it. The Israeli government under Ariel Sharon seemed, however, not interested in conducting any peace negotiations with Syria which might lead to Israeli withdrawal from the Golan Heights.

It should be mentioned in this connection that throughout the 1990s there were clear signs of Israel's desire or even enthusiasm to promote the peace process for a number of reasons. First, there was Israel's fear of a surprise Syrian attack on the Golan Heights (marauding), considered to be a definite possibility in Israel at that time.

Thus Israel wanted to remove this threat by negotiating with Syria. Second, Israel wanted to stop the continuous spilling of its soldiers' blood in South Lebanon, where the Israeli army was engaged in a long battle with Hizballah. As is known, this organization enjoyed the assistance and backing of the Syrians, who openly used it as a bargaining chip against Israel. Third, Israel hoped, despite everything and when all was said and done, to enjoy some political and economic gains, mainly the normalization of relations with the Arab world, first and foremost with Syria itself, through a peace agreement with that country. Finally, Israel hoped that by promoting negotiations with Syria it could improve its bargaining position in negotiations with the Palestinians.

However, with the passage of time and especially in the wake of the conquest of Iraq by the United States, Israel's desire to promote negotiations with Syria diminished. Firstly, the Syrian army was getting progressively weaker as time went by, in addition to which the technological and qualitative gap between it and the Israeli army also widened. The presence of American military forces on Syria's eastern border reduced even further Syria's options for action and thus the option that Syria would launch a war against Israel was no longer a concern for Israel. Secondly, while Israel's withdrawal from South Lebanon did not solve the Hizballah issue, it did diminish the urgency of its threat in Israeli public opinion. Thirdly, Israel no longer expected to reap political or economic advantages from an Israeli–Syrian peace agreement; it was clear to everyone that it would enjoy only limited advantages, if at all. Finally, it transpired that the Syrian track did not necessarily influence what was happening on the Palestinian track.

Moreover, even the American administration, a key player in promoting the peace process, does not appear to be overly enthusiastic about lending the full measure of its weight to the promotion of Syrian–Israeli peace. In the 1990s the Americans believed that a solution to the Israeli–Syrian conflict would lead to the solution of the other issues relating to Washington's problems with Damascus, including Syria's support for terrorism. However, in the wake of September 11 and especially after the war in Iraq in spring 2003, the American administration changed its attitude toward Syria. It views the question of Syria's support of terrorism as an American–Syrian problem relating to the national security of the United States. Furthermore, the Americans are not interested in promoting their relations with the Syrian regime, which they view as a threat and as one of a series of evil regimes worthy of being reviled and not showered with favors, totally unlike the manner in which the Americans regarded the regime in Damascus in the early 1990s after the Gulf War, when Syria was viewed as a potential ally of the United States. Indeed, it was President Bush who declared in early 2005 that Bashar was no better then Yasir 'Arafat and therefore should not be trusted.[43] The conclusion many analysts drew from this statement was that the U.S. was actually opposing any resumption of the Syrian–Israeli peace talks.

Conceivably, the conditions outlined above could develop, thereby permitting both sides to return to their negotiating positions of December 1999, i.e. at the brink of readiness to attain peace, from which both Israel and Syria had retreated to hostility bordering on the prospect of war. A comment by Bashar's wife, Asma, in an interview with the *Observer* in December 2002 shows that such a possibility was not out of the question. Asked about the challenge of raising the couple's son Hafiz under the constant threat of war, she replied as any mother raising children in the region, whether Arab or Israeli, would: "This is part of our life, it exists, but we ask ourselves how much longer we will have to live this way and how can we ensure that we will continue to move forward."[44]

CHAPTER 8

Syria in Lebanon – the end of an era?

An end that constitutes a beginning

On April 26, 2005, the last of the Syrian troops left Lebanese soil, thereby ending Syria's 29-year military presence there. The withdrawal of the Syrian forces from Lebanon was announced by Bashar al-Asad in an unusual address to the Syrian People's Assembly on March 5, 2005. Bashar explained in the speech that the withdrawal was simply a direct and logical extension of the policy he had followed regarding the Lebanese question ever since his accession to the leadership of Syria, and that it was an independent Syrian decision which served both Syria's and Lebanon's interests.[1] However, it was clear to the entire audience that the withdrawal of the Syrian forces from Lebanon was a desperate move made under international, and even Lebanese, pressure, and was aimed at preserving the Syrian regime in Damascus at the price of relinquishing Lebanon.

Indeed, a series of Syrian errors had led to the expulsion of Syria from Lebanon. First and foremost was the decision by Damascus in September 2004 to force an extension of Lebanese President Emile Lahhud's term of office, a step that evoked U.N. Security Council Resolution 1559 calling for the withdrawal of the Syrian forces from Lebanon. The next crisis was the assassination of Lebanese Prime Minister Rafiq al-Hariri in February 2005. Even if the Syrians were not directly responsible for the murder, the opinion in Lebanon was that they were involved in it. The assassination aroused unprecedented agitation in Lebanon, resulting in international pressure on Syria to leave.[2]

The withdrawal of the Syrian forces prompted debate over whether Syria would be able to maintain its influence in Lebanon even without a military presence there. Bashar al-Asad himself announced explicitly that Syria would continue to play a role in Lebanon, and that no one could prevent it from doing so.[3] Yet perhaps the most telling response to this question was demonstrated by the Lebanese crowds who rushed into the streets throughout the country to pull down and destroy the symbols of Syria's presence. First and foremost, they destroyed statues of Hafiz al-Asad and his dead son, Basil, smashing and removing them from their pedestals, along with portraits, signs and memorial plaques.[4]

These scenes appeared to be persuasive evidence that the Syrian era in Lebanon had indeed ended once and for all, underscoring the question all the more acutely of how Lebanon had slipped away from Syria's grasp. Damascus's errors in Lebanon during the year preceding the withdrawal account for this development only partially, for three other factors were also involved: Israel's withdrawal from South Lebanon in May 2000; the deterioration in relations between Damascus and Washington with the start of the war in Iraq in the spring of 2003; and, most saliently, the passing of Hafiz al-Asad in June 2000, which ushered in the end of an era in the history of the two countries, Syria and Lebanon.

Hafiz al-Asad's legacy

The telephone conversation between the presidents of Syria and Lebanon, Hafiz al-Asad and Emile Lahhud, on Saturday morning, June 10, 2000, was hardly unusual. Both leaders talked with each other frequently, as behooved their close alliance and, it may be said, the total dependence of the Lebanese president and his government on their patron in Damascus. That particular conversation, however, ended uncharacteristically and unexpectedly, as described later by Emile Lahhud:

> We talked about the situation in the region, about the issues of concern to Syria and Lebanon, and, of course, we extolled the victory we attained in the struggle for the liberation of South Lebanon. The last sentence that President Asad managed to say to me was that we must guarantee a better future for our children and leave them a much better reality, upon our passing, than that which we had received. However, having said this, he was suddenly silent, and immediately thereafter the conversation was cut off. A little later, I learned that he had turned over command to his son Bashar, and that I had been privileged to be the last person to speak with him the moment before his death.[5]

The fact that Hafiz al-Asad died while dealing with Lebanese affairs was symbolic, for the co-option of Lebanon into Syria's sphere of influence, and even more so its transformation into a protectorate responsive to the dictates of Damascus, constituted the outstanding, and in effect sole, achievement of the Syrian president's foreign policy during his prolonged rule.

Whether, as was often claimed, Asad sought to promote or even realize the vision of a "Greater Syria" – the vision of establishing a Syrian sphere of influence and control, or even a political entity stretching over the ancient lands of *bilad al-sha'm* (the Syrian Lands), which would include Lebanon, Jordan and the Palestinians – or whether all he wanted was to promote Syrian political interests in Lebanon is irrelevant. The fact is that he was able, in the wake of the outbreak of civil war in Lebanon in April 1975, and later in the wake of Israel's failed intervention in that country in the summer of 1982, to exploit the golden opportunity that came his way to impose his control over Lebanon, Syria's backyard, or perhaps its front gate. Asad was able to end the bloody civil war in Lebanon, which lasted a decade and a half (1975–89), rehabilitate Lebanon's political system and governmental institutions, which had been paralyzed throughout the war, and breathe new life into the country after it was long perceived as moribund. These achievements allowed him to turn Lebanon into a client state, under Syria's full control, and reap political, security and especially economic benefits from Damascus's extensive investment in it.

This accomplishment was not self-evident. During the first years following the entry of Syrian forces into Lebanon in June 1976, Syria's involvement in Lebanese affairs did not appear to be productive. Instead of extracting Lebanon from the civil war raging within it, and exerting control over Lebanon from Damascus, Syria seemed to be sinking into the Lebanese morass, as had many other invading forces in that country in the past. Several factors accounted for this state of stagnation.

First, Damascus had difficulty recruiting a majority of the power bases in Lebanon to its side. Most of the Lebanese regarded (and continue to regard) Syria's hegemonic ambitions in Lebanon with suspicion. Notably, the Syrian forces that entered Lebanon in June 1976 did so at the request of the then president of Lebanon, Sulayman Franjiyya, a friend and ally of Hafiz al-Asad. Franjiyya, backed at the time by the heads of the Christian camp in Lebanon, hoped that the Syrians would be able to force a cease-fire on the warring hawks and thereby rescue the Christians, who were at the brink of a military defeat by their rivals. However, the Syrian forces met with strong resistance by a broad coalition that included the P.L.O., leftist elements, and Sunni and Druze forces, who were able to block the advance of the Syrian troops and prevent them from taking control of Lebanon in its entirety. Significantly, even the Christians, who ostensibly were being aided by the Syrians, changed their minds in midstream, turned their backs on Damascus and linked up with

Israel. It took Syria more than ten years to take control of most of the centers of power in Lebanon, Muslim and Christian alike, and only after these elements had been worn down by the prolonged, bloody civil war and had no other alternative but to submit to the dictates of Damascus.[6]

Secondly, from the late 1970s to the early 1980s (1977–82), Syria waged a struggle with Israel over control of Lebanon. Israel wanted to supplant Syria in that country, a step that posed a strategic threat to Syria's status in the region as well as to the stability of the Ba'th regime at home. The confrontation between Israel and Syria reached a climax with the Israeli invasion of Lebanon in June 1982 when the Israeli army dealt a severe blow to the Syrian forces deployed there. The Israelis reached the Beirut–Damascus road, brought about the election of Israel's ally in Lebanon, Bashir Jumayyil, as president, and ultimately forced the P.L.O. and the Syrian forces to evacuate Beirut. However, the Syrian-sponsored assassination of Jumayyil in September 1982 caused the collapse of the "new order" which Israel hoped to establish in Lebanon, and a peace agreement signed by the Israeli and Lebanese governments on May 17, 1983 soon became a dead letter. Under pressure from a wave of terror led by the radical Shi'ite Hizballah organization, which burst on to the Lebanese scene in 1983, Israel began an exodus from Lebanon. Its retreat was completed in September 1985, except for a security strip that Israel held in South Lebanon until May 2000.[7]

Thirdly, Syria faced international intervention on the Lebanese issue, primarily by the United States, which aimed to remove it from that state. Following the Israeli withdrawal from the Lebanese capital, a multinational force was dispatched to Beirut in the summer of 1982, consisting of American, French and Italian troops. Presumably, the American administration under Ronald Reagan sought to replicate the step taken by Dwight Eisenhower in July 1958 when he sent U.S. marines to the Lebanese capital, thereby ending the civil war there at that time. However, Lebanon in the 1980s was a different country from that encountered by the American soldiers in the summer of 1958. As if to demonstrate this difference, Hizballah suicide bombers blew themselves up at the American Embassy compound in Beirut and thereafter at the marines' headquarters in the city, in April and in October 1983, possibly with the encouragement or at the very least the knowledge of the Syrians, causing hundreds of civilian and American military fatalities. These attacks, followed by additional ones perpetrated by Hizballah against the Americans and the French, led to the withdrawal of the entire multinational force from Lebanon, leaving the Lebanese arena under the sole control of Damascus.[8]

From the mid-1980s onward, therefore, Syria was the only force in Lebanon. Having learned from the failure of its intervention in the latter part of the 1970s, Damascus now moved cautiously and patiently to realize its long-range goal: the full subjection of Beirut to its dictates. This time, it accomplished its aim rapidly, with the signing of the Ta'if agreement by all Lebanon's communal leaders on October 22, 1989. The agreement, which ended the civil war, also enabled the start of a process of rehabilitation in Lebanon along lines laid out by Syria and under its supervision and control.[9]

The Ta'if agreement constituted an updated and expanded version of the National Charter of 1943, this time formalized by signatories. It included a series of reforms in the format of the Lebanese governmental system, such as reducing the authority of the Maronite president and equalizing his status to that of the Sunni prime minister and the Shi'ite parliamentary speaker, and enlarging the parliament and instituting numerical parity between Christian and Muslim delegates. The agreement also stipulated that the scope of the Syrian forces deployed in Lebanon would be determined in coordination and with the agreement of both countries and that, within two years at the latest from the implementation of the constitutional reforms in the agreement, the Syrian forces would withdraw from Beirut and deploy in the Lebanese Biqa'.

Underlying the agreement was a recognition by the leaders of the Lebanese communities, especially the Maronite and Sunni communities, that the continuation of the civil war not only did not serve their communal and personal interests, but was liable to threaten these interests. Undoubtedly, the threat posed by the Shi'ite community to the Maronites and Sunnites contributed to this awareness. The threat stemmed not only from the military superiority of the Shi'ite militias, and especially from Hizballah, which had become their ally, but more importantly from the demographic reality that the Shi'ites had become the largest community in the country. According to various estimates, the Shi'ites constituted approximately 40 percent or more of the population in the late 1990s, in contrast to the last census (1932) figure of 18 percent.

The signing of the Ta'if agreement was followed by the rehabilitation of Lebanon's political system and governmental bodies. Presidential elections were held in 1989 (and again in 1995 and 1998); parliamentary elections were held in 1992 (and again in 1996 and 2000); and elections to local councils were held in 1998 for the first time in 35 years. The reform of governmental bodies led to a surprising revival of the state. Although Hizballah, based in South Lebanon, continued to attack Israel, with the consent of the Syrians, order and stability were restored in the rest of the country, and the Lebanese resumed their lives almost as if they had not been caught up in a bloody war in which communities attacked and massacred each other for over a decade.

This rehabilitative process took place under the complete supervision of Syria. As if to assure their special authoritative status in Lebanon, the Syrians initiated an agreement of "brotherhood, cooperation and coordination" between the two states. Signed on May 22, 1991, the agreement granted legitimation and a formal status to the Syrian presence in Lebanon and to Damascus's growing involvement in Lebanon's domestic affairs.[10]

With the rejuvenation of its political system during the 1990s, Lebanon shifted from constituting a burden for Syria to becoming a worthwhile investment, in several areas:

Political benefits. Lebanon obediently followed Damascus's dictates in the areas of foreign policy and security. It supported all Syria's moves in the inter-Arab and international arenas fully and in effect automatically. This commitment to Damascus was especially pronounced in the area of the Israeli–Arab peace process. Ostensibly, the finalization of an Israeli–Lebanese peace agreement could have been achieved relatively easily, as Israel did not have any territorial claims on Lebanon, and vice versa. Moreover, such a step was desirable to Beirut, which hoped that regional peace would bring economic prosperity to Lebanon. However, fear of Syria led to Lebanese avoidance of promoting their own talks with Israel and in effect created a linking of the Lebanese to the Syrian tracks. This reality was aptly described by the prime minister of Lebanon during most of the 1990s, Rafiq al-Hariri: "Our moves are coordinated entirely with Syria's moves. If Syria takes a step forward, we follow suit, and if Syria takes even one step backward, we step backward in its wake."[11]

Retrospectively, this linkage between the Syrian and Lebanese negotiating tracks led to a hardening of Lebanon's stance on a series of key issues. First was the question of the Palestinian refugees living in Lebanon, whom Lebanon refused to settle in its territory. Later, new issues arose, such as the Israeli demand to bring Hizballah's military activity on Lebanese soil to an end. Ultimately, the attainment of an Israeli–Lebanese peace agreement appeared to be no less complicated, and possibly even more so, than the attainment of an Israeli–Syrian agreement.

Economic benefits. The rehabilitation of Lebanon's economy benefited Syria as well. Indirect profits were obtained by Syrian army officers and politicians from commissions and protection payments turned over by Lebanese merchants and businessmen. Direct profits were derived from smuggling and from the cultivation and trade of drugs. More importantly, hundreds of thousands of Syrian workers were employed in Lebanon, thereby easing the major unemployment problem in Syria, estimated in the early 2000s at 20 percent of the workforce or more. Salary transmissions from Syrian workers in Lebanon to Syria amounted to approximately $2 billion and possibly $3 billion annually, constituting a significant contribution to the Syrian economy.[12]

The actual data regarding the number of Syrian workers in Lebanon soon became a state secret. The Lebanese government – and the Syrian government as well – had a clear interest in minimizing these figures, while opponents of the Syrian presence in Lebanon circulated inflated figures. Estimates varied from 600,000, according to Prime Minister Hariri, to 800,000, according to Syrian sources, and 1.5 million as claimed by the Christian opposition in Lebanon – a figure that exceeded the total Lebanese workforce (estimated as approximately 1.26 million).[13] The difficulty in estimating the true number of Syrian workers in Lebanon stemmed primarily from the fact that most were employed in temporary work, sometimes on a per diem or a seasonal basis. Furthermore, many Lebanese employers refrained from reporting hiring Syrian workers so as to avoid paying welfare benefits for them.

Complaints were widely heard in Lebanon that these workers were taking jobs away from the Lebanese, especially as unemployment in Lebanon rose in the 1990s. Still, most of the Syrian workers were employed in jobs such as construction or sanitation or domestic work – fields that were unattractive to most Lebanese, who preferred receiving unemployment compensation from the government. In turn, the Syrian workers, most of whom were young men who sought temporary or seasonal work, including students seeking employment during school vacations, complained about the humiliating attitude of the Lebanese employers, low pay, and the absence of any welfare benefits.[14]

An additional, albeit marginal, aspect of the economic importance of Lebanon to Syria was the idea discussed in Syria at various times to turn Lebanon into a Syrian Hong Kong, i.e. an economic buffer zone that would ease Syria's integration into the world economy without necessitating its exposure to world market and globalization forces which could jar its economic and political stability.

From the start, Syria's involvement in Lebanon evoked the widespread view that its intention was to annex Lebanon as a step in realizing the vision of a Greater Syria, to which Hafiz al-Asad ostensibly was committed. Once Syria took control of Lebanon following the signing of the Ta'if agreement, this suspicion was heightened. Syria, it was thought, planned to swallow up Lebanon, and as a first step initiate a process of "Syriazation" of that country which would lead to de facto annexation. The presence of hundreds of thousands of Syrian workers in Lebanon who in time were likely to settle there permanently with their families and become citizens reinforced this fear.

However, this prediction appeared to be unfounded, for whether Hafiz al-Asad considered annexing Lebanon to Syria remained unknown. Apparently, he was satisfied with subjecting it to Damascus's complete control. Every student of Lebanese history – and Asad clearly was familiar with the history of that country – understood that annexing Lebanon to Syria was impractical and that, if the Syrians tried to move in this direction, they would once again sink into the quicksand from which they had extracted themselves with great difficulty in the mid-1980s, in no small measure as a result of Israel's invasion there.

Notably, all the power brokers in Lebanon opposed annexation to Syria and the loss of their country's independence. They did, however, view cooperation with the Syrians as being in the Lebanese interest or, more precisely, in their own interest and were therefore prepared to submit to Damascus's dictates – certainly in the area of strategic issues such as the relationship with Israel. Yet, they opposed any infringement of Lebanon's independence and sovereignty, or any violation of its way of life or its political system. In this context, it should be noted that all the Arab states, as well as the international community, with the U.S. and France in the lead, were opposed to any Syrian move in Lebanon that would jeopardize that country's independent existence. Moreover, the Syrians themselves seemed to retreat from the notion of annexing Lebanon, primarily for fear that such a move could lead to the "Lebanonization" of Syria, i.e. that the typically Lebanese factionalism and separatism based on socioeconomic, religious, ethnic and clan divisions would spread to Syria as well and bring back the state of domestic instability and weakness that had prevailed there in the 1940s and 1950s.

The withdrawal of the Israeli army from South Lebanon, May 2000: the beginning of the countdown

In Damascus's view, another important advantage of the Syrian presence in Lebanon, and particularly in South Lebanon, was that it provided Syria with an arena for active confrontation with Israel. The campaign against Israel conducted by Hizballah with the support and encouragement of Damascus – and, notably, with no call for Syrian accountability for this situation over the years – proved to be a winning strategy for the Syrians. It prompted many Israelis to accept the Syrian linkage of peace and quiet on Israel's northern border with the signing of an Israeli–Syrian peace agreement which would include a full Israeli withdrawal from the Golan Heights. Notably, the Syrians themselves appeared to be surprised at the success of this strategy, i.e. the effectiveness of the Hizballah campaign against Israel with Syrian encouragement and support. They never expected that what the Syrian army had failed to achieve in its concerted attack on the Golan Heights (in October 1973) would be attained by several hundred Hizballah fighters carrying on a limited campaign against Israel along its border with Lebanon.

By the late 1990s, a sizable majority of Israeli citizens supported reaching a peace settlement with Syria even at the cost of full withdrawal from the Golan Heights, as part of an inclusive agreement that, inter alia, would bring quiet to Israel's northern border. This development was evident to the newly elected Israeli prime minister, Ehud Barak, in May 1999, and prompted him to promote such an arrangement. Apparently, however, the Syrians demanded more than the Israeli government, let alone the Israeli public, could accept, namely a withdrawal not to the international boundary between Israel and Syria but to the more disadvantageous June 4, 1967 line. Conceivably, too, it was the Syrians' grudging attitude, and not necessarily the stringent conditions laid down by Damascus, that pushed Israeli public opinion to reject the outline of the proposed Israeli–Syrian settlement that emerged between Asad's and Barak's envoys.

The Syrians failed to take advantage of the window of opportunity opened by Hizballah in order to achieve a settlement with Israel that met their conditions. Moreover, Hizballah's campaign succeeded beyond anyone's expectations, leading to the collapse in the late 1990s of the security zone in South Lebanon held by Israel with the assistance of its ally, the South Lebanese Army commanded by General Antoine Lahad. Essentially, Hizballah's accomplishment was psychological rather than military: it was not the Israeli military that weakened but rather Israeli public opinion, which found the ongoing bloodletting in South Lebanon (averaging 30 Israeli fatalities annually) no longer tolerable. Notably, the decisive blow to Israel's determination to hold on to the security zone came from Ehud Barak, who, running for election as prime minister in March 1999, promised to pull the Israeli forces out of Lebanon within a year. That announcement started a snowball that could not be stopped. Barak estimated that he could attain a peace agreement with Syria within a few months, which under any circumstances would include a settlement of the Lebanese problem and a guarantee of quiet along Israel's northern border. Retrospectively, when he failed to attain an agreement with the Syrians, he had no choice but to fulfill his promise to the Israeli electorate and order the withdrawal.[15]

The withdrawal of the Israeli army from South Lebanon removed Syria's only bargaining chip against Israel, namely its ability to keep up the bloodletting of Israeli soldiers stationed in the security zone. Not surprisingly, the Syrians tried to prevent the prospect of a withdrawal by veiled threats that a unilateral withdrawal without attaining an Israeli–Syrian peace agreement which would involve a parallel Israeli withdrawal from the Golan Heights would not produce the desired quiet on the northern border.[16] Reports from Lebanon just before the withdrawal pointed to efforts by the Syrians to encourage Palestinian elements to act against Israel. The head of the Palestinian Islamic Jihad, Ramadan Shallah, in an announcement that evoked protests by many Lebanese but which may have been inspired by Syria, stated that his movement viewed South Lebanon as part of the battlefield with Israel.[17]

On May 24, 2000, Israeli forces completed their withdrawal from South Lebanon. It is easy to understand why Ehud Barak, the Israeli prime minister who led Israel's unilateral withdrawal from South Lebanon, described the pullout as a substantial achievement. Barak believed that, by withdrawing, Israel had extricated itself from "the Lebanon complex," also known as "the Lebanon syndrome," and ensured peace and quiet – at least relatively – along the Israeli–Lebanese border. Barak repeated this conviction even after he was driven from office, and described the withdrawal as "one of the greatest triumphs of my term."[18] And yet, in contrast to the sense of satisfaction and triumph that Barak sought to express, many in Israel were left with a feeling of anxiety and even defeat after the withdrawal; many felt that the Lebanese saga, including Hizballah's ongoing struggle with Israel, was far from over.

In Lebanon, Hizballah activists led celebrations at what they considered a huge victory for the organization. After all, the struggle against Israel had been a major reason for the group's establishment in 1983 and been one of the main factors making it a leading force within the Shi'ite community in Lebanon. One cannot easily downplay this achievement by Hizballah, since throughout the 1990s it had remained almost the sole group in any Arab state committed to implementing an armed struggle against Israel. It would be argued that Hizballah achieved what no other Arab country or army had been able to do: oust Israel from Arab territory without the Arab side committing to any concession. No wonder that spokespersons of the organization tried to present their victory over Israel as a turning point in the history of the Arab–Israeli conflict. Indeed, the organization's secretary-general, Hasan Nasrallah, declared:

> A few hundred Hizballah fighters forced the strongest state in the Middle East to hoist the white flag.... The era when the Zionists frightened the Lebanese and the Arabs has ended. The Zionist entity lives in fear after the defeat suffered by the army of occupation at the hands of the Islamic resistance fighters in Lebanon. This fear prevails not only in occupied northern Palestine but also in the heart of Tel Aviv and deep in occupied Palestine.... Israel, which has nuclear weaponry and the strongest air force in the region, is weaker than spiderwebs.[19]

As an Islamist movement seeking influence and power within Lebanon in order to transform Lebanese society, however, Hizballah's victory brought it serious problems and decisions about its future. After all, it was the long, successful struggle against Israel that maintained the group, bolstered its standing within the Shi'ite community and made it strong in Lebanon's public opinion and political system. The same factor gave it foreign support, especially from Iran and Syria. Now, following the Israeli withdrawal, the organization lost some of its luster in the face of day-to-day challenges from Lebanese life and the harsh choices of Lebanese domestic politics.

It should be mentioned that, alongside maintaining its armed struggle against Israel during the 1990s, the Hizballah organization began integrating itself into Lebanon's governmental bodies, which were rejuvenated following the signing of the Ta'if agreement – an agreement it had vehemently opposed at the time. The organization ran in each of the Lebanese parliamentary election campaigns held after the agreement came into effect, on a list titled *kutlat al-wafa lil-muqawama* (Loyalty to the Resistance Bloc). The list won approximately ten of the 128 parliamentary seats in the three elections through 1992–2000. Additionally, Hizballah expanded its activity in the Shi'ite population, with substantial Iranian backing, establishing educational and cultural networks, a media organization, economic institutions and health and welfare services.

A lively debate among observers of Lebanon has focused on the question of whether Israel's withdrawal from South Lebanon in 2000 marked the end of Hizballah's violent militant agenda, or whether the Lebanonization challenge facing the organization would impel it to search for new ways to continue its struggle against Israel.[20] A reflection of Hizballah's dilemma was evident in its election campaign for the Lebanese parliament in 2000, which failed to translate the organization's achievements vis-à-vis Israel into a reinforcement of its status and power in the Lebanese domestic scene. The campaign focused almost entirely on domestic issues, especially in the socioeconomic realm, which headed the Lebanese agenda.

The calm which prevailed along the Israeli–Lebanese border, however temporary, presented another unexpected difficulty to the Syrians, in addition to the loss of their bargaining chip with Israel (i.e. the Hizballah attacks against the Israeli forces in South Lebanon). The withdrawal of the Israeli army caused a shift of public concern in Lebanon, in the region and internationally, away from the Israeli presence in Lebanon to the Syrian presence there. Soon, to the surprise of the Syrians, demands began to be made within Lebanon for the removal of the Syrian forces too, and the restoration of Lebanese independence and sovereignty.

It was at this point that President Hafiz al-Asad died, while conversing on the telephone with the president of Lebanon, leaving behind mounting questions regarding the indisputable achievement of his rule – the subjection of Lebanon to Syrian control.

Syria in Lebanon following Bashar's ascent to power

Once Bashar al-Asad assumed power, in an atmosphere of doubt regarding his capability to fill his father's shoes, it was the Lebanese arena, not unexpectedly, that put his leadership capacity to the first test. The challenge he faced was twofold: growing criticism in Lebanon of the Syrian presence in and control of the country; and fear in Syria of a military confrontation with Israel in light of renewed Hizballah attacks against Israel in October 2000.

Lebanon was not an unknown quantity to Bashar, for as far back as the mid-1990s he had been given responsibility for the "Lebanese file," i.e. for managing Syria's ongoing involvement there, and especially for assuring Damascus's continued presence and control in the country. This task was part of Bashar's training for his eventual role as heir to the presidency. Presumably, his involvement in the Lebanese arena helped him gain an understanding of the complexity of this neighboring country. However, his handling of Lebanese affairs was not viewed as impressive either within Lebanon or outside it. Many Lebanese perceived him as trying to combine a didactic approach (playing the role of a teacher who expected his pupils to learn their lessons) with a bureaucratic or technocratic approach (transmitting instructions through administrative channels and expecting them to be carried out explicitly). Bashar gave the impression of minimizing the human element in the conduct of Syria's affairs in Lebanon. Indeed, no sooner was the responsibility for Lebanese affairs transferred to him than his close associates promptly announced that he intended to "end the pilgrimage campaign of Lebanese personalities to Damascus and that, from now on, the Lebanese would have to solve their problems themselves and not take them to Syria for clarification and resolution."[21]

The result, however, was a disconnection between the Syrian and the Lebanese ruling elites, which served to heighten internal disputes among the Lebanese politicians. Ultimately, the Lebanese leaders ended up seeking Damascus's intervention for the resolution of their conflicts anyhow, sometimes when these disputes had reached explosive proportions. Bashar discovered that any attempt to operate in Lebanon through the channels of governmental authority – the president, the prime minister, the speaker of the parliament, or the military elite – was destined to fail, as it evoked extraneous antagonism among the Lebanese communal leaders, including those who were expressly aligned with Syria. Eventually, Bashar, like his father, was compelled to relent and receive an endless procession of Lebanese notables who arrived to lay their troubles before him and in effect use him in their intercommunal rivalries in time-honored Lebanese fashion. Clearly, Lebanon's political culture overrode Bashar's bureaucratic, "scientific" approach.

Nevertheless, Bashar, possibly acting on his father's advice, did develop ties with several Lebanese notables. These included Sulayman Tony Franjiyya, grandson of the former president of Lebanon (1970–76) Sulayman Franjiyya, a close friend of Hafiz al-Asad. It had been President Franjiyya who had requested Syria's active intervention in Lebanese affairs. His son Tony Franjiyya, a close friend of Rif'at al-Asad, Bashar's uncle, was murdered by activists of the Lebanese Phalanges in 1978. Thereafter, the family's affairs were run by Tony's young son, Sulayman Tony Franjiyya, who had been a friend of Basil al-Asad and later established close ties with Bashar. Another Lebanese notable with whom Bashar developed ties was Talal Arslan of the prominent Druze Arslan family, whom the Syrians promoted as a counterweight to the Junblatt family, the historic rivals of the Arslans for primacy in the Druze community.[22] Yet another close associate of Bashar was Tah Miqati, of the merchant Sunni Miqati family in Tripoli, who became prominent in the wake of the Ta'if agreement. Tah's father, Najib Miqati, was elected to parliament as a delegate from northern Lebanon and was named Minister of

Communications in 2000. The family was engaged in extensive commercial activity, including significant investment in one of Syria's mobile communications companies, Space-Tel.[23]

An additional connection worthy of mention is the close link established by Bashar with Hasan Nasrallah, leader of the Hizballah movement. By his own admission, Nasrallah had never met Hafiz al-Asad personally,[24] presumably because Asad Sr. saw no need for such a meeting, as in his view Nasrallah was simply another of the many Lebanese who carried out Syria's dictates there. Bashar, however, met with Nasrallah frequently, possibly because he viewed him as a victorious hero for harassing the Israeli forces in South Lebanon and a role model worthy of emulation. Once Bashar assumed the presidency, Nasrallah demonstratively offered his patronage to the young leader, stating on various occasions that Hizballah was prepared to assist him in entrenching his status.[25] Later on, it was reported that Bashar had permitted preachers linked with Hizballah to base themselves in the Alawite communities in northern Syria, a step aimed at enhancing the religious legitimation of the Alawites, and by extension that of Bashar and his regime, within the majority Sunni population in Syria. At the same time, however, this step increased Bashar's dependence on Hizballah and its leaders.[26]

Ultimately, Bashar did not acquire the role of kingmaker in the Lebanese arena during the period that preceded his father's death, a role that had been filled in the past by such dominant Syrian political figures as 'Abd al-Halim Khaddam and Hikmat Shihabi. This lacuna, along with doubts about Bashar's ability to fill his father's shoes once he took over the reins of power, promoted many Lebanese to view the change of regime in Syria as an opportunity to alter the power balance between the two states and reinforce the status of Lebanon vis-à-vis Syria. Conceivably, even the strongest critics of Syria's involvement in Lebanese affairs, and particularly of its military presence in Lebanon, did not actually intend to bring about the removal of the Syrians from Lebanon, at least not immediately. However, their challenge to Damascus, which was meant to enhance their importance, was interpreted in Lebanon and outside it as evidence of Syria's weakness now that Hafiz al-Asad was gone and his son Bashar had taken his place.

Notably, even before Asad's death, a growing antagonism toward the Syrian presence in Lebanon was palpable within the Lebanese population. While this mood was rooted in the traditional Lebanese suspicion of Syria's intentions in Lebanon, distrust appeared to grow as the Syrian hold on Lebanon became entrenched and in its wake increased daily friction between the Lebanese and the Syrians. A glance at Lebanese newspaper headlines in the late 1990s illuminates the background and circumstances of this growing antagonism. Many Lebanese resented the setting up of 26 polling stations throughout their country in March 1999 to allow the hundreds of thousands of Syrian workers there to take part in a referendum to ratify President Hafiz al-Asad's candidacy for a fifth term of office and, a year later in July 2000, another referendum to ratify Bashar's candidacy for the presidency. For many Lebanese, these acts were insulting and represented a violation of Lebanese sovereignty. Maronite Patriarch Butrus Nasrallah Sufayr warned that the setting up of these polls could be interpreted as turning Lebanon into a Syrian province.[27]

Another move that evoked anger was an order issued by the Lebanese Minister of Education in the summer of 2000, possibly under pressure by Damascus, easing the entrance requirements for Syrian students applying to Lebanese universities. The order prompted vehement protest demonstrations by Lebanese students, who feared that their Syrian counterparts would be given preference in acceptance to the universities.[28] An additional cause of resentment against the Syrians was a decision in 2000 by the Lebanese government, under Syrian pressure, to reduce customs on Syrian agricultural imports into Lebanon, a step that hurt Lebanese farmers. Protesting, the farmers blocked the main roads in the country.[29] Yet another issue that soured the atmosphere between Beirut and Damascus was the question of Lebanese prisoners held in Syrian jails. Damascus freed 50 Lebanese prisoners in November 1999, claiming that no others were held in Syria, but according to the Lebanese many more were in custody there and their fate was uncertain.[30]

These and many other issues, however, were overshadowed by three major issues:

1. *Syria's involvement in domestic Lebanese politics.* This stung many Lebanese, especially those who opposed the Syrian presence in Lebanon and Syrian patronage of those Lebanese who supported that presence. Notably, this pattern of relationships between the Lebanese and a foreign patron was not new, for a similarly complex and problematic relationship had existed between the Lebanese and France during the French Mandate period, and with Israel during that country's involvement in Lebanon in the early 1980s.

2. *Syria's military involvement in Lebanon.* The presence of Syrian military and security forces was a harassing factor for the population. In this context, the measures taken by the representative of Syrian military security, Ghazi Kana'an, who was replaced in 2002 by Rustum Ghazzala, and their forces, were less intrusive than the

behavior of the thousands of Syrian soldiers spread throughout the country. They became noxious to the Lebanese not necessarily for political or security reasons but because of their practice of demanding protection money from every driver who passed through the checkpoints they manned along the Lebanese roads.

3. *The presence of hundreds of thousands of Syrian workers in Lebanon.* They were viewed as stealing the livelihoods of the Lebanese and even as a kind of Trojan horse sent by the Syrians in anticipation of the annexation of Lebanon to Syria. Reports from Beirut cited numerous incidents of attacks against these workers involving physical abuse, theft and murder.[31]

Parliamentary elections in Lebanon in the summer of 2000, held in an atmosphere of anticipation following the withdrawal of the Israeli army from South Lebanon as well as the passing of Hafiz al-Asad, resulted in a defeat for the representatives of the outgoing government under Salim al-Huss and the return of Rafiq al-Hariri as prime minister. Hariri, who had held that post during 1992–98, had been forced to resign because of friction with his colleagues in the Lebanese ruling elite and possibly because of pressure by Bashar al-Asad as well. Hariri was known to have close ties with the Saudi royal family, having made his fortune as a building contractor and developer in Saudi Arabia. He was also known to be close to 'Abd al-Halim Khaddam, the Syrian appointee in charge of Lebanese affairs during the 1980s, which may have accounted for his strained relationship with Bashar. (Asad Sr. as will be recalled, replaced Khaddam with Bashar in this role as part of the grooming of the heir apparent.)

The electoral victory of parliamentary delegates identified with Hariri's camp (though not necessarily politically loyal to him or under his patronage) reflected purely domestic Lebanese developments. Nevertheless, it was perceived outside Lebanon as a protest against the current Lebanese government, and by extension against the Syrians, who were the patrons of that government. This perception was widespread even though Hariri himself denied that his victory had any such significance, immediately expressed his commitment to Syria and the Syrian presence in Lebanon and promptly traveled to Damascus to declare his loyalty to Bashar al-Asad.[32]

This undisguised obeisance to Syria was the spark that set off broad public protest against the Syrian presence in the country shortly after the death of Hafiz al-Asad and the Lebanese parliamentary elections in the summer of 2000. The signal for the protest was given by the editor of the Beirut daily *al-Nahar*, Jubran Ghassan Tuwayni, in a series of editorials focusing on the assertion that "Lebanon will not be a free and sovereign state until all the foreign forces leave it."[33] Tuwayni, who was known as a supporter of General Michel 'Awn, and had been in exile in Europe until 1993, became, upon his return to Lebanon, the most outspoken of the critics of Syria's presence there. Tuwayni's criticism of the Syrians was soon echoed by the Maronite patriarch, Butrus Nasrallah Sufayr, another long-time critic of the Syrian presence, and in his wake the Council of Maronite Bishops, which, in an unprecedented declaration in September 2000, announced that, with the withdrawal of Israel, the time had come to re-examine the question of the Syrian presence in Lebanon.[34]

The voices of protest that began to be raised against the Syrians, primarily by the Maronite community, were accompanied by large-scale demonstrations of Christian, mostly Maronite, students and activists in Maronite political parties, such as the Free Liberals led by the Sham'un family, or supporters of Michel 'Awn. Syrian flags were burned during the demonstrations and pictures of the late President Asad and his son Bashar were destroyed.[35] Additionally, the appearance of posters calling for the removal of the Syrians from Lebanon was reported throughout the country, statues of Hafiz al-Asad were demolished,[36] and Syrian workers were attacked.

In another surprising development, the leader of the Druze community in Lebanon, Walid Junblatt, joined the anti-Syrian critics, declaring that, while he acknowledged the need for the presence of Syrian forces in strategic areas in Lebanon because of the ongoing Israeli–Arab conflict, the Syrian army must be removed from Beirut and its forces deployed in the Biqa', as stipulated in the Ta'if agreement. Moreover, the Syrians would have to end their involvement in domestic Lebanese affairs.[37] Challenging both the Lebanese government and the Syrians, Junblatt stated:

> The explanations given to us by our leaders, as by the Syrian leaders, regarding the need for the continued Syrian presence in Lebanon as stemming from the shared destiny of both nations, are unsatisfactory. After all, we have a democracy in Lebanon, while Syria has a one-party system [the Ba'th Party], and therefore we cannot understand what this shared destiny is that Bashar al-Asad preaches to us.[38]

Junblatt's defiance of the Syrians is noteworthy in light of his personal history. His father, Kamal Junblatt, was known for his opposition to the entry of the Syrian forces into Lebanon in June 1976, and paid for his stance with his life when he was shot in an ambush in March 1977 by "unknown" assailants who had undoubtedly been dispatched by the Syrian security services. Walid, then about 30, succeeded his father as head of the family and of the Druze community, and immediately made headlines by visiting the Presidential Palace in Damascus as soon as the 40-day mourning period for his father was over. There he met with Hafiz al-Asad, who presumably had ordered his father's death, and who embraced the young leader, promising that he would be a father to him from then on.[39] Ever since, Walid obeyed Damascus's dictates meticulously. However, with Asad's death in June 2000, he changed course abruptly and joined the anti-Syrian camp in Lebanon, motivated apparently by a new political development: the need to recruit personal support from the Maronite electorate in the Shuf Mountains. This was necessitated by governmental plans to unify the Shuf region into a single electoral district, which would put the Maronites in a position to tip the scales in any contest between the Junblatt clan and their rivals in the Druze community.

The Syrians reacted to the protests in Lebanon with relative restraint. Walid Junblatt was notified that he was no longer welcome in the corridors of power in Damascus, yet the Syrians made a point of explaining that he would not be prevented from visiting Syria as a private person and that he could keep the villa in the Syrian capital that had been given to him by Hafiz al-Asad. In the event, Junblatt returned to the embrace of the Syrians. His political acumen led him to the conclusion in the summer of 2001 that the winds of war blowing in the region in the wake of the Palestinian Intifada and the events of September 11 in the United States dictated a reconciliation with Syria. Retracting his criticism of the Syrians, he made a pilgrimage to Bashar al-Asad's palace in May 2002 and had a lengthy reconciliation meeting with him.[40]

The Syrians also showed restraint toward the Christian camp, revealing a clear preference for dialogue rather than confrontation with the hard-core anti-Syrian Maronite opposition led by the Maronite Church under Patriarch Sufayr. The Syrians tried unsuccessfully to arrange a meeting between Bashar and the patriarch, but the Maronite prelate remained immutable in his demand for a Syrian exodus from the country. Moreover, declaring that he would not visit Syria until Lebanon became an independent state, he declined, for that reason, to accompany the Pope on his historic visit to Damascus in May 2001. Notably, the patriarch was a harsh critic of the Americans' intention to go to war against Iraq in the spring of 2003, for which he was praised by the Syrians. However, his intent at that time seemed to be to please France rather than Damascus.[41]

Hoping to reduce friction with the Lebanese population, the Syrians began redeploying their forces in Lebanon in the wake of the withdrawal of the Israeli army from South Lebanon in May 2000. Apparently, Bashar grasped that it was the Syrian military presence that was at the root of the deteriorating relations between the two states. He acknowledged on several occasions that, "if Syrian military forces were deployed in the streets of Damascus for a prolonged period, this would evoke objection and revulsion toward their presence in the Syrian public too, as has occurred in Lebanon."[42] Furthermore, the Syrians apparently adopted this move as a way of deflecting inter-Arab and international pressure on them to withdraw their forces from Lebanon in the wake of Israel's withdrawal from South Lebanon. The Syrians must have also realized that the redeployment of their forces in Lebanon would in any case not weaken their control of the country, for that control was implemented by the loyal Lebanese ruling elite itself – first and foremost the Lebanese president, his government and Lebanon's military and security forces.

The Syrian deployment began in June 2000 with a reduction in the number of Syrian army checkpoints along the Lebanese roads,[43] followed later on by the evacuation of most of the Syrian forces from Beirut and the other Lebanese cities, which was completed in April 2002. In January 2003, the Syrians evacuated additional forces from northern Lebanon. The completion of the withdrawal of the forces from Beirut and other Lebanese cities was projected by the Syrians as the completion of the implementation of the Ta'if agreement, which mandated removing the Syrian forces from Lebanon's cities, mainly Beirut, and concentrating them in the Lebanese Biqa'. Damascus reported that, in contrast to the approximately 40,000 Syrian soldiers stationed in Lebanon in early 2000, only 10,000–15,000 remained after the completion of the redeployment.[44] These moves, however, were interpreted by Syria's critics as a sign of weakness and submission to pressure. The steps taken by Syria in April 2002 and in January 2003 were seen as a reflection of Syria's fear of a military conflagration with Israel as a result of the escalation of violence along the Israeli–Lebanese border. According to this thinking, the Syrians sought to reduce that danger by demonstratively thinning out their forces in the anticipated arena of confrontation.

The Syrians, for their part, emphasized that the move was truly a redeployment of their forces in Lebanon and not a comprehensive withdrawal, which, they reiterated, would take place only when an overall peace agreement was attained in the region. Bashar himself repeatedly explained:

No senior Syrian official ever stated, since the entry of the Syrian forces into Lebanon in 1976, that a permanent presence is involved.

On the contrary, Syria keeps reiterating that its forces entered Lebanese territory in order to assist that country's government, and when the presence of these Syrian forces in Lebanon is no longer needed, they will return to Syria. This is not a new position. Syria has said these things from the start, and therefore we in Syria are surprised each time we are asked about the future of our presence in Lebanon.[45]

Notably, Bashar arrived in Beirut in March 2002 for his first visit as president of Syria, just prior to the Arab summit to be held there. He had intended to take part in the summit in any event, but, conceivably, arrived early to visit Lebanon in the context of his "patron" role.[46] The visit was also aimed at conveying a message of reconciliation to the Lebanese Christians, the country's most implacable opponents to the Syrian presence, for the visit was the first ever to Beirut by a Syrian president, and implied Syrian recognition of Lebanon's independent existence. The Syrians had consistently refrained from posting an ambassador in Beirut, thereby demonstrating their rejection of the notion of Lebanese independence. Two Syrian presidents who preceded Bashar had met with their Lebanese counterparts on Lebanese soil in the town of Shatura – Syrian President Shukri al-Quwatli, who met with Lebanese President Bishara al-Khuri in 1947, and Hafiz al-Asad, who met with Sulayman Franjiyya in 1975 – but never in Beirut.

Syria, however, failed in its attempts to halt the growing criticism in Lebanon of its presence there. Opposition mounted partly in light of a perceived confusion in Syria's response. The intensification of anti-Syrian criticism was led by Maronite Church circles close to Patriarch Sufayr. An unprecedented sharp attack was issued against the Syrian presence in Lebanon at the close of the annual conference of Maronite bishops in September 2000, constituting an official and binding platform for the Maronite Church.[47]

In the spring of 2001, Syria's opponents in the Christian camp convened the Qurnat Shahwan Forum, named for the Maronite monastery where the first meeting was held. The forum's activity accelerated quickly to the point of creating a common front, which later proved to be baseless but which swept up the Lebanese public, and especially the Maronite Christians, in a wave of anti-Syrian sentiment.[48] This atmosphere was reflected in a historic visit on August 2001 by Patriarch Sufayr to southern Mount Lebanon in the Shuf region, the heartland of the Druze community, where he was received at the home of Walid Junblatt. The meeting was projected as a sign of reconciliation between the Druze and the Maronites, who had waged a savage war against each other in the region – the "war of the Mountain" – during 1983–84. However, the encounter between the two leaders soon turned into an anti-Syrian protest, with thousands of Druze and Christian demonstrators who had arrived to welcome the prelate shouting anti-Syrian slogans. Lebanese security forces hastily dispersed the demonstrators, arresting several dozen of them.[49]

The heightened anti-Syrian criticism in the summer of 2001 prompted Syria, along with its allies in Lebanon, to respond more aggressively than previously, along the same lines it took at home against the reformist camp in Syria when it demanded change during this period. Reports from Beirut indicated the arrest, on August 7, 2001, of dozens of former Lebanese military personnel, led by Tawfiq al-Hindi, an advisor to the commander of the Lebanese forces. Hindi and other detainees were charged with spying for Israel.[50] In reality, many Lebanese Christians and others had cooperated with Israel or maintained contact with representatives of Israel during that country's prolonged involvement in Lebanon in the 1970s and 1980s. However, the sudden accusations of spying for Israel constituted a dangerous precedent and, furthermore, revealed the incident to be trumped up in order to conceal the intent to deter and frighten Syria's critics in Lebanon. The fact that it was the Lebanese security bodies, responsible to President Lahhud, who ordered the arrests, bypassing Prime Minister Hariri and Minister of Defense Khalil al-Hirawi, who were abroad at the time, also pointed to panic in Damascus and among its allies in Lebanon, prompting them to act hastily.

As a result, the main Christian struggle against the Syrian presence in Lebanon shifted to the international arena. In June 2002, a world Maronite conference was held in Los Angeles, in which the patriarch's representatives played a dominant role. The conference called on Syria to withdraw from Lebanon. Thereafter, Maronite supporters joined the Israeli lobby in Washington, the America–Israel Public Affairs Committee, in an effort to promote anti-Syrian legislation in Congress (the Syrian Accountability and the Restoration of Lebanon's Sovereignty Law, focusing, inter alia, on the "Syrian conquest" of Lebanon, in the wording of the initiators of the legislation).[51]

Ultimately, however, the anti-Syrian criticism that swelled after the Israeli withdrawal from the security zone in South Lebanon, and after Hafiz al-Asad's death, gradually waned following the outbreak of the Palestinian Intifada in October 2000, the events of September 11, 2001, and especially the American attack on Iraq in 2003. While these events intensified the dilemmas faced by Syria and Lebanon in terms of their backing of Hizballah and other Palestinian terrorist organizations, nevertheless they impelled the anti-Syrian camp to lower its profile. Druze leader Walid Junblatt distanced himself from the Christian camp, as noted above, and returned to the embrace of Damascus. Moreover, prior to the American attack on Iraq, the Maronite Church leaders, undoubtedly influenced by the French and the Vatican stance, called for the prevention of the war, praising none other than Bashar al-Asad for his efforts in this direction.[52]

The expulsion of Syria from Lebanon

Despite pressure within Lebanon on Syria to evacuate its troops from Lebanon, Syria in early 2004 still appeared destined to maintain its control and influence there. However, the storm that had begun in Iraq in the spring of 2003 ultimately spread to Lebanon, leading to the eviction of the Syrians. This was but another clear expression of the disastrous result for Damascus from the worsening of Syria's relations with the U.S. The U.S joined up with France, its sworn rival in the international scene, and together the two countries led a move that would pose a threat to the future of Syria's presence in Lebanon. The arena was Lebanon, but Syria was called upon to pay a price in Lebanon, for its acts, or rather its failure to act, in Iraq.

On September 3, 2004, the Lebanese parliament approved, with a large majority, an amendment to the Lebanese constitution. Out of the 128 members of the parliament, 96 supported the amendment and only 29 opposed it, with three members left who preferred not to attend the session. According to the amendment the term of the Lebanese president, Emile Lahhud, was to be extended, under exceptional terms, for another three years.[53]

The parliamentary vote came after Resolution 1559 had been adopted by the U.N. Security Council only the day before, on September 2, 2004. It actually ignored or even challenged this resolution. The resolution, which was passed with the support of nine members of the Security Council, while the other six abstained, called for the respecting of Lebanon's sovereignty and constitution, the withdrawal of all foreign forces from Lebanon and the dismantling of all Lebanese and non-Lebanese militias. The final resolution was softer in comparison with the original version and, for example, did not mention Syria by name, referring to the Syrian forces deployed in Lebanon as foreign forces. The French and American representatives in the Security Council, however, made it clear to whom the resolution was directed.[54]

Since early 2004 the political system in Lebanon had been busy guessing the identity of the new president of Lebanon who was to replace the incumbent president, Emile Lahhud, at the end of his six-year term in office. It should be mentioned that the term length of six years, as written in the Lebanese constitution, is a sacred value in Lebanon and any effort in the past to change it had been faced with firm opposition. Indeed the efforts of previous presidents like Bishara al-Khuri (1943–52) and Kamil Sham'un to change the constitution had led Lebanon into political turmoil and, in the case of Kamil Sham'un, even into civil war in 1958. Only President Lahhud's predecessor, Ilyas al-Hirawi, received in 1995, with Syrian backing and Western blessing, and with the approval of prominent Lebanese figures, an extension of three years to his six-year term in office.

For some time it seemed that the Syrians had doubts regarding the identity of the next president and for the way to lead to his election. President Lahhud proved eventually to be the easy choice, because he was known to be a weak president with no real bases of power either within or outside Lebanon. And therefore the Syrian decision was eventually to bring about his re-election. Once the decision was made, the top leaders of Lebanon were summoned one by one to the Presidential Palace in Damascus, where they were told by President Bashar that the Syrians had decided that Lahhud was to be the next president of Lebanon.[55]

In full contradiction of the past, the Syrians did not bother to lay the ground for their choice of Lahhud inside Lebanon. With a little attention and care, they could have encouraged the emergence of authentic Lebanese voices from within Lebanon calling for the re-election of Lahhud, thus saving themselves from harsh criticism inside Lebanon. Nor did the Syrians bother to contact their Arab allies and prepare the international arena. The result was that their move caused strong and unprecedented reaction even inside Lebanon but also in the international arena. Indeed, in Lebanon there was strong reaction from the Christian Maronite leadership headed by the Maronite patriarch, Butrus Nasrallah Sufayr, and from leaders of the Christian opposition parties and supporters of the exiled general Michel 'Awn, and finally from Walid Junblatt, the Druze leader. There was also protest at the popular level, for example demonstrations in the streets of Beirut.[56]

But the "Syrian success" was mainly in the international arena. The Syrians succeeded for the first time in uniting France and the United States, something no one had done before them since the war in Iraq. The draft resolution the two countries submitted to the Security Council was eventually softened, not necessarily because of the efforts invested by Syrian diplomacy but because of the fear of countries like Russia or China that such a resolution, if adopted, could be used in the future as a precedent against them. It is worth mentioning that even countries like Algeria refused to vote against the resolution and preferred to abstain, a fact that proves the lack of readiness in the Arab world to support Syria.

The assassination of Rafiq al-Hariri

At the last meeting between Rafiq al-Hariri and Syrian President Bashar al-Asad in August 2004, Bashar al-Asad asked Hariri to support the Syrian demand to extend the term of Lebanese President Emile Lahhud for another three years. Later on, Hariri related that Bashar had even threatened that he "would rather break Lebanon over the heads of Hariri and Junblatt than see his word in Lebanon broken."[57]

On February 14, 2005, a few months after receiving this threat, Hariri died in a car bombing. The Lebanese opposition was quick to put the blame on Syria as having responsibility for the assassination of Hariri. After all, it was argued in Lebanon, Syria had every reason to want him out of the way. In recent months, Hariri had kept a low profile and allowed Walid Junblatt, the leader of the Druze in Lebanon, to carry the banner of Lebanese opposition to Syria. Nevertheless, Hariri enjoyed virtually unlimited personal resources, broad popularity in Lebanon and very good ties with the Saudi royal family, the president of France and even the American administration. He was therefore able to play a central role behind the scenes in crafting the American–French axis that, in September 2004, produced U.N. Security Council Resolution 1559, which called for the withdrawal of all foreign forces from Lebanon and even established a mechanism for U.N. monitoring of developments in order to ensure that Lebanon remained a focus of international attention. For these reasons, Hariri was seen as the biggest Lebanese bone in Syria's throat.[58]

The killing of Hariri provoked unprecedented reaction, both in Lebanon and abroad. Rather than hunker down, the Lebanese opposition stepped up its denunciations of Syria and its local Lebanese allies. The most prominent opposition spokesman has been Walid Junblatt, who didn't hesitate to put the blame for the killing squarely on Syria and its "collaborationist regime" in Beirut. Junblatt and his colleagues demanded the withdrawal of all Syrian forces from Lebanon and even endorsed the idea of a foreign protection force. Their campaign drew widespread support from various sectors of the Lebanese population – Maronites, Sunnis and Druze – who were fed up with the Syrian presence and now wanted to exploit the murder of Hariri in order to get the Syrians out of their country.[59]

This domestic protest was encouraged by international reaction to Hariri's killing. Although the United States was careful not to charge Syria with direct responsibility, it made its attitude known by quickly recalling its ambassador in Damascus "for consultations." French President Jacques Chirac went to Beirut on a condolence visit to the Hariri family but pointedly refrained from meeting any senior government officials. The U.S. and France together initiated a demand by the Security Council to bring the killers to justice, and the U.N. Secretary-General, Kofi Annan, announced the dispatch of an independent team to investigate the circumstances of the assassination.[60]

If the Syrians hoped that the inflamed passions aroused by the assassination of Hariri would soon subside, they were disappointed. Some two weeks after the murder, under the pressure of massive demonstrations by hundreds of thousands of supporters of the anti-Syrian opposition, Lebanese Prime Minister 'Umar Karami, a Syrian protégé, made a surprise announcement of his resignation in light of accusations that his government was responsible, even if indirectly, for the murder. Syria still had a considerable number of allies in Lebanon, who hurriedly organized huge demonstrations of their own in Riyad al-Sulh Square in Beirut under the leadership of the Hizballah movement, calling for support for the Syrian presence in the country. However, a counter-demonstration of even larger proportions – nearly a million people – demonstrated that the opposition had a majority in terms of Lebanese public opinion.[61]

The massive demonstrations in Lebanon, featuring unprecedented sharp attacks against Syria, encouraged intensified pressure by the West on Damascus to fulfill the terms of Security Council Resolution 1559 and remove its forces from Lebanon. With the horses having fled the stable, Bashar called a special session of the Syrian People's Assembly, on March 5, 2005, and announced the evacuation of all Syrian troops from Lebanon. The withdrawal was completed on April 26, 2005, whereupon the Syrians announced that they viewed themselves as having complied with the Security Council resolution. U.N. Secretary-General Kofi Annan quickly responded, however, that, as long as Hizballah did not disarm, Syria could not be viewed as having fulfilled the totality of the conditions of the resolution.[62]

The completion of the withdrawal of the Syrian forces from Lebanon brought the nearly three-decade-long Syrian military presence there to an end. Despite attempts by Damascus and its allies in Lebanon to give the withdrawal an aura of dignity, the farewell ceremonies for the Syrians could not conceal the humiliation involved in their eviction from Lebanon, an eviction forced on them by an international consensus and, even more, by a broad Lebanese consensus.

Afterword

The Syrian withdrawal from Lebanon undoubtedly marks the end of an era. Clearly, Damascus will have difficulty conceding its prolonged control in Lebanon, along with the political, military and especially economic benefits and profits accrued by its rule there. The Syrians are likely, therefore, to try to retain a certain amount of their influence in the country, using whatever cards they have left. Notably, the distance between Beirut and Damascus is only an hour's drive, and the Syrians still have a considerable number of allies in Lebanon, especially Hizballah. That organization has already become the next target of the Lebanese "Cedar Revolution", and Hasan Nasrallah, its leader, is unequaled in his ability to sense a noose tightening around his neck. Indeed, many Lebanese leaders, backed by France and the U.S., have emphasized their expectation that Hizballah will disarm, although as part of an internal Lebanese dialogue and not under external pressure. The stated willingness of Hizballah's leaders to consider this possibility, which they had rejected out of hand in the past, reveals both the organization's distress and its preparedness to adopt a pragmatic approach in order to survive. In fact, the organization had already started its campaign with the intent of winning a victory in democratic elections in Lebanon. Significantly, Nasrallah has projected himself as an ardent supporter of the implementation of full democracy in Lebanon,[63] as he is likely to be the main beneficiary by virtue of the demographic advantage of the Shi'ite community, which constitutes approximately 40 percent of the Lebanese population. Nasrallah must now decide whether to risk his accomplishments thus far in an electoral campaign for the control of Lebanon, or sustain the use of violence and fly in the face of the internationally backed Lebanese consensus which seeks the organization's disarmament.

While Syria may try to preserve its status in Lebanon, it is, nevertheless, on the defensive, and with the passage of time has lost the ability to initiate political or military processes in Lebanon or in the Middle East generally. The Syrian regime is weaker than it has ever been, isolated internationally and even regionally, and in effect fighting for its survival. Meanwhile, the security forces in Lebanon, in coordination with the departing Syrian troops, systematically dismantled all the statues, monuments, memorial plaques, signs and pictures showing the likenesses of Bashar al-Asad and his father, Hafiz al-Asad. In locations where crowds of young Lebanese had preceded them, the statues had been smashed, the memorial plaques destroyed and the pictures of those who had been the masters of Lebanon for the preceding 30 years torn up, truly marking the end of an era.[64]

Why Bashar? Because there is no one else

Bashar al-Asad's ascent to power in Damascus in June 2000 evoked great expectations in Syria and beyond that, in light of the young ruler's familiarity with Western thinking and the Western way of life, he would initiate a revolution in Syria's domestic policy and, even more significantly, in its foreign policy.

The years that have passed since then have shown that Bashar did not aspire to such a revolution. Even if he realized the need to introduce change and reform in Syria, and perhaps even attempted to introduce steps in this direction, he was not strong enough to face down the ruling elite old guard, which was intent on retaining the generation-long status quo. Furthermore, the widespread image of the young leader as dynamic, open and pro-West was revealed to be hollow. Although he made many high-visibility visits abroad, as well as several throughout Syria (in stark contrast to his father, who spent most of his years in power cloistered in his palace), reports in the Western and the Israeli press indicated that Bashar spent most of his time playing computer games, and in other pursuits unrelated to the management of the affairs of state.

Moreover, once he assumed the presidency, the moderate tone of his earlier statements was quickly replaced by militant, inflammatory positions on domestic and especially regional and international issues which he adopted or was pressured to adopt. Such rhetoric was particularly pronounced in connection with the Palestinian Intifada and the Israeli–Arab conflict, and later became even more explicit regarding the impending war in Iraq. This conduct, in the view of many observers, revealed inexperience and a lack of self-confidence, and possibly the absence of an orderly decision-making system or of experienced advisors close to him. All these factors led the young president into situations his father had carefully avoided.

Nevertheless, in the first years after Bashar took control of Syria in June 2000, internal calm and stability were preserved. Moreover, the transfer of power to him was accomplished smoothly and without necessitating the young president to face any challenge or threat to his rule. He was even able, for a while, to project a sense of vigor and vitality that promised active change. Ultimately, even though he made many mistakes in his decisions and his performance, in the view of Western and Israeli analysts (mostly as a result of inexperience and immaturity), they were not fateful errors that affected the stability or the survival of his regime.

Bashar's success in surviving in power in the first years that followed his father's death impelled a reassessment of the widely skeptical predictions at the start of his rule that his days in office would be numbered. An Israeli analyst wrote in the Israeli daily *Ma'ariv*, in early 2003:

> Two and a half years after he inherited the regime in Damascus, some in Israel still believe that the Syrian president is a weak leader. The series of insults that have been hurled at him by Israeli analysts comes straight from a kindergartener's lexicon of reprimands. They have said he acts like a little child, that he is immature, that he behaves foolishly, and mainly he has been accused of being swept up by Hasan Nasrallah's charisma. All this because Asad does not behave as the masters of this country expect.... But Asad reveals himself to be a smart leader who plucks the fruits of his moves.[1]

Another view, expressed in the spring of 2003 by a critic of the Syrian regime living in Paris, Subhi Haddad, held that:

> Bashar al-Asad is a devotee of the past and at the same time a hostage to it. He is an active participant in preserving the past, in commemorating it and in sanctifying it.... The regime, which Bashar represents, is not only incapable of developing [and] leading [a process of] modernization, change and reform, but by its very nature it opposes any change and loathes any thought of change and reform.... From this we may deduce that Asad Jr. has no intention of bringing down the dictatorial, corrupt regime that his late father built up during the 30 years of his rule.[2]

Curiously, the reaction to Bashar by the Syrian street, and apparently by the Syrian political system itself, appeared to remain the same as it had been from the day he took office. Then, the Syrian public replied to the question: Why Bashar as president? with the response: *Ma fi ghayru* (There is no one else), reflecting the perception of a lack of alternative to accepting his rule in order to preserve the political stability that existed in the country for a whole generation, and possibly also to advance Syria socially and economically. The fact that this response has remained the same over several years reveals that, since taking over the regime, Bashar has been unable as yet to provide the man in the street with additional reasons to show that he was worthy of succeeding his father. Apparently, Syrians who had become accustomed to the iron fist used by the regime in the past tended to view Bashar as a weak ruler who lacked the killer instinct so vital to anyone seeking to rule Syria, while others who hoped for change were disappointed with Bashar for not ushering in concrete reform in domestic policy, society and the economy.

While it was true that there was no immediate danger to Bashar's rule in his first years in power, it was clear from the beginning that he had not yet firmly entrenched himself in the presidency.

First, it is lonely at the top. Bashar was surrounded for most of his first six years in power by the same entrenched power brokers – the boon companions of his late father. True, there had been some personnel changes, but these involved nothing more than the replacement of one or another senior figure with his deputy. Thus, the shake-up was simply the replacement of old-guard party hacks and officials with younger party hacks and officials, products of the same "schools" as their predecessors, and for the most part committed to the dogged preservation of the status quo.

Indeed, Bashar appeared to have consolidated a personal staff to assist him in promoting his goals and leading Syria toward change, however limited. This staff consisted of young men his age who shared his world view, some of whom, like him, were previously unidentified politically. Some members of this group, whom Bashar brought with him from the Syrian Computer Society where they had been involved in disseminating computer and Internet awareness, were appointed to the cabinet. This group, however, was unlikely to be able to assist Bashar in ruling the country, as they lacked power bases of their own and were not influential in governmental circles.

Second, there is a lack of agenda for the present or vision for the future. Bashar has failed in his attempt to formulate an orderly political agenda according to which he wants to lead and rule Syria. His answers to the question of where Syria is headed for the future have been generalized and vague, relating to the preservation of his regime and in a broader sense the preservation of the status quo, and in even broader terms the preservation of the political and socioeconomic realities in the country, while making some cosmetic changes of a technical nature (improvement in the functioning of the administrative and governing apparatuses) and adherence to his father's basic positions in the sphere of foreign policy. After all, it was Bashar who admitted in a speech he delivered in the People's Assembly in March 2003 that "There were those who turned my inauguration speech into a flag or even an operational plan. But the truth is that these were merely thoughts and there is a big difference between thoughts and an operational concrete plan."[3]

Nevertheless, the developments in Syria during Bashar's first years in power were best described by Ibrahim Hamidi, *al-Hayat*'s correspondent in Damascus, who wrote in March 2004: "The progress of reform in Syria may be likened to the hands of a clock. If you don't look away from them, you don't notice any movement, but when you look away for awhile, you see progress."[4] Incontrovertibly, in Syrian terms the country had begun to undergo a process of change. The rejuvenation of the ruling elite, and especially of the governmental bureaucracy, after decades of stagnation, was beginning to be palpable. The weakening of the Ba'th Party's grip, and a detachment from the radical revolutionary legacy that typified the Ba'th regime, were evident, if slow-moving, beginnings. A series of governmental decisions in this context may be noted, including the decision in 2003 to change the mandatory school uniform from khaki to light and dark blue (although the discovery that most Syrian families were unable to bear the costs involved impelled Bashar to order a special salary increment for public service employees for this purpose).[5] Similarly, military instruction was canceled in the public school system and was significantly cut back in institutions of higher education; compulsory instruction in Ba'thist ideology in the universities was discontinued; and military service was reduced from two and a half years to two years in January 2005.[6]

Lastly, Bashar has shown an awareness of the need eventually to define himself separately from his father, reflected in his observation: "The difference between my father and my grandfather was amazingly slight, for life changed slowly then. In contrast, the difference between me and my father is very great, and the difference between me and those younger than me by only a decade is even greater."[7]

Furthermore, asked in an interview he granted to the *NYT* in late 2003, about the way he deals with the legacy of his late father, Bashar answered:

I am his son just inside the house. I am going to be different from him. This is normal. The son is not a copy of his father. He takes some things from his parents but he will get many things from the society; and the father is not an isolated picture. Part of him is from the society. So it is a mixture. It is very theoretical to say how much of you is part of your father and how much is independent. But as a president, the first thing is to make your decisions and your vision based on the society, the country and the people. This is one of the things that President Assad used to do. That is why we can converge. Let's talk about the vision of Syrian society about the Golan Heights. It has been now 36 years. It is two generations. We don't differ about this subject.

The needs of modernization are quite different between the 1960s and 2003. So we don't have to converge in this. It is a different field. We converge in certain fields but we don't converge in others because we have different needs and different circumstances. So, this is how we can compare. In his time, in the late sixties he was considered a great modernizer. Maybe if you just want to move from 2000 another ten years, I won't be considered as a modernizer like today because I am going to be from a different generation. That depends on the circumstances and on myself, so this is how I look at it. But it is not inhibiting because at the end I am doing my job towards the country. It is not a family affair.[8]

However, Bashar did not have the luxury of functioning as if he were president of Switzerland, a country without grave problems and without enemies. He found himself ruling over Syria, a pivotal state in a complex and volatile region. Indeed, whenever a regional crisis erupted – whether the Palestinian Intifada, the war against terror, or the war in Iraq declared by the U.S. – Bashar found himself helpless in the face of a challenge that was clearly beyond his capacity.

Bashar's main problem was clearly external, primarily his deteriorating relationship with the U.S., the supreme power in the world and in the Middle East in particular. This crisis in relations with Washington was not, as Bashar chose to believe, decreed from above, or the product of evil conniving by Israel or Zionism. The crisis was self-created, the result of errors and poor judgment, which had cost him sanctions by the Americans and eventually the loss of control of Lebanon.

Now it appeared that the danger was drawing closer to home and was affecting the stability of the regime domestically. Notably, the immediate challenge to the regime did not come from the Islamists, as had been generally assumed, but rather from the minority communities, especially the Kurds, together with reformist elements who demonstrated a steadfast resolve in the struggle against the regime despite their weakness. Ultimately, however, Bashar's real problem was his evident weakness. Because the Syrian system was intrinsically based on personal power, Bashar's weakness was liable to prompt someone within the regime – a relative or some other member of the Alawite community, or even someone in the ruling elite – to force him out with the specific aim of saving the regime from the dangers that his weakness might incur.

To sum up, six years after taking office Bashar has not filled the void his father left, nor has he consolidated his own rule. His image, weak from the beginning, has suffered still further. Thus, it is doubtful whether he enjoys the same respect and "acceptance" his father did. While it is true that there is no immediate domestic threat to Bashar's rule, it is clear that he has not yet firmly entrenched himself in the presidency.

Bashar is ostensibly in charge since he has the formal authority to make decisions, and it is difficult to identify any competing locus of power that poses a real threat to him or makes decisions in his stead. It seems, thus, that the Syrian state is in the grip of inertia, which is the trademark of Hafiz al-Asad's old cronies. The power of these people lies not only in their seniority and experience, but in the fact that they are the authentic representatives of the real power bases of the regime: the military officers, the government bureaucracy and the party activists. This senior echelon is in no rush to depose Bashar. But, at the moment of truth, they did not hesitate to intervene when they felt that the young president's reformism threatened their status and the regime in general.

In his first three years in power many observers asked themselves whether Bashar really did rule Syria. This question was altered with the start of the war in Iraq in the spring of 2003, and became a question of whether Bashar would manage to survive in power in the face of the challenges to him, especially the American challenge. Syrian Foreign Ministry spokeswoman Bushra Kanfani explained that "of course Syria is under difficult pressures and faces existential challenges, but when didn't it face challenges and threats such as these?," pointing out that 40 years previously the country had also experienced existential problems, but had managed to deal with them and survive them.[9] Possibly, Bushra Kanfani was right, and adhering to principles and policy lines in the face of the storm overtaking Syria, as its leadership under Hafiz al-Asad had done for so many years, would prove successful. However, such a policy could also prove to be disastrous.

Meanwhile, problems piled up at Bashar's door. Along with regional and international challenges which required the wise and careful conduct of Syrian foreign policy was the domestic reality of a depressed socioeconomic system and, even more unnerving to the Syrian regime, the Islamic threat, however latent.

Still, Bashar is a young leader with his future before him. He has refrained from making irrevocable mistakes. He was endowed with a good grasp of events, curiosity and a readiness to learn. He appeared to understand the need for change.

Will Bashar grow to be a worthy and admired leader who radiates power and steadfastness? Notably, his late father was not endowed with an excess of charisma, yet he was revered by the Syrian people and respected abroad. Or will Bashar's era become a passing, and marginal, episode in Syrian history, and thereby bring the Asad dynasty founded by his father to an end? If so, it would mark the end of a dynasty but not necessarily the end of the Ba'th regime, and certainly not the end of the Syrian state. The coming years will provide the answer to this question.

Will Bashar al-Asad survive in power?

When Bashar al-Asad took power in Damascus in June 2000 many in Syria and abroad raised the question of how long it would take before Bashar would implement the political, social and economic reforms he had promised. At that time many Syrians perceived Bashar as the great hope for Syria's taking a new path, different from that upon which his father, Hafiz al-Asad, had led the country.

However, as the months and years passed it became clear that Bashar was incapable of bringing about the hoped-for changes. His efforts to introduce limited political openness (the "Damascus Spring") ended in a fiasco, with Bashar himself repudiating the forces of reform in Syria that he had encouraged in their struggle. The attempt to bring about social and economic changes also failed. Against this background many Syria-watchers began to raise the question of whether Bashar was really in charge of the Syrian state. They speculated that perhaps the regime was actually in the hands of the "old guard," the friends of Bashar's father who were still in control of the reins of power and would ensure that nothing changed in Syria.

However, six years after Bashar's accession to power, it would seem that the question that troubles people in Syria, and observers and researchers abroad as well, is whether Bashar will survive in power for a long time. This question became acute in the wake of the strategic difficulties in which Syria has found itself, and there are those who would argue that Bashar brought these difficulties upon himself and his country.

It is indeed true that during the past six years Bashar destroyed many of his father's achievements. There are even those who would argue that he destroyed his life's work. Syria is no longer the stable and strong state it was when Hafiz al-Asad died. It is subject to pressures and even threats from within and without. Its network of relations with its surroundings is in a state of crisis. Domestically, attacks against the regime by Muslim fundamentalists have increased, and Syria has lost its hold in Lebanon. The intimate relations with

Saudi Arabia and Egypt no longer exist. Europe, headed by France, has turned its back on Damascus, while the American administration does not hide its aspiration to bring about a change of regime in Damascus, even if at this stage Washington may still hope that the change will come about by itself, as a result of domestic developments within Syria.

It has been said repeatedly about Bashar that he lacks charisma, leadership ability, experience and political skill. It is possible that he lacks another commodity badly needed by politicians – luck. On his 36th birthday, which fell precisely on September 11, 2001, he was informed of al-Qa'ida's terrorist attacks on New York City and Washington, D.C. Because of these attacks, Bashar pays a heavy daily price, which may cost him his seat of power. Meanwhile, on New Year's Day 2006, Bashar received a "holiday present," in the form of declarations made by former Syrian Vice-President 'Abd al-Halim Khaddam, unprecedented in their severity, to the effect that Bashar was involved in, or at least bore responsibility for, the murder of former Lebanese Prime Minister Rafiq al-Hariri.

'Abd al-Halim Khaddam was a close personal friend of Hafiz al-Asad from their high school days. He accompanied Bashar's father during the whole duration of his political career, for nearly 50 years. He held a long series of key positions in the highest ranks of the Syrian government, the pinnacle being the post of vice-president, which he held from 1985 to June 2005. In short, he was one of the most important mainstays of the Syrian regime. It was Khaddam, indeed, who was appointed Hafiz al-Asad's temporary replacement in June 2000 after Hafiz al-Asad died, and it was Khaddam who issued the decrees that made possible the choice of Bashar as president.

In an interview Khaddam granted to the Saudi-owned al-'Arabiyya satellite television channel, he accused Bashar of being responsible, even if only indirectly, for the murder of Rafiq al-Hariri. Khaddam also argued that Bashar had instituted one-man rule in Syria, and that his regime was infected with corruption. He added that Bashar was an emotional and impulsive man not fit to be president. Khaddam also called upon the Syrian people to rebel against Bashar and estimated that he would not finish the year 2006 in office.

It is doubtful that Khaddam's declarations will have a domino effect in Syria. Over the years his power has faded, and he certainly does not now enjoy any real support in the Ba'th Party or Syrian military circles. Nor does he enjoy any great sympathy or support among the Syrian public, since he was one of the most visible symbols of Hafiz al-Asad's regime for many years.

Nevertheless, something bad is happening to Bashar and his regime. In September 2005, Ghazi Kana'an, the Minister of the

Interior, committed suicide. Kana'an was an important figure in Syria's security establishment. He served as head of Syria's military security in neighboring Lebanon for nearly 20 years. His death took place against the background of the investigation into the assassination of former Lebanese Prime Minister Rafiq al-Hariri in Beirut in February 2005. In October 2005, the German prosecutor Detlev Mehlis submitted his interim report on the investigation. There he accused the Syrian regime of involvement in the murder, charging, indeed, that it had been organized by senior Syrian officials. At their head he placed Mahir al-Asad, younger brother of President Bashar, and Asaf Shawkat, brother-in-law of the president, married to Bashar's sister, Bushra. Shawkat serves as head of the Military Security Department in Syria, the most central and important domestic security body in the country, and in this respect he is Bashar's right-hand man in all matters involving the security and survival of the Syrian regime. Apart from Mahir and Asaf Shawkat, other senior Syrian officials, most prominently Foreign Minister Faruq al-Shar', were mentioned in the report as being implicated in the crime. They were charged with concealing the truth and giving false testimony to the Mehlis committee. The Mehlis report submitted thus far is only an interim account. The investigation is continuing, and it could cause Syria many additional complications.

Bashar al-Asad, meanwhile, has shown no readiness to act in order to extricate himself and his country from the crisis in which they find themselves in their relations with the United States and the international community. It would seem that Bashar is not relating to the possibility that the Americans will act against him with the seriousness demanded. It is possible that he believes that, just as his father survived the difficulties he faced in the 1970s and 1980s on account of his tough policies and his refusal to consider any compromises or concessions, so will he, Bashar, survive the American storm.

However, it would seem that the dilemma is not only Bashar's, but also, and even more so, U.S. President George Bush's. For, in spite of the weakness of Bashar's regime, it is difficult to conceive that it will fall without an American military operation such as was launched against Saddam Husayn. The question is whether President Bush is prepared to enter into a new military adventure in the Middle East before extricating the U.S. from the Iraqi morass in which it has been stuck for several years.

Against the background of the difficulties in which the Syrian regime finds itself, opposition forces are raising their voices both at home and abroad calling for democratization. However, these forces carry no real weight among the Syrian public. The public still prefers to continue the existing situation for fear of what the future might bring and for lack of a real alternative to Bashar's regime. Thus, on the streets of Damascus people are especially concerned about the possibility that the Iraqi scenario might repeat itself in their country, with the state breaking apart, anarchy developing in the realms of security and government, the strengthening of the fundamentalist Muslim foundations in Syrian society, and unrestrained outbreaks of fundamentalist terrorism led by al-Qa'ida.

The most serious threat that Bashar needs to be concerned about would seem to come from within the regime, from among powerful elements in the army and the Ba'th Party, and almost certainly from among the members of the 'Alawi community, who are liable to come to the conclusion that the continuation of Bashar's regime endangers them and their standing. Alternatively, the most serious threat could come from those who might seek to exploit the vacuum in the highest echelons of the Syrian regime that has not been filled since the death of Hafiz al-Asad. In any case, it is the nature of internal processes such as these, taking place within the highest echelons of a regime like the one in Syria, to be concealed, and also to progress slowly and gradually.

Does this mean that Bashar will continue to hold on to his seat as president for a long time despite the weaknesses of his regime? It is, of course, difficult to give an answer to this question. It can be assumed that he will find it very difficult to repeat the achievement of his father and rule the country for the next 30 years. Moreover, one may recall the bombshell placed by 'Abd al-Halim Khaddam at the end of 2005, which is, so to speak, one more "straw" placed on the back of the legendary camel. By itself it is not enough, but sooner or later the array of difficulties being experienced by Syria is liable to accumulate and become a critical mass – critical and dangerous for Bashar al-Asad and his regime.

Notes

List of abbreviations

AFP – Agence France Presse (Paris)
AP – Associated Press (New York)
CF – Country Profile (Economist Intelligence Unit)
CR – Country Report (Economist Intelligence Unit)
FT – *Financial Times*
MECS – *Middle East Contemporary Survey*
MEIB – *Middle East Intelligence Bulletin*
MENA – Middle East News Agency (Cairo)
MEQ – *Middle East Quarterly*
MM – *Middle East Mirror*
NYT – *New York Times*
SANA – Syrian Arab News Agency (Damascus)
WP – *Washington Post*
WT – *Washington Times*

Preface

1. Al-'Arabiyya TV channel, 31 December 2005.
2. Reuters, 21 October 2005.
3. *Al-Sharq al-Awsat*, 4 July 2000.
4. See *Yedi'ot Aharonot*, 17, 19 December 2005. See also Syrian TV, 22 December 2004; *Ma'ariv*, 14 March 2005; *al-Sharq al-Awsat*, 15 March 2005.
5. See *al-Sarq al-Awsat*, 10 January 2005.
6. *La Repubblica*, 6 March 2005.
7. Voice of Israel, 18 June 2000, 1 July 2001.
8. An interview by the author with a British diplomat, Tel Aviv, 22 March 2005.
9. *Al-Nahar*, 18 August 2000. See also *WP*, 27 April 2000.

Introduction *The legacy of the late leader*

1. Syrian TV, 11 March 1999.
2. *Al-Hayat*, 21 December 1998.
3. *Tishrin*, 12 March 1999.
4. R. Damascus, 11 March 1999; *Tishrin*, 12 March 1999.
5. Patrick Seale, *Asad of Syria: The Struggle for the Middle East* (London: I.B.Tauris, 1988), p. 341.
6. Eyal Zisser, *Asad of Syria: The Leader and the Image* (Tel Aviv: Tel Aviv University, Moshe Dayan Center for Middle Eastern Studies, 1994), p. 17.
7. Patrick Seale, *Asad of Syria*, pp. 328–329.
8. An interview by the author with a Syrian diplomat, Washington, DC, 23 June 1999. See also Patrick Seale, *Asad of Syria*, pp. 340–342.
9. James A. Baker, III, *Politics of Diplomacy, Revolution, War and Peace, 1989–1992* (New York: Putnam's Sons, 1995), pp. 447–450.

10. See *Ha'aretz*, 1 May 2000; *al-Quds al-'Arabi*, 29 May 2000. See also an interview by the author with Patrick Seale, Tel Aviv, 13 March 2000.

11. *Ha'aretz*, 6 March 2000.

12. See an interview by the author with an American diplomat who took part in the Geneva Summit, Washington, DC, 25 November 2002. See also *Yedi'ot Aharonot*, 31 March 2000.

13. *Tishrin*, 11 June 2000.

14. *Al-Ahram*, 15 July 2000.

15. *Al-Safir*, 13 June 2000.

16. See *al-Hayat*, 25 April 2000.

17. Patrick Seale, *The Struggle for Syria* (Oxford: Oxford University Press, 1965).

18. For more on the power struggles in Syria in 1946–63, see Patrick Seale, *The Struggle for Syria*; Nikolaos Van Dam, *The Struggle for Power in Syria* (London: I.B.Tauris, 1994); Michael H. Dusen, "Intra- and Inter-generational Conflict in the Syrian Army" (Unpublished thesis, Johns Hopkins University, 1971); Andrew Rathmell, *Secret War in the Middle East: The Covert Struggle for Syria, 1949–1961* (London: I.B.Tauris, 1994).

19. Itamar Rabinovich, *Syria under the Ba'th, 1963–66: The Army–Party Symbiosis* (Jerusalem: Israel Universities Press, 1972), pp. 11–25.

20. For more on the Ba'th Party and the Neo-Ba'th regime in Syria, see Kamal Abu-Jaber, *The Arab Ba'th Socialist Party: History, Ideology and Organization* (Syracuse: Syracuse University Press, 1966); Nikolaos Van Dam, *The Struggle for Power in Syria*, pp. 34–89. See also Eyal Zisser, "June 1967: Israel's Capture of the Golan Heights," *Israel Studies*, Vol. 7, No. 1 (Spring 2002), pp. 168–194.

21. See Moshe Ma'oz's lecture on "Asad of Syria," which was delivered in the framework of the seminar "Syria after Asad," held by the Moshe Dayan Center for Middle Eastern Studies, Tel Aviv University, 19 June 2000 (the lecture can be found in the Center's Library).

22. See Eyal Zisser, *Decision Making in Asad's Syria* (Washington, DC: Washington Institute for Near East Policy, 1998), pp. 17–27. See also Eyal Zisser, *Asad's Legacy: Syria in Transition* (New York: New York University Press, 2000), pp. 29–35.

23. For more, see Eyal Zisser, *Asad's Legacy*, pp. 196–203. For more on state and Islam in Syria, see Umar F. Abdallah, *The Islamic Struggle in Syria* (Berkeley, CA: Mizan Press, 1983), pp. 83–103.

24. See Moshe Ma'oz, *Asad: The Sphinx of Damascus* (London: Weidenfeld Nicolson, 1988), pp. 119–157.

25. See *al-Nahar*, 17 June 2000. See also Hanna Batatu, *Syria's Peasantry, the Descendants of its Lesser Rural Notables and their Politics* (Princeton, NJ: Princeton University Press, 1999), pp. 178–180.

26. See Onn Winckler, *Demographic Developments and Population Policies in Ba'thist Syria* (Brighton: Sussex Academic Press, 1999), p. 52.

27. See Eyal Zisser, *Asad's Legacy*, pp. 37–50.

28. See *Davar*, 8 March 1990. See also Eyal Zisser, "Syria," in Ami Ayalon (ed.), *MECS*, Vol. XIV (1990), p. 653.

29. Eyal Zisser, *Asad's Legacy*, pp. 179–203.

30. *Al-Thawra*, 17 February 1998.

31. See Itamar Rabinovich's lecture on "Syria after Asad," which was delivered in the framework of the seminar "Syria after Asad," held by the Moshe Dayan Center for Middle Eastern Studies, Tel Aviv University, 19 June 2000 (the lecture can be found in the Center's Library).

Chapter 1 *The road to the top*

1. See an interview with Dr. Edmund Schulenburg, *Ha'aretz*, 9 February 2001. See also *NYT*, 2 July 2000.

2. *Al-Hayat*, 11 June 2000; *Tishrin*, 19 June 2000.
3. Patrick Seale, *Asad of Syria*, pp. 37–39.
4. *Al-Hayat*, 11 June 2000.
5. *Ha'aretz*, 9 February 2001.
6. Patrick Seale, *Asad of Syria*, pp. 54–55, 68–71.
7. Ibid., p. 179.
8. Ibid., pp. 329–331.
9. *Al-Safir*, 5 August 2001.
10. *Al-Shira'*, 11 December 2000. See also *al-Safir*, 30 December 2000.
11. See *Tishrin*, 18 September 2002.
12. See Eyal Zisser, *Asad's Legacy*, pp. 1–13. See also an interview by the author with Patrick Seale, Tel Aviv, 11 March 2000.
13. *Al-Hayat*, 11 June 2000; *Tishrin*, 19 June 2000.
14. *Al-Watan al-'Arabi*, 22 July 2001; *Foreign Report*, 11 November 2001; *Yedi'ot Aharonot*, 11 March 2000.
15. *MEIB*, Vol. 2 (2001), pp. 206–207. See also an interview by the author with Patrick Seale, Tel Aviv, 11 March 2000.
16. *Al-Watan*, 1 December 2000.
17. *Ha'aretz*, 9 February 2001.
18. Ibid.
19. Ibid. See also an interview with Bashar al-Asad, *WP*, 27 April 2000.
20. AP, 9 July 2000.
21. See Syrian TV, 16 December 2002.
22. *Al-Hayat*, 19 December 2002.
23. Ibid.
24. *Observer*, 16 December 2002.
25. *Ha'aretz*, 9 February 2001.
26. *Al-Hayat*, 15 January 2001; *Ha'aretz*, 9 February 2001; *WP*, 15 April 2001.
27. *Observer*, 16 December 2001.
28. See, for example, *Ruz al-Yusuf*, 25 June 2000; *Ha'aretz*, 6 August 2000; AFP, 20 August 2000.
29. *Observer*, 16 December 2002.
30. *Yedi'ot Aharonot*, 27 May 1999.
31. Bernard Lewis, *The Middle East: 2000 Years of History – From the Rise of Christianity to the Present Day* (London: Weidenfeld Nicolson, 1995), p. 87.
32. Patrick Seale, *Asad of Syria*, pp. 421–440. See also Eyal Zisser, *Asad's Legacy*, pp. 152–178.
33. Eyal Zisser, *Asad's Legacy*, pp. 155–160.
34. Ibid., pp. 155–157.
35. *Al-Hayat*, 22 January 1994; *Tishrin*, 23 January 1994; *Ha'aretz*, 24 January 1994.
36. See *Yedi'ot Aharonot*, 27 May 1999.
37. Syrian TV, 22, 23, 25 January 1994.
38. See an interview by the author with an American diplomat who served in Damascus during these years, Tel Aviv, 24 January 1995.
39. See an interview by the author with an American army officer who served in Damascus during the years 1991–95, Washington, DC, 23 June 1996.
40. See an interview by the author, London, 7 October 2005.
41. See, for example, *al-Ba'th*, 17 April 1996. See also Eyal Zisser, *Asad's Legacy*, pp. 155–156.
42. *Al-Wasat*, 14 August 1997.
43. R. Damascus, 11 June 2000.
44. Eyal Zisser, *Asad's Legacy*, pp. 155–158.
45. *Al-Hayat*, 12 October 1997.
46. *Al-Usbu'*, 23 May 2000; the interview was quoted in *al-Ba'th*, 24 May 2000.

47. *Al-Thawra*, 19 January 1997.
48. See Syrian TV, 21, 23 January 1999.
49. *Sunday Telegraph*, 14 March 1999. See also R. Damascus, 14 July 1999.
50. *Al-Kifah al-'Arabi*, 3 February 1999.
51. AP, 4 February 2000.
52. AFP, 7 November 1999.
53. *WP,* 24 April 2000.
54. Ibid.
55. *Yedi'ot Aharonot*, 27 May 1999.
56. R. Damascus, 12 February 1999.
57. Syrian TV, 11 March 1999.
58. See an interview by the author with an American diplomat, Washington, DC, 25 November 2002. See also *Ha'aretz*, 1 May 2000; *al-Quds al-'Arabi*, 29 May 2000.
59. *Ha'aretz*, 4 February 1997; *al-Nahar,* 30 June 1999.
60. SANA, 8 February 1998; *NYT,* 10 January 1999.
61. See Eyal Zisser, "Syria," in Bruce Maddy-Weitzman (ed.), *MECS*, Vol. XXIII (1999), pp. 555–556.
62. AFP, 14 November 1999; *al-Sha'b al-'Arabi*, 19 November 1999.
63. *Al-Hayat*, 25 April 2000.

Chapter 2 *Taking the reins of power*

1. Syrian TV, 10 June 2000.
2. R. Damascus, 10 June 2000; *Tishrin*, 11 June 2000. For the Syrian constitution, see *al-Thawra*, 1 February 1973.
3. *Tishrin*, 12 June 2000.
4. Lebanese News Agency, 10 June 2000.
5. See an interview by the author with a Western diplomat who serves in Damascus, Washington, 23 November 2002.
6. Syrian TV, 18, 19 June 2000.
7. *Al-Ba'th*, 26 June 2000.
8. R. Damascus, 25 June 2000.
9. *Tishrin*, 27 June 2000. See also al-Jazira TV channel, 10, 11 June 2000.
10. R. Damascus, 12 July 2000; *Tishrin*, 13 July 2000.
11. *NYT,* 10 July 2000; *al-Hayat*, 13 July 2000.
12. R. Damascus, 17 July 2000.
13. R. BBC, 13 June 2000.
14. *Al-Hayat*, 13 July 2000.
15. ANN TV channel, 30 July 2000.
16. R. BBC, 13 June 2000.
17. AFP, 20 June 2000; *Ha'aretz*, 27 November 2000; ANN TV channel, 30 November 2000.
18. See, for example, *al-Ra'y al-'Amm*, 22 December 2000; *al-Hayat*, 13 February 2002.
19. *Le Monde*, 28 June 2000.
20. *Independent*, 13 June 2000. See also *WP,* 18 June 2000.
21. See an interview by the author with Patrick Seale, Tel Aviv, 11 March 2000.
22. *Yedi'ot Aharonot*, 23 June 2000.
23. *Ha'aretz*, 9 February 2001.
24. See, for example, *al-Sharq al-Awsat*, 13 June 2000; *al-Quds al-'Arabi*, 15 June 2000.
25. An interview with a Syrian academic, Orlando, FL, 23 November 2000.
26. Egyptian TV, 15 July 2000.
27. *Christian Science Monitor,* 18 June 2001.

Chapter 3 *Bashar al-Asad – the man and his regime*

1. See Eyal Zisser, "The 'Alawis, Lords of Syria: From Ethnic Minority to Ruling Sect," in Ofra Bengio and Gabriel Ben-Dor (eds.), *Minorities and the State in the Arab World* (Boulder, CO: Lynne Rienner Publishers, 1999), pp. 129–148.
2. See Eyal Zisser, *Asad's Legacy*, pp. 20–24.
3. For Bashar's inaugural speech, see R. Damascus, 17 July 2000.
4. *Al-Mustaqbal*, 5 April 2001.
5. *Al-Sharq al-Awsat*, 8 February 2001.
6. See *al-Hayat*, 17 January 2000; *al-Quds al-'Arabi*, 26 June, 21 July 2000.
7. *Al-Hayat*, 16 July 2000.
8. *Tishrin*, 19 July 2000.
9. *Al-Majd*, 13 May 2002.
10. *Al-Liwa'*, 1 July 2002.
11. *Al-Qabas*, 21 July 2003.
12. *Observer*, 16 December 2002. See also an interview by the author with a British diplomat, Tel Aviv, 22 March 2005.
13. An interview with Peter Mendelson, Ramat Gan, 12 November 2001; an interview with a German diplomat, Tel Aviv, 15 March 2002. See also an interview by the author with a British diplomat, Tel Aviv, 22 March 2005.
14. R. BBC, 11 June 2000. See also *al-Hayat*, 7 December 2000.
15. *Al-Shira'*, 21 November 2000. See also *al-Safir*, 30 November 2000.
16. *Al-Nahar*, 18 August 2000.
17. *Al-Shira'*, 21 November 2000.
18. *Times*, 15 December 2002.
19. *WP*, 27 April 2000.
20. R. Damascus, 25 June 2000.
21. *Tishrin*, 10 July 2000.
22. *Tishrin*, 12 July 2000.
23. *Al-Qabas*, 21 July 2003.
24. *Al-Sharq al-Awsat*, 28 January 2001; *Izvestia*, 24 January 2005. See also SANA, 24 January 2005.
25. *Yedi'ot Aharonot*, 15 September 2002. See also an interview by Ephraim Halevi, former head of the Israeli Mossad and of the National Security Council, upon his retirement, *Yedi'ot Aharonot*, 22 August 2003.
26. Syrian TV, 20 June 2002.
27. See *Akhbar al-Sharq*, 23 January 2005; SANA, 24 January 2005.
28. Syrian TV, 29 November 2002.
29. See *Ha'aretz*, 27 June 2001; Reuters, 27 June 2001.
30. *Al-Sharq al-Awsat*, 8 February 2001.
31. *Daily Telegraph*, 6 January 2004; for the Syrian response, see *al-Hayat*, 10, 12, 15 January 2004.
32. See Bashar's interviews to *al-Sharq al-Awsat*, 18 December 2003; *NYT*, 30 December 2003.
33. *Tishrin*, 16 December 2002.
34. R. Damascus, 28 November 2002.
35. for the Society's website, see www.scs-syria.com.
36. See Martin Kramer, "Syria's Alawis and Shi'ism," in Martin Kramer (ed.), *Shi'ism, Resistance and Revolution* (Boulder, CO: Westview Press, 1987), pp. 203–204. See also *Ha'aretz*, 15 January 2003.
37. R. Damascus, 14 July 2000.
38. *Ha'aretz*, 9 February 2001.
39. Patrick Seale, *Asad of Syria*. See also an interview by the author with Syrian academics, Washington, DC, 23 November 1996, 11 June 1998. See also *al-Nahar*, 4 January 2001.

40. *Akhbar al-Sharq*, 15, 27 May 2003.
41. SANA, 2 January 2001; *al-Sharq al-Awsat*, 2 January 2001. See also the announcement of their engagement, *al-Watan*, 29 November 2000.
42. *Al-Sharq al-Awsat*, 16 January 2002; AFP, 27 October 2003; *al-Sharq al-Awsat*, 24 December 2004; *al-Hayat*, 3 January 2004.
43. See also *Tishrin*, 24 May 2002; *al-Hayat*, 15 December 2003.
44. *Observer*, 16 December 2002.
45. Ibid.
46. See, for example, *Le Point*, 12 May 2000; *al-Shira'*, 29 May 2001; SANA, 13 December 2001; *al-Hayat*, 14, 16 December 2001; *Akhbar al-Sharq*, 26 May 2002; *Yedi'ot Aharonot*, 15 September 2002; Eyal Zisser, "Who Really Rules Syria?," *MEQ*, Vol. X, No. 1 (Winter 2003), pp. 15–23.
47. *Al-Watan*, 17 December 2004; *al-Hayat*, 26 September 2004; *Akhbar al-Sharq*, 14 June 2004; *al-Khalij*, 29 April 2005.
48. *Al-Watan*, 1 December 2000; *Foreign Report*, 11 November 2001. See also *al-Watan*, 17 December 2004; *Akhbar al-Sharq*, 14 June 2004; *al-Hayat*, 29 September 2004.
49. *Ma'ariv*, 13 May 2003, 17 October 2003.
50. Reuters, 18 February 2005; *Yedi'ot Aharonot*, 29 April 2005.
51. See Eyal Zisser, *Asad's Legacy*, pp. 25–36.
52. *Ha'aretz*, 27 November 2001, 14 April 2002; *Yedi'ot Aharonot*, 15 September 2002.
53. Al-'Arabiyya TV channel, 9, 10 June 2003.
54. See http://all4Syria.org, 29 July 2004; *al-Hayat*, 25 January 2005.
55. AFP, 18, 19 February 2005.
56. See http://all4Syria.org, 29 July 2004.
57. See Eyal Zisser, "Syria," in Bruce Maddy-Weitzman (ed.), *MECS*, Vol. XXIV (2000), pp. 535–536. See also Eyal Zisser, "Who Really Rules Syria?," pp. 21–23.
58. SANA, 13 December 2001; *al-Hayat*, 14, 16 December 2001.
59. SANA, 13 December 2001.
60. *Al-Hayat*, 16, 27 September 2003.
61. *Tishrin*, 27 September 2003; SANA, 27 September 2003; *Wall Street Journal*, 14 September 2003. See also *al-Hayat*, 27, 28 September 2003.
62. *Tishrin*, 27 September 2003.
63. *Tishrin*, 25, 27 September 2003; SANA, 6 February 2005.
64. *Tishrin*, 5 October 2004.
65. *Tishrin*, 6 March 2003; *al-Hayat*, 13 March 2003. The Assembly's members from within the National Progressive Front were split as followed: the Ba'th Party – 132; the Arab Socialist Union (of Safwan al-Qudsi) – 7; the Socialist Democratic Union (of Fa'iz Isma'il) – 7; the Communist Party (the Bakdash Faction) – 4; the Communist Party (the Yusuf Faysal Faction) – 4; the Arab Unionists (the 'Uthman Faction) – 2; the Socialist Democratic Union (the Fadlallah Nasir al-Din Faction) – 4; the Arab Socialist Union (the Ahmad Ahmad Faction) – 3.
66. Syrian TV, 18 January 2003; *al-Sharq al-Awsat*, 27 January 2003; R. Monte Carlo, 4, 5 March 2003.
67. R. Damascus, 18 March, 7 October 2003.
68. For the constitution, see *al-Thawra*, 1 February 1973.
69. *Al-Nahar*, 16 June 2000; *al-Hayat*, 17 June 2000; *al-Ra'y al-'Amm*, 20 August 2004; *al-Hayat*, 10 March 2005. See also Hanna Batatu, *Syria's Peasantry, the Descendants of its Lesser Rural Notables and their Politics*, p. 178.
70. *Al-Nahar*, 16 June 2002; *al-Hayat*, 17 June 2000.
71. R. Damascus, 18 June 2000.
72. *Al-Hayat*, 4 July 2003; *Tishrin*, 5 July 2003.
73. *Al-Ra'y al-'Amm*, 10 July 2003; *al-Hayat*, 11 July 2003.
74. *Al-Ba'th*, 3 July 2003.
75. *Al-ra'y al-'Amm*, 11 August 2004.

76. *Abyad Aswad*, 18 August 2004; *al-Ra'y al-'Amm*, 20, 24 August 2004.
77. *Al-Watan*, 5 April 2004.
78. *Al-Hayat*, 10 March 2005.

Chapter 4 *A false spring in Damascus*
1. For more on Mundhir al-Muwassali, see *al-Majalla*, 8 April 2001.
2. See Syrian TV, 26 June 2000. For the Syrian constitution, see *al-Thawra*, 1 February 1973.
3. R. Monte Carlo, 26 June 2000; Reuters, 27 June 2000.
4. For Bashar's inaugural speech, see R. Damascus, 17 June 2000.
5. *Al-'Ittihad*, 31 August, 15 September 2000.
6. *Al-Hayat*, 23 July 2002.
7. *Al-Zaman*, 1 May 2001.
8. *Al-Hayat*, 3 February 2001; *al-Usbu' al-'Arabi*, 2 April 2001; *al-Zaman*, 6 April 2001. See also R. BBC, 14 May 2000.
9. *Al-Hayat*, 17 April 2001.
10. *Al-Hayat*, 7 January 2001.
11. *Al-Mustaqbal*, 8 January 2001.
12. *Al-Zaman*, 14 January 2001; *al-Hayat*, 16 January 2001.
13. *Al-Zaman*, 11 June, 21 August 2001; *al-Ra'y al-'Amm*, 2 September 2001.
14. See *Al-Aman*, 13 May 2001; *al-Hayat*, 4 July 2001.
15. *Al-Hayat*, 2 September 2001. See also *al-Safir*, 31 December 2000; *al-Wasat*, 19 February 2001.
16. *Al-Hayat*, 27 September 2000; *al-Safir*, 29 September 2000.
17. *Al-Hayat*, 29 September 2000.
18. *Al-Ba'th*, 14 September 2000.
19. *Tishrin*, 12 September 2000.
20. *Al-Safir*, 12 January 2001.
21. *Al-Hayat*, 16 April 2001.
22. *Al-Hayat*, 4 May 2001.
23. *Al-Hayat*, 23, 25 August 2002.
24. See *al-Sharq al-Awsat*, 8 February 2001, 2 November 2003.
25. *Al-Hayat*, 17 February 2001.
26. *Al-Hayat*, 4 February 2001.
27. *Al-Hayat*, 30 March 2001; *al-Zaman*, 11 May 2001.
28. AFP, 9 July 2001.
29. *Al-Hayat*, 26 April, 22, 26 July 2001; *al-Dustur*, 26 June 2001. See also *al-Nahar*, 17 July, 5 September 2001.
30. *Al-Hayat*, 11 May 2001.
31. *Al-Zaman*, 23 May 2001.
32. AFP, 7 September 2001.
33. *Tishrin*, 21 November 2001.
34. *Tishrin*, 27 December 2001.
35. *Al-Raya*, 7 August 2001.
36. *Al-Watan*, 14 August 2001. See also AFP, 6 September 2001, 4 April 2002; *al-Zaman*, 9 September 2001; *al-Hayat*, 13 September 2001.
37. AP, 30 January 2002; AFP, 19 March 2002. See also http://www.lijan.de; Reuters, 12 October 2001, 28 August 2002; *al-Zaman*, 4 December 2001.
38. *Al-Hayat*, 7 March, 15 November 2002; AFP, 19 March 2002.
39. *Akhbar al-Sharq*, 17 December 2002.
40. See *al-Hayat*, 17 June 2000; *al-Nahar*, 16 June 2000.
41. *Al-Hayat*, 4, 7, 13 March 2001.
42. *Al-Hayat*, 12, 19 January 2002; Reuters, 3 January 2002.

43. *FT,* 15 May 2001.
44. *Al-Hayat,* 14 July 2001.
45. SANA, 26 December 2002; *al-Hayat,* 29 December 2002, 10 April 2005; *al-Watan,* 26 May 2003.
46. *Al-Quds al-'Arabi,* 25, 31 May 2002.
47. Syrian TV, 9 April 2003; *Akhbar al-Sharq,* 11 April 2003.
48. *Al-Nahar,* 24 August 2003.
49. See the Muslim Brothers website, www.shrc.org, 10 May 2003. See also *al-Siyasa,* 6 November 2003.
50. *Al-Hayat,* 10 June 2003; *al-Nahar,* 10 June 2003.
51. *Al-Quds al-'Arabi,* 11 February 2004.
52. See http://www.reformsyria.org, 13 March 2005; *al-Hayat,* 21 March 2005.
53. *Akhbar al-Sharq,* 20 December 2004; *al-Hayat,* 26 December 2005.
54. *Al-Hayat,* 9, 10 March 2004.
55. Ibid.; Reuters, 9, 10 March 2004.
56. Reuters, 10, 11, 12 March 2004; *al-Hayat,* 10, 11 March 2004.
57. For more, see Eyal Zisser, *Faces of Syria* (Hebrew) (Tel Aviv: Hakibutz Hameuchad, 2003), pp. 195–205.
58. AFP, 3 April 2005; *al-Hayat,* 4 April 2005.
59. *Al-Hayat,* 13 March 2004; *al-Ba'th,* 13 March 2004.
60. *'Ilaf,* 4 November 2004; AP, 1 December 2004; *Akhbar al-Sharq,* 5 April 2005; *al-Hayat,* 6 April 2005.
61. *Akhbar al-Sharq,* 3 September 2004; *'Ilaf,* 7 February 2005.
62. *La Repubblica,* 28 February 2005; *Tishrin,* 28 February 2005.

Chapter 5 *Society and economy in the age of globalization*

1. *Tishrin,* 20 April 2000.
2. *Tishrin,* 10 September, 10 December 2000; *al-Mustaqbal,* 18 September 2000.
3. R. Damascus. See also *al-Watan,* 22 April 2001; *Tishrin,* 15 May 2002. The Syrian authorities updated the income tax law as well, which had been unchanged since 1949. According to the existing law, income tax was as follows: 5% for the first £SY1,000; 8% for the second £SY1,000; 11% for the third £SY1,000; 14% for the fourth £SY1,000; 18% for the fifth £SY1,000. According to the change, the first 2,000 pounds were exempted from the tax. See *Tishrin,* 19 March, 6 August 2002, 11, 12 May 2004.
4. CR, *Syria – 2000,* No. 2, 3, pp. 2, 9.
5. *Tishrin,* 10 August 1998; see also Eyal Zisser, "Syria," in Bruce Maddy-Weitzman (ed.), *MECS,* Vol. XXII (1998), pp. 574–575. See also an interview with Syrian Deputy Prime Minister for Economic Affairs, *al-Usbu',* 23 December 2002.
6. CR, *Syria – 1998,* No. 2, 3, pp. 2, 9; CR, *Syria – 1989,* No. 2, 3, pp. 2, 9–11.
7. CR, *Syria – 1991,* No. 1, 3, pp. 2, 9; CR, *Syria – 1992,* No. 1, 3, pp. 2, 9.
8. *Al-Thawra,* 16 May 2002; *al-Safir,* 1 November 2004.
9. *Al-Bayan,* 8 September 2001; *Akhbar al-Sharq,* 29 September 2002, 7 May 2004; *Tishrin,* 10 March 2004; *al-Thawra,* 8 November 2004.
10. *Al-Mustaqbal,* 25 November 2002.
11. Ibid. See also *al-Thawra,* 8 November 2004.
12. *Al-Safir,* 23 February 2001.
13. *Tishrin,* 2 June 2002.
14. See Eyal Zisser, "Syria," in Bruce Maddy-Weitzman (ed.), *MECS,* Vol. XXIV (2000), p. 536. See also *Tishrin,* 5 June 2002; *al-Quds al-'Arabi,* 22 May 2002.
15. SANA, 10 April 2001; *al-Hayat,* 14 April 2001.
16. *Al-Safir,* 5 June 2002; R. Monte Carlo, 5 March 2003.
17. See CR, *Syria – 2002–2003,* pp. 2, 3, 9. See also *al-Hayat,* 29 October 2002.

18. See also CR, *Syria – 1986*, No. 2, pp. 5–9; CR, *Syria – 1987*, No. 2, pp. 9–11.
19. See Eyal Zisser, *Asad's Legacy*, pp. 188–195. See also *al-Ba'th*, 26 April 2000; *al-Hayat*, 18 March 2002; SANA, 22 May 2002, 2 July 2003; AFP, 15 February 2004.
20. See Eyal Zisser, "Syria," in Bruce Maddy-Weitzman (ed.), *MECS*, Vol. XXI (1997), p. 661. See also ANN TV channel, 30 November 2000; *al-Hayat*, 2 December 2001.
21. *Tishrin*, 22 October 2002; *al-Hayat*, 29 October 2002. Many of the moneychangers were released following an amnesty declared by Bashar al-Asad in November 2000; *al-Hayat*, 21 November 2000.
22. *Al-Ba'th*, 5 September 2001, 22 May 2002; *Al-Thawra*, 20 June 2002, 14 October 2004; *al-Mustaqbal*, 14 November 2002; *Tishrin*, 31 December 2002, 3 April 2005; *al-Sharq al-Awsat*, 1 March 2003.
23. *Tishrin*, 28 July 2001.
24. AFP, 3 March 2001; *al-Nahar*, 14 May 2002.
25. *Tishrin*, 3 December 2000.
26. *Al-Hayat*, 18 March 2001; Syrian TV, 30 March 2002.
27. *Tishrin*, 21 April 2002; *al-Hayat*, 13 July 2002; *al-Ba'th*, 14 March 2001. See also *al-Ba'th*, 21 December 2002; AFP, 7 January 2004.
28. *Al-Quds al-'Arabi*, 25 May 2002.
29. See *al-Sharq al-Awsat*, 14 February 2001; *al-Hayat*, 14 March 2001, 7 June 2004. See also *al-Ba'th*, 21 December 2002, 23 February 2005.
30. *Al-Ahram*, 25 November 2002.
31. See al-Jumhuriyya al-'Arabiyya sl-Surriyya, Ri'asat Majlis al-Wuzara, al-Maktab al-Markazi lil-Ihsa, *al-Majmu'a al-Ihsa'iyya liSanat 1993, lisanat 2000* (Damascus, 1993, 2001). See also CF, *Syria – 1993–94*; CF, *Syria – 2000–01*; Steven Plaut, "The Collapsing of the Syrian Economy," *MEQ*, Vol. VI, No. 3 (September 1999); World Bank, World Development Indicators, 1999; *Tishrin*, 8, 9 March 2000, 16 November 2001.
32. See Raymound A. Hinnebusch, *Authoritarian Power and State Formation in Ba'thist Syria: Army, Party and Peasant* (Boulder, CO: Westview Press, 1990), pp. 127–275.
33. *Al-Hayat*, 14 March 2001; AFP, 11 April 2001.
34. See Volker Perthes, *The Political Economy of Syria under Asad* (London: I.B.Tauris, 1994).
35. See al-Jazira TV channel, 13 March 2001. See also Onn Winckler, "Hafiz al-Asad's Socio-Economic Legacy: The Balance of Achievements and Failures," *Orient*, Vol. 3, No. 41 (2000), pp. 449–467.
36. See CR, *Syria – 1986*, No. 2, pp. 5, 9; CR, *Syria – 1987*, No. 2, pp. 9–11. See also Eliyahu Kanovski, *What's behind Syria's Current Economic Problems?* (Tel Aviv: Tel Aviv University, Moshe Dayan Center for Middle Eastern Studies, May 1985).
37. Reuters, 1 May 2002; CF, *Syria, 2002–2003*, pp. 2–4.
38. Onn Winckler, *Demographic Developments and Population Policies in Ba'thist Syria*. See also al-Jumhuriyya al-'Arabiyya sl-Surriyya, Ri'asat Majlis al-Wuzara, al-Maktab al-Markazi lil-Ihsa, *al-Majmu'a al-Ihsa'iyya liSanat 2000*, pp. 59–60. For the 2002 and 2005 figures, see *al-Thawra*, 10 August 2002, 15 April 2005.
39. AP, 28, 30 February 2001. See also *Tishrin*, 18 October 2000, 18 January, 10 November 2001.
40. Eyal Zisser, "Syria," in Bruce Maddy-Weitzman (ed.), *MECS*, Vol. XVII (1993), pp. 640–641; Vol. XVII (1994), pp. 619–653.
41. *Tishrin*, 27 May 2002.
42. *Al-Ba'th*, 14 May 2002, 3 November 2004.
43. CR, *Syria – 2001*, No. 2, pp. 5, 9; CR, *Syria – 2002*, No. 2, pp. 9–11. See also an interview with the Syrian Deputy Prime Minister for Economic Affairs, *al-Usbu'*, 23 December 2002. For the Russian–Syrian agreement to settle the debts, see *al-Hayat*, 24 January 2005.

44. CR, *Syria – 2002*, No. 2, pp. 5, 9; CR, *Syria – 2005*, No. 2, pp. 5, 9.
45. Ibid.
46. Reuters, 22 May 2001; *Tishrin*, 22 May 2001.
47. *Al-Hayat*, 26 July 2001. See also *al-Ra'y al-'Amm*, 10 April 2002; *Tishrin*, 12 April 2004.
48. CR, *Syria – 2002*, No. 2, pp. 5, 9; CR, *Syria – 2005*, No. 2, pp. 5, 9.
49. *Al-Ba'th*, 16 March 2001.
50. *Tishrin*, 22 July 2001.
51. *Tishrin*, 6, 12 June 2002; *al-Hayat*, 7 June 2002.
52. *Al-Bayan*, 30 June 2002; *al-Watan*, 7 July 2003.
53. *Al-Thawra*, 22 May 2002.
54. *Al-Watan*, 4 April 2001; R. Damascus, 2 October 2002; *Tishrin*, 3 October 2002; *Akhbar al-Sharq*, 3 October 2002.
55. See *Tishrin*, 10 September 2000; *al-Hayat*, 13 July 2003; *Tishrin*, 22 August 2004.
56. *Al-Hayat*, 13 February 2002.
57. *Al-Hayat*, 26 April 2002; *al-Ra'y al-'Amm*, 26 April 2002.
58. *Tishrin*, 24 July 2002; *Akhbar al-Sharq*, 24 July 2002; *al-Hayat*, 26 July 2003.
59. See *Tishrin*, 12 January 2005; *al-Safir*, 13 January 2005.
60. *Al-Hayat*, 27 February 2004.
61. *Al-Hayat*, 6 August 2001.
62. *Al-Safir*, 5 December 2000; *al-Wasat*, 13 November 2001; *al-Mustaqbal*, 9 January 2002.
63. *Tishrin*, 30 July 2000; *al-Usbu'*, 25 November 2000.
64. SANA, 6 January 2005.
65. See *Tishrin*, 13 January, 15 April 2000, 21 December 2002, 14 October 2004; R. Damascus, 5 December 2000; *al-Thawra*, 30 November 2001, 14 October 2005; *Akhbar al-Sharq*, 18 December 2002.
66. *Tishrin*, 14 May 2000.
67. *Al-Hayat*, 10 December 2002, 14 January 2003.
68. *Al-Hayat*, 17, 18 September 2003.
69. *Al-Ba'th*, 10 January 2002.
70. SANA, 29 September 2002.
71. See *al-Tahwra*, 1 November 2004. See also *al-Hayat*, 8 November, 2 December 2004.

Chapter 6　*Bashar al-Asad in the international arena – the al-Aqsa Intifada, the September 11, 2001 events, and the war in Iraq*

1. Syrian TV, 11 September 2001.
2. Syrian TV, 9 April 2003.
3. Syrian TV, 21, 27, 28 February 2005.
4. See *Weekly Standard*, 11 December 2004; *WT*, 5 January 2005; *NYT*, 5 January, 4 February 2005.
5. See Eyal Zisser, *Asad's Legacy*, pp. 67–98.
6. *Tishrin*, 13 March 1992.
7. See Robert Olson, *Turkey's Relations with Iran, Syria, Israel and Russia, 1991–2000* (Costa Mesa, CA: Mazda Publishers, 2001), pp. 105–124.
8. See an interview by the author with Peter Mendelson, Ramat Gan, 12 November 2001; an interview with a German diplomat, Tel Aviv, 15 March 2002.
9. See an interview of Bashar al-Asad to *WP*, 27 April 2000.
10. See *Yedi'ot Aharonot*, 27 May 1999.
11. See, for example, interviews with Bashar al-Asad which were published in *al-Fais* before his visit to Madrid in May 2001; *Le Monde* before his visit to Paris in June 2001; *Der Spiegel* before the visit to Berlin in July 2001; to the Italian media before

his visit to Rome in February 2002; and *The Times* before his visit to London in December 2002. All these interviews were also published in their Arabic version in the Syrian press. *Tishrin*, 1 May 2001; *Tishrin*, 26 June 2001; *al-Ba'th*, 10 July 2001; *al-Ba'th*, 17 February 2001; *Tishrin*, 16 December 2002.

12. See *al-Zaman*, 5 May 2001; *MM*, 20 August 2001; Reuters, 29 January 2002. See also CR, *Syria – 2001*, No. 2, pp. 2–4; CR, *Syria – 2002*, Vol. 1, pp. 2–5.

13. *Al-Quds al-'Arabi*, 16 November 2000. See also Bashar's remarks in an interview to *The Times*, 16 December 2002. See also *al-Safir*, 15 February 2002.

14. Reuters, 17 April 2001; *al-Safir*, 15 February 2002.

15. Reuters, 7 May 2001; R. Damascus, 8 May 2001.

16. *Tishrin*, 13 September 2001.

17. *Tishrin*, 27 March 2002.

18. R. Monte Carlo, 1 October 2001; *al-Hayat*, 21 April, 25 November 2002; *WP*, 25 July 2002.

19. See also George Bush's cable to Bashar al-Asad on the occasion of the al-Adha fest., *al-Watan*, 24 February 2002. See also *WP*, 25 July 2002.

20. Reuters, 28 October 2001.

21. See *Ha'aretz*, 2 September 2002; *Yedi'ot Aharonot*, 15 September 2002.

22. *Al-Hayat*, 3 January 2001; *al-Safir*, 3 March 2002.

23. SANA, 31 January 2002; *al-Khalij*, 31 January 2002. See also al-Jazira TV channel, 13 May 2001.

24. See Reuters, 11 October 2001; al-Jazira TV channel, 13 May 2001.

25. Reuters, 10, 11 September 2002.

26. *Al-Hayat*, 20 April 2001; Reuters, 22 May 2002.

27. *The Times*, 13 December 2002.

28. *Al-Zaman*, 28 July 2001; *al-Hayat*, 31 July 2001.

29. *Al-Ba'th*, 14 October 2002; *al-Sharq al-Awsat*, 18 October 2002.

30. AFP, 13 February 2003. See also *al-Safir*, 12 February 2003.

31. See, for example, Reuters, 8 October 2000; *NYT*, 1, 5 December 2000; *al-Hayat*, 22 December 2001, 16 January 2002; *al-Quds al-'Arabi*, 16 November 2002.

32. See *Daily Star*, 15 May 2002. See also an interview with an American diplomat, Tel Aviv, 1 June 2002.

33. *Ha'aretz*, 25 May 2002.

34. *Al-Hayat*, 16, 19 October 2003.

35. Reuters, 8, 9 November 2002. See also *Tishrin*, 13 November 2002; *al-Hayat*, 11 November 2002.

36. SANA, 6 September 2002.

37. *Al-Hayat*, 14 November 2002.

38. *Akhbar al-Sharq*, 18 April 2002; *al-Hayat*, 21 April 2002.

39. See *al-Hayat*, 21 April, 13 August 2002; *al-Safir*, 25 April 2002; Reuters, 12 September 2002.

40. R. Damascus, 10 March 2003.

41. R. Damascus, 9 March 2003.

42. *WP*, 17 March 2003.

43. SANA, 27 March 2003.

44. This comparison was made during a joint press conference by the Syrian Foreign Minister and his French colleague, Dominique de Villepan. See Reuters, 12 April 2003; *al-Ray al-'Amm*, 13 April 2003.

45. *Al-Safir*, 27 March 2003.

46. R. Damascus, 22 March 2003.

47. R. Damascus, 23 March 2003.

48. See AP, 28 March, 13 April 2003; Fox News, 14 March 2003.

49. *Al-Safir*, 15 May 2003; *al-Hayat*, 27 May 2003.

50. LBC TV channel, 16 September 2003.

51. *Al-'Ittihad*, 29 July 2003.
52. *Al-Hayat*, 23 October 2003; *NYT*, 24 October 2003.
53. CNN, 6 October 2003.
54. AP, 14 October 2003; al-Jazira TV channel, 16 October 2003; *al-Hayat*, 24 October 2003.
55. SANA, 13 September 2003.
56. Reuters, 12 December 2003; CNN, 13 February 2004.
57. Reuters, 12, 15 December 2003.
58. *Al-Hayat*, 14, 15 December 2003; Reuters, 15 December 2003.
59. *Al-Sharq al-Awsat*, 19 December 2003; *al-Ra'y al-'Amm*, 29 December 2003.
60. *Al-Hayat*, 29 December 2004; *al-Riyyad* (Riyyad), 17 January 2005.
61. See Bashar's interview to al-Jazira TV, 1 June 2004.
62. Ibid.
63. See *al-Khalij* (Kuwait), 13 April 2004; see also *al-Watan* (Kuwait), 4 July 2004.
64. See *Daily Telegraph*, 2 December 2004.
65. AFP, 25 December 2004.
66. Al-'Arabiyya TV channel, 17 December 2004.
67. See *al-Ba'th*, 7 November 2004; *Tishrin*, 9 November 2004.
68. Reuters, 12 May 2004; *WT*, 26 May 2004.
69. See *Weekly Standard*, 11 December 2004; *WT*, 5 January 2005; *NYT*, 5 January 2005.
70. *Yedi'ot Aharonot*, 19, 20 December 2004.
71. *Ma'ariv*, 14 March 2005.
72. Reuters, 15, 16 February, 2 March 2005.
73. See *al-Nahar*, 20 December 2004; *NYT*, 4 December 2004.
74. *La Repubblica*, 28 February 2005; *Tishrin*, 28 February 2005.
75. Turkish CNN, 6 April 2004; *al-Hayat*, 7 April 2005.
76. *Al-Hayat*, 25 February 2004.
77. Al-Jazira TV, 11 September 2004.
78. Lebanese News Agency, 14 May 2004.

Chapter 7 *Syria and Israel in Bashar's era*

1. *Ha'aretz*, 9 December 1999. See also remarks made by Itamar Rabinovich, former Israeli Ambassador to Washington and head of the Israeli delegation to the peace negotiations with Syria; Israeli TV, Channel 1, 9 December 1999.
2. See Eyal Zisser, "What Went Wrong," *Orient*, Vol. 42, No. 2 (2001), pp. 25–49. For historical background on the Israeli–Syrian peace negotiations, see Itamar Rabinovich, *Brink of Peace* (Tel Aviv: Yedi'ot Aharonot, 1998); Moshe Ma'oz, *Syria and Israel from War to Peace-Making* (Oxford: Oxford University Press, 1996). See also Eyal Zisser, *Asad's Legacy*, pp. 99–128; Helena Cobban, *The Israeli–Syrian Peace Talks, 1991–1996 and Beyond* (Washington, DC: United States Institute of Peace Process, 1999). See also an interview with former Syrian Ambassador to Washington, Walid al-Mu'allim, *Journal of Palestinian Studies*, Vol. XXVI, No. 2 (Winter 1997), pp. 401–412.
3. See an interview with Ehud Barak to *Ha'aretz*, 19 May 2000. See also Raviv Drucker, *Harakiri, Ehud Barak: The Failure* (Hebrew) (Tel Aviv: Mishkal, Yedi'ot Aharonot Books, 2002), pp. 167–178; Ran Edelist, *Ehud Barak Fighting the Demons* (Hebrew) (Tel Aviv: Kineret Publishing House; Zmora-Bitan Publishers; Mishkal, Yedi'ot Aharonot Books, 2003), pp. 134–174. See also *al-Nahar*, 28 March 2000; an interview with Syrian Defense Minister Mustafa Talas to R. al-Sharq, 10 July 2000. See also an interview by the author with former American Ambassador to Israel Martin Indyk, Tel Aviv, 6 March 2001.
4. See Israeli TV, Channel 2, 10, 17 June 2000; *Ha'aretz*, 11, 16 June 2000; *Yedi'ot Aharonot*, 11 June 2000.

5. R. Damascus, 4 October 2000; Reuters, 6 October 2000; R. Monte Carlo, 23 November 2000.
6. *Al-Zaman*, 28 July 2000.
7. *Tishrin*, 25 December 2002.
8. *Al-Safir*, 27 March 2003.
9. R. Damascus, 22 October 2000.
10. R. Damascus, 16 January 1994.
11. R. Damascus, 6 May 2001.
12. R. Damascus, 8 May 2001.
13. *Tishrin*, 24 June 2001.
14. *Tishrin*, 28 March 2002.
15. *Yedi'ot Aharonot*, 18 April 2001; *Ha'aretz*, 18 April 2001.
16. *Ha'aretz*, 2, 6 July 2001; an interview with an American diplomat, Tel Aviv, 16 July 2001.
17. See Bashar's interview to the German *Der Spiegel*. The interview was published in full in the Syrian press; see *al-Ba'th*, 10 July 2001.
18. *Yedi'ot Aharonot*, 26 June 2002; *Ha'aretz*, 28 June 2002.
19. *Yedi'ot Aharonot*, 26 June 2002, 15 September 2002.
20. *Ha'aretz*, 24 January 2001; *Yedi'ot Aharonot*, 15 September 2002.
21. *Yedi'ot Aharonot*, 15 September 2002. See also Eyal Zisser, "Who Really Rules Syria?," pp. 15–24.
22. See *Ha'aretz*, 27 November 2000; *Yedi'ot Aharonot*, 15 September 2002.
23. *Al-Majd*, 19 March 2001.
24. *Ha'aretz*, 27 November 2001.
25. *Al-Hayat*, 18, 20 December 2002.
26. See an interview of Bashar al-Asad to al-'Arabiyya TV channel, 9, 10 June 2003.
27. Ibid.
28. *Ma'ariv*, 13 May, 17 October 2003.
29. Reuters, 5 October 2003; *Ha'aretz*, 17 October 2003.
30. See an interview with Amos Gilad, head of the political branch in the Israeli Defense Ministry, Israeli TV, 6 October 2003. See also *Ha'aretz*, 7 October 2003; *Yedi'ot Aharonot*, 7 October 2003.
31. Reuters, 6 October 2003; *Ha'aretz*, 17 October 2003.
32. See an interview of Faruq al-Shar' to the *Daily Telegraph*, 26 October 2003.
33. *Al-Thawra*, 25 October 2003; R. Monte Carlo, 26 October 2003.
34. *NYT*, 30 December 2003.
35. Israeli TV, Channel 1, 5 January 2004.
36. *Ma'ariv*, 5, 6 January 2004.
37. Israeli TV, Channel 1, 11, 12 January 2004; *Ma'ariv*, 11, 12 January 2004.
38. *Al-Watan*, 8 September 2004; *Ha'aretz*, 8 September 2004.
39. See *al-Hayat*, 14 October 2004.
40. *Ha'aretz*, 28 September 2004; *al-Thawra*, 28 September 2004.
41. See *Ha'aretz*, 27, 28 February 2004.
42. See an interview of Bashar al-Asad to the Spanish newspaper *al-Fais*. The interview was published in the Syrian press, *Tishrin*, 1 May 2001.
43. See *Ma'ariv*, 14 March 2004.
44. *Observer*, 16 December 2002.

Chapter 8 *Syria in Lebanon – the end of an era?*

1. SANA, 5 March 2005; *Tishrin*, 6 March 2005.
2. See *al-Mustaqbal*, 15, 16 February 2005; *al-Hayat*, 15 February 2005; *al-Nahar*, 16, 17 February 2005.
3. SANA, 5 March 2005.

4. See AFP, 21 March 2005; *al-Safir*, 14 April 2005.

5. Lebanese News Agency, 10 June 2004.

6. For a historical background, see Reuven Avi-Ran, *Syrian Involvement in Lebanon (1975–1985)* (Hebrew) (Tel Aviv: Ma'archot, 1986); William W. Harris, *Faces of Lebanon: Sects, Wars and Global Extensions* (Princeton, NJ: Marcus Weiner Publishers, 1997).

7. For more, see Ze'ev Schiff and Ehud Ya'ari, *Milhemet Sholal* [Israel's Lebanon War] (Tel Aviv: Schoken Publishing House, 1984). For the English version, see Ze'ev Schiff and Ehud Ya'ari, *Israel's Lebanon War* (New York: Simon Schuster, 1994).

8. See Anthony McDermont and Kjell Skejelsback (eds.), *The Multinational Force in Beirut 1982–1984* (Miami: Florida International University, 1991); Hala Jaber, *Hezbollah: Born with Vengeance* (New York: Columbia University Press, 1997), pp. 75–96.

9. See William W. Harris, *Faces of Lebanon*, pp. 279–322.

10. See Eyal Zisser, *Asad's Legacy*, pp. 129–151.

11. R. Beirut, 10 May 1995.

12. *Al-Nahar*, 31 January 2000; *al-Hayat*, 13 February 2001.

13. See also *al-Usbu' al-'Arabi*, 27 March 2000; *al-Watan al-'Arabi*, 12 May 2000; *al-Mustaqbal*, 18 November 2000; *al-Nahar*, 31 May, 26 November 2000, 21 March 2001; *al-Thawra*, 14 June 2001; R. Monte Carlo, 16 November 2001.

14. *Al-Hayat*, 13 February 2001.

15. See Ran Edelist, *Ehud Barak Fighting the Demons*, pp. 303–306, 313–321; Raviv Drucker, *Harakiri, Ehud Barak: The Failure*, pp. 129–137.

16. *Al-Ba'th*, 20 April 2000; *al-Hayat*, 27 April 2000.

17. *Al-Hayat*, 12 November 1999; see also *al-Diyyar*, 13 November 1999.

18. Israeli TV, Channel 2, 25 May 2000.

19. Al-Manar TV, 6 June 2000.

20. See Eyal Zisser, "The Return of Hizballah," *MEQ*, Vol. IX, No. 4 (Fall 2002), pp. 3–12; Eyal Zisser, "Hizballah at a Crossroads," in Bruce Maddy-Weitzman and Efraim Inbar (eds.), *Religious Radicalism in the Greater Middle East* (London: Frank Cass, 1997), pp. 90–110; Bahman Baktiari and Augustus Richard Norton, "Lebanon End-Game," *Middle East Insight* (March–April 2000), at www.mideastinsight.com.

21. See *al-Mushahid al-Siyasi*, 14 March 1999.

22. See Eyal Zisser, "Syria," in Bruce Maddy-Weitzman (ed.), *MECS*, Vol. XXIII (1999), pp. 564–565.

23. See *al-Safir*, 26 October 2000; *al-Mustaqbal*, 27 November 2000; *Yedi'ot Aharonot*, 15 September 2002.

24. R. Damascus, 10 June 2001.

25. See al-Manar TV, 11 June 2000; R. al-Nur, 12 June 2000; Syrian TV, 9 June 2002.

26. *Ha'aretz*, 15 January 2003. See *al-Sharq al-Awsat*, 12 February 1999; AFP, 8 August 2000.

27. AFP, 6 February 1999; *al-Nahar*, 22 August 2000.

28. *Daily Star*, 14 November 2000.

29. *Tishrin*, 12 December 2000; *al-Sharq al-Awsat*, 16, 29 December 2000.

30. See, for example, *al-Nahar*, 18 November 2000; *Daily Star*, 23 November 2000; *al-Safir*, 24 November 2000; R. Monte Carlo, 7 December 2000.

31. See Eyal Zisser, "Syria," in Bruce Maddy-Weitzman (ed.), *MECS*, Vol. XXIII (1999), pp. 550–552.

32. *Al-Hayat*, 8 September, 26 October 2000.

33. *Al-Nahar*, 22 March, 24 May 2000.

34. *MM*, 22 September 2000.

35. *Al-Hayat*, 22 April, 4 November 2000; AFP, 25 June 2000; *al-Nahar*, 28 August 2000.

36. Reuters, 4 April 2000; R. Monte Carlo, 12 April 2000; AFP, 7 September 2002.

37. *Al-Hayat*, 17, 19 March 2001.
38. AFP, 16 March 2001.
39. See Patrick Seale, *Asad of Syria*, pp. 284–285.
40. *Al-Hayat*, 24 May 2002. See also R. al-Nur, 17 August 2002.
41. *Al-Watan*, 1 May 2001; *al-Diyyar*, 11 July 2001.
42. *Al-Nahar*, 25 November 2000.
43. MENA, 6 June 2000; Lebanese TV, 7 June 2000; *al-Hayat*, 17 February 2003.
44. *Al-Hayat*, 5, 7 April 2000.
45. See *al-Quds al-'Arabi*, 31 May 2002. See also an interview with Bashar to the French *Le Figaro*. The interview was published in *Tishrin*, 26 June 2001.
46. *Al-Hayat*, 3 March 2002.
47. *Al-Nahar*, 6 September 2001.
48. *Al-Safir*, 3 May 2001.
49. Lebanese News Agency, 4, 7 August 2001.
50. Reuters, 7 August 2001; *al-Hayat*, 8, 9 August 2001.
51. *Daily Star*, 15 May 2002; *al-Watan*, 2 June 2002; *al-Safir*, 24 June 2002.
52. *Al-Safir*, 7 March 2003.
53. Reuters, 3 September 2004; *al-Nahar*, 5 September 2004.
54. Reuters, 2 September 2004; *NYT*, 3 September 2004.
55. See *al-Safir*, 18 August 2004; *al-Nahar*, 19 August, 1 September 2004.
56. *Al-Safir*, 30 August 2004; *al-Nahar*, 29 August 2004; Lebanese News Agency, 2, 4 September 2004.
57. Al-Jazira TV, 27 March 2005; *al-Hayat*, 1, 2 April 2005.
58. *Al-Mustaqbal*, 15, 16, 18 February 2005.
59. See *al-Hayat*, 15, 16, 27, 28 February 2005.
60. *Al-Hayat*, 15, 17, 19 February 2005.
61. AFP, 28 February, 8, 10 March 2005.
62. SANA, 5 March, 26 April 2005; *al-Hayat*, 5 May 2005.
63. See *al-Nahar*, 7 July 2004; al-Manar TV, 9, 19 July, 3 August, 7 September 2004.
64. See AFP, 21 March 2005; *al-Safir*, 14 April 2005.

Conclusion *Why Bashar? Because there is no one else*

1. *Ma'ariv*, 15 December 2002.
2. *Al-Quds al-'Arabi*, 20 March 2003.
3. R. Damascus, 10 March 2003.
4. See *al-Hayat*, 2 March 2004.
5. See *al-Hayat*, 6 June, 17 July 2003.
6. *'Ilaf*, 6 June 2004; SANA, 6, 29 January 2005.
7. *WP*, 27 April 2000.
8. *NYT*, 30 December 2003.
9. *'Ukaz*, 12 January 2005.

Index

'Abd al-Nasir, Jamal 82
'Abdallah II, King of Jordan 34, 36, 52–4, 63, 130–1
'Abdallah, Crown Prince and King of Saudi Arabia 36, 163
al-Abrash, Mahmud 70
Abu Basil 28
Abu Dhabi TV 150
Abu Rumana 118
Abu Sulayman 28
Afghanistan 132, 136
'Aflaq, Michael 7, 58
Agriculture Cooperative Bank 97
Aipac 129, 181
Air Force Security Directorate 66
Airbus 102
al-Akhras, Asma 24–5, 52, 56–60, 62, 171
al-Akhras, Fawaz 24–5
al-'Alawi, Iyad 144
'Alawite mountain see 'Alawite region
'Alawite region 6, 20, 36–7, 48, 57, 117
'Alawites 6–10, 12, 20, 22, 26, 31, 36–7, 44, 47, 58, 61, 63, 65, 73, 117, 125, 202
Aleppo 6, 12, 32, 55, 66–7, 71, 82, 93, 117–8
Aleppo, University 68, 71, 95
Algeria 12, 94, 195
Alliance for the Democracy 95
America-Israel Public Affairs Committee – see Aipac
American Express 105
al-'Ammash, Tawfiq 1182
Annan, Kofi 196
Ankara 130–1
ANN (Arab News Network) 36, 42, 62
Appolodoros of Damascus 57
al-Aqsa Intifada xi, 92, 125–32, 150–4, 156–7, 161, 168, 189, 192, 198, 202
al-Aqsa Mosque 157
Arab Revolutionary Workers Party 83

Arabian Peninsula 6
al-'Arabiyya TV 64
Arad, Ron 89
'Arafat, Yasir ix, 37, 145, 161, 171
Armitage, Richard 137
Arslan, family 184
Arslan Talal 184
al-Asad, Anisa 20, 58, 62
al-Asad, Basil viii, 19–22, 26–32, 63, 173, 184
al-Asad, Bushra 19–22, 62, 207
al-Asad, Hafiz vii–xi, 1–16, 19–22, 26, 28–33, 36, 38, 40, 42–5, 47, 49, 52–3, 58–9, 61, 65–7, 70, 73, 78, 80–1, 90, 94, 106–111, 120, 126–7, 130, 148–9, 151–3, 158, 166–8, 171, 173–4, 179, 183–9, 191–2, 197, 203, 205–6, 208
al-Asad, Hafiz (son of Bashar) 59
al-Asad, Hafiz (son of Bushra) 22
al-Asad, Jamil 27, 36, 42, 62
al-Asad, Karim 59
al-Asad, Mahir 20–2, 61–2, 164, 207
al-Asad, Majid 20
al-Asad, Mundhir 62
al-Asad, Na'isa 36
al-Asad, Naya 22
al-Asad, Rif'at 9, 22, 24–5, 36–7, 42, 61–2, 67
al-Asad, Sumar 36–7, 42
al-Asad, Zayn 59
Aslan, 'Ali 39, 63, 65
Association Agreement 121
Assyrians 98
'Ata, Muhammad 135–6
al-'Atari, Naji 68, 70, 118, 121
al-Atasi, Jamal 82, 89–91
al-Atasi, Suhayr 82, 89–90
Athens 131, 143
Atlantic Ocean 56
al-Atrash, Muhammad 67

'Awn, Michel 188, 194
'Ayn Sahab 165
al-'Azm, Sadiq 84–5, 94

Bab Tuma 140
Baghdad 94–5, 122, 125, 133
Bahrain 33
Baker, James 4, 15
Balfour declaration 140
Banyas 133
Barak, Ehud 37, 148, 180–1
Bakdash, Khalid 214
al-Ba'th, daily 40, 69, 72, 84, 113, 115
Ba'th Party vii, viii, 4, 5, 7, 11–14, 21, 27,
   30, 32, 37, 40, 43, 47, 49, 53–4, 58, 60,
   63, 66–71, 73, 77, 81–3, 88–9, 91, 93,
   102, 105–6, 113, 152, 167, 188, 200–3,
   208
Ba'th Revolution 7, 9, 27, 40, 47, 86, 96,
   99, 101, 104, 107, 110
al-Ba'th, University 71, 93
Beirut vii, 84, 98, 110, 125, 134, 154, 158,
   175, 177, 186–8, 190–2, 194–7, 206
Berlin 131
Bethlehem 157
Biqa' valley 160, 176, 188, 190
Bin Ladin, Najwa 136
Bin Ladin, 'Umar 136
Bin Ladin, Usama 126, 133, 134–6, 138
al-Bitar, Salah al-Din 7
Botswana 117
Britain 24–26, 51–2, 163, 165
Brotherhood, Cooperation and Coordi-
   nation Agreement 177
Buckingham Palace 24
al-Buni, Kamal 91
Burg, Yosef 3
Burns, William 136
Bush, W. George ix, 92, 126, 133–4, 136,
   138, 140–7, 154, 171, 207
Bush, George, the father 126
Buzi, Walid 91

Cairo 20, 154
Ceausescu, Nicolae 13, 26
Center for Islamic Studies 83
China 101, 121, 194
Chirac, Jacques 33, 92, 196
Christians 6, 48, 174, 191–2
Church of Nativity 157
Church of the Holy Sepulcher 157

Clinton, Bill 4, 148, 156
Collins, Phil 23, 34
Communist Party 43, 82, 91
Communist Party – Political Bureau 43, 91
Constitution, al-Ba'th Party 37
Constitution, Lebanese 193–4
Constitution, Syrian 5, 33, 38–40, 42, 49–
   50, 65–6, 70, 78, 90, 95
Council for Currency and Credit 105

Daghram, Durayd 61
Dahr al-Baydar 159
Daily Telegraph 56
Dakhlallah, Mahdi 69, 72, 144
Dalila, 'Arif 84–5, 91
Damascus vii, ix, x, 6, 12, 13, 19–22, 25–8,
   30, 32, 35, 37, 40, 42–5, 48, 50, 52, 54–9,
   61–2, 68, 70–2, 78–82, 89, 91–8, 100–1,
   108, 112, 115–21, 125–30, 132–4, 137–
   46, 150, 156–7, 159, 163–71, 177, 179,
   183–4, 187, 189–99, 201, 205–8
Damascus Commerce Bureau 106
Damascus, Radio 140, 157
Damascus, University 19, 22, 45, 61, 68,
   71, 82, 91–3, 97, 101
Dar'a 67, 112
al-Darakzali, Ma'mun 135
al-Dardari, Durayd 61
Defense Squadrons Division 27
Defensive Shield, operation 139, 150
Democratic Awaking Party 96
Department of Military Security 22, 62,
   65, 186, 207
Diaspora Bank 106
Druze 6, 48, 176, 184, 188–9, 191–5
al-Duri, 'Izzat Ibrahim 144

East Europe 8, 11–14, 71, 95, 114
Egypt 7, 12, 26, 58, 107, 109, 110–1, 129,
   166, 206
Eisenhower, Dwight 175
England see Britain
Europe 14, 27, 36, 44, 51, 81, 92, 95–6,
   100, 105, 110, 113, 115, 121, 129, 131–2,
   188, 206
European-Lebanese Bank of the Middle
   East 105
European Union 81, 92

al-Fajr, rocket 160
Faluja 144

Far East 115
Faysal Yusuf, 214
Fayyad, Shafiq 66
FBI 137
Finland 139
Fiorini, Marc 81
Firdus, foundation 59
Firuds, Square (Baghdad) 125
Forum for National Dialogue 79
France 6, 22, 33, 55, 90, 92, 121, 146, 157, 166, 175, 179, 286, 189, 193–7, 206
Franjiyya, Sulayman 174, 184, 191
Franjiyya, Tony Sulayman 174, 184, 191
Friends of Civil Society 81
French Mandate 6, 22, 88, 186

Gates, Bill x
General Saving Bank 103
General Security Directorate 66–7
Genesis 23
Geneva 4, 148, 156
Germany 136, 158
Ghab region 109, 115
al-Ghadiri, Farid Nahid 95
Ghazzal, Iyad 61
Ghazzala, Rustum 186
Golan Heights 5, 85, 128, 150, 154, 163, 165, 167, 169, 180–1, 202
Gouraud Henri 90
Graham, Bill 136
Gulf War 13, 111, 171

al-Habash, Muhammad 83
Habib, 'Ali 61, 63, 65
Habib, 'Isa 82, 91
Habib, Salah 115
Haddad, Ibrahim 115
Haddad, Subhi 199
Hadera 160
al-Hafiz, Amin 77
Haifa 165
Halevi, Ephraim 54
Hama 43, 55, 91, 97, 115
Hamas 165, 167
Hamidi, Ibrahim 94, 201
Hamud, 'Ali 67, 69
Harba, Muhammad 67
al-Hariri, Rafiq vii, 98, 172, 177–8, 187, 192–6, 206–7
Harvard Business School 25
Hasaka 67, 82, 96, 98, 108, 112

Hasan, king of Morocco 36
Hasan, Ahmad 68–9, 146, 165
al-Hayat, daily 19, 31, 94, 201
Haydar, 'Ali 9
Haydar, Haydar 84
Hill, Faith 34
al-Hindi, Tawfiq 192
al-Hirawi, Ilyas 194
al-Hirawi, Khalil 192
Hitler, adolf 140
Hizballah 56, 58, 64, 126, 131–7, 141, 150, 153–4, 159–167, 170, 175–6, 180–5, 196–7
Homs 24, 61, 67–8, 71, 93
Hong Kong 121, 178
al-Humsi, Ma'mun 83, 90–2
al-Huriyya, School 21
al-Husayn, Muhammad 69, 107, 121
King Husayn (of Jordan) 54
Husayn, Saddam 95–7, 125–6, 129, 138, 141–4, 161, 207

Idlib 108
al-'Imadi, Muhammad 67, 105
Indyk, Martin 167
Internet 31, 34, 52, 57, 61, 67, 92, 95, 130–1, 200
Intifada, 143 see also al-Aqsa Intifada
Investment Bank 103
Iran 13, 58, 97, 110, 126, 117, 129–30, 132–3, 136, 161–2, 167, 182
Iraq ix, x, xi, 6, 94–8, 103, 108, 110–1, 114–5, 121–2, 125–147, 153–4, 161, 164, 170, 179, 189, 192–5, 198, 202–3, 207–8
'Isa, faruq 66
Islamic Jihad 165–7
Islamic Rebellion see Islamic Revolt
Islamic Revolt 9–10, 20, 59, 66–7, 93
Isma'ilis 6, 48, 110
Israel x, xi, 3, 7, 10, 12, 13, 15, 20–1, 29, 37, 42–3, 51–2, 54, 56, 59, 62, 64, 71, 85, 89, 91–2, 98, 105–6, 109–10, 126–9, 132–4, 137, 139–46, 148–71, 173–83, 188, 190–2, 198–202
Izvestia, daily 54
'Izz al-din, Fa'iz 93
'Izz al-din, Khalil 167
'Izz al-din, Isma'il 66

Jadid, Salah 7, 8
Jaladat Badrakhan 82, 89

Jallul, Taqwfiq 66
Jarmana 83
Jazira, region 6, 97, 109, 117
al-Jazira TV, 137, 150
Jerusalem 44, 163, 167–8
Jesus 156–7
Jews 55, 134, 15–8
John Paul II, the Pope 55, 89, 134, 156–7, 167
Jordan 33–4, 50, 52, 55, 58, 63, 100, 108, 112, 130, 132, 174
Jumayyil, Bashir 175
Junblat, Kamal 188
Junblat, family 184, 189
Junblat, Walid 188–9, 191–5

Kabas, Damascus 117
al-Kaftaru, Ahmad 83
Kalbiyya 47, 61, 63
Kalasa, Aleppo 117
Kana'an, Ghazi 64, 69, 187, 207
Kanafani, Bushra 203
Karami, 'Umar 98, 196
al-Kasm, Ra'uf 67
Katzav, Moshe 167–8
Kerry, John 145
Khaddam, 'Abd al-Halim vii, 9, 29–30, 35, 39, 45, 63, 72, 87, 101, 139, 185, 187, 206, 208
al-Khaymi, Sami 61
Khayr Bak, Mahdi 83
al-Khuri, Bishara 181, 194
al-Kifah al-'Arabi, weekly 32
Kim Il Sung 26
King's College 25
Kirkuk 133
Knesset 143
Kulthum, Faysal 82
Kurds 6, 82, 89, 96–8, 107, 130, 200
Kuwait 33, 51 126, 128, 139

Ladhiqiyya 62, 69, 71, 82–3, 89, 93, 163, 165
Lahhud, Emile 39, 172–3, 192–5
Law no. 10 (1991) 104–120
Law no. 24 (1986) 98, 104
Lebanon ix, xi, 5, 35, 43, 58, 64, 85, 91, 98, 100, 104, 106, 110, 117–8, 121–2, 125–6, 128, 131, 133, 136–8, 141, 146, 148, 150, 153–62, 170–197, 202, 205, 207

Lebanon War (1982) 91, 151, 153, 159, 174
Leningrad Polytechnic 68
Lewis, Bernard 26
Liberal foundation 98
Libya 146
Likud 140
London x, 19–25, 31–3, 36, 42, 49, 51, 59, 61, 67, 86–7, 131
London, University 67
Los Angeles 192
Lubrani, Uri 47
Lutfi, 'Amir 68

Ma'ariv, daily 199
al-Madani, 'Abd al-Rahman 116
Madrid 128, 131, 169
Madrid Conference 128, 169
al-Maghrabi, 'Akif 26
al-Mahyani, Muhammad Khalid 67
al-Majd, daily 50
Makhluf, family 21, 59, 61
Makhluf, Rami 23, 28, 61
Mamluks 26
al-Mani', Haytham 95
Manasra, Muhammad 66
Maronites 176, 186, 188, 192–5, 189–91
Mashariqa, Zuhayr 63
Ma'tuq, Khalil 82, 89
Mehlis, Detlev vii, 207
Migdal, Clive 23
Miqati, family 184
Miqati, Najib 184
Miqati, Tah 184
Military Committee 7
Milham, Munif 83
Miru, Mustafa 67–8, 119–21, 151
Misyaf 68, 82, 98
Morgan J.P. 25, 60
Morocco 36, 130
Moscow 131, 137
Mossad 54
Mount Druze 6
Mount Lebanon 154, 159, 193
al-Mufid, 'Abd al-Karim 102–3
Mughaniyya, 'Imad 136
Muhajirun Quarter 50
Muhammad, the Prophet 156
Muhammad V, King of Morocco 130–1
Mujtahid, Muhammad Mahir 61
al-Munjid, Bashir 68

Murtada, Hani 68
Muslim Brotherhood 3, 20, 42, 85–6
Mustafa, Zuhayr 'Imad 61, 68, 146
al-Muwassali, Mundhir 77–8, 81

al-Nahar, daily 187
Najaf 144
Nasrallah, Hasan 131, 182, 185, 197–9
National Charter of 1943 176
National Council for Truth, Justice and
    Reconciliation 82
National Progressive Front 10, 69–70, 83,
    167
Nayyuf, Nizar 89
Neo Ba'th 7, 109, 111
New York 125–6, 132–3, 135, 206
New York Times, daily 166, 200
North Korea 26, 111, 114, 132, 136

Observer, daily 51, 60, 171
October 1973 War 10, 20, 151, 155, 165
Oslo Accords 169

Paddington 25
Palestine 85, 106, 110, 142, 152, 154–7,
    163, 169, 182
Palestinian Authority 37
Palestinians 137, 150, 152–7, 170, 174
Paris 55, 68, 89, 131, 157, 199
el-Pais, daily 77
Peking 131
Pentagon 127, 145
People's Assembly 1–2, 10, 14, 35, 37–41,
    48, 58, 62–70, 77–8, 81, 90–1, 103, 120,
    140, 172, 206, 220
People Saving Bank 103
Philippines 102
Picard, Elizabeth 30
PKK 131
PLO 174–5
Political Security Directorate 66, 69, 89
Postal Authority Saving Fund 103
Powel, Collin 56, 133, 137, 141–2
PPS see SSNP

al-Qabas, daily 51
Qaddah, Sulayman 40
Qaddura, 'Abd al-Qadir 70
Qadmus 98
al-Qa'ida 126, 133–6, 138, 206, 208
al-Qal'a, Sa'dallah Agha 67

Qamishli 82, 89, 96–7
Qardaha 59
Qatar 142
al-Qudsi, Bari'a 90
al-Qudsi, Safwan 214
Queen's College 25
al-Quwatli, Shukri 191

Ramadan Fast 55
Raqqa 112
Real Estate Bank 103, 105
Reagan, Ronald 175
Reform Party 95
La Repubblica, daily ix
Republican Guard Division 28, 30
Rice, Condoleeza 145
al-Rifa'i, Ghassan 67
al-Ris, Suhayr 82
Risha, Hasan 68
Riyad al-Sulh Square, Beirut 196
Riyaq 159
Road Map 164
Roed-Larssen Terje 167
Roman Empire 57
Romania 13, 26
Rome 131, 167
Rumsfeld, Donald 137, 140
Russia 54, 111, 114–5, 129, 137, 194

Sa'ada, Antun 21
Sa'd, 'Adnan 'Ali 68
Sadat, Anwar 109, 167
Sadr, Musa 9
Sagi, Uri x
Safi, Ibrahim, 66
al-Safir, daily 140, 153
al-Saqr, Turki 40
Salah al-Din 148
Sanqar, Ihsan 83
Saudi Arabia 27, 33, 36, 42, 129, 158, 163,
    187, 195, 206
Sawasiyya 98
Saydaniyya 81, 117
Sayf, Riyad 81–5, 90–3
al-Sayyad, 'Abd al-Rahman 66
Schulenburg Edmond 19–20, 22–5, 44
Seale, Patrick 2, 3, 6, 27, 52
Security Council vii, 132, 138, 142, 172,
    193–6
Security Council Resolution No. 1559
    172, 193–6

See of Galilee 148–9, 169
Sha'aban, Buthayna 4, 68, 143
Shab'a Farms 133, 150, 159
Shaddud, Majid 152
Shalish, Dhu al-Himma 61
Shallah, Ramadan 165, 181
al-Shallah, Ratib 106
al-Shami, Khalid, 93
Sham'un, family 188, 194
Sham'un, Kamil 194
al-Shar', Faruq 51, 63, 95, 134, 139–40,
    143, 148, 151, 165, 207
Sharon, Ariel 92, 153–6, 159, 162–3, 167,
    169
al-Sharq al-Awsat, daily ix, 49, 54, 59, 87,
    143
Shawkat, Asaf 22, 61–2, 65, 207
Shaykhu, Marwan 38
Shepherdstown 148
Shihabi, Hikmat 29–30, 35, 185
Shi'ites 10, 58, 175–6, 182, 197
Shu'aybi, Fawzi 146, 152
Shuf mountains see Shuf region
Shuf, region 189, 191
Shukri, Muhammad 'Aziz 45, 93
Six Day War 8, 148, 150, 161
Skobie Margaret 143
Social Peace Party 81, 83, 85
Socialist Arab Democratic Union Party 82
Soros, George 105
South Africa 82, 152
South Lebanon 64, 153–4, 159–60, 170,
    173, 175–6, 179–81, 183, 185, 187, 190,
    192
Soviet Union viii, 11–15, 114, 126–9, 134,
    164
Spain 42, 62
Sri Lanka 103
SSNP (Syrian Socialist National Party) 21

Stalin, Joseph 91
State Department 96, 134, 137–8, 143
Sudan 103, 107
Sufayr, Butrus Nasrallah 178, 186–9, 191,
    194
Sulayman, Bahjat 32, 65
Sulayman, Nabil 89
Sunnis 6, 7, 9, 24–5, 47–8, 58–9, 61, 63, 73,
    111, 174, 176, 184–6, 195
Sussex, University 67
Suwayda 82, 117

Sykes–Picot Agreement ix, 140
Syrian Arab Society 24–5
Syrian Card 105
Syrian Central Bank 105
Syrian Commercial Bank 61, 100, 103
Syrian Computer Society 28, 31, 57, 61,
    67, 200,

Tadmur 89
Ta'if Agreement 176, 179, 182, 184, 188,
    190
Talas, Mustafa 4, 9, 39, 45, 63, 87
Taliban 132
Tartus 22, 67, 82, 91, 117
al-Tawhid, Mosque 55
Tehran 68, 133, 167
Tel Aviv 182
Thatcher, Margaret 23
al-Thawra, daily 32, 101
Third Reich 140
Tishrin, daily 48, 51, 56, 84, 90–1, 105
Tishrin, University 71, 99
al-Turk, Riyad 43, 81, 91–2, 95
Turkey 96–7, 115, 130, 132, 146
Turkmani, Hasan 63, 142
Turkomans 6
Tuwayni, Jubran Ghassan 187

UAE (United Arab Emirates) 33
UAR (United Arab Republic) 7
Ukraine 98
'Umar Ibn al-Khattab, mosque 55
'Umran, 'Adnan 38, 68, 139
UNESCO 108
United Kingdom see Britain
United States, viii, 7, 13, 33, 52, 94–6,
    125–7, 132–7, 139–40, 143, 148, 164,
    166, 180–1, 175, 189, 194, 196, 207
al-Usbu', weekly 31

Vatican 193
Virginia 148

War of the mountain (1983–1984) 192
al-Wasat, magazine 33
Washington ix, 4, 61, 68, 95–6, 125–7,
    129, 132–46, 148, 163–8, 170, 173, 192,
    202, 206
Washington Post, daily 33, 53
West Bank 155, 160

World Bank 67, 102

Yarmuk, refugee camp 151
Yasin, Salim 90, 102–3
Yemen 103, 107
Yom Kippur War see October 1973 War
York, university 68

al-Za'im, 'Isam 67, 69, 106, 115, 121
Zamar, Haydar 136
al-Zarqawi, Mus'ib 144
Zayzun, dam 55, 115–6
Ze'evi, Aharon 62
al-Zu'bi, Husayn 93
al-Zu'bi, Mahmud 67, 112